THE CREATOR
BEYOND TIME & SPACE

20th Century Evidence
for a Transcendent
Creator and the
Supernatural Origin
of the Bible

MARK EASTMAN, M.D.
CHUCK MISSLER

THE WORD
FOR TODAY

P.O. Box 8000 · Costa Mesa, CA 92628 · www.twft.com · E-mail: info@twft.com

Scriptural quotations based on the New King James and King James versions of the Bible unless otherwise specified. Translational emendations, amplifications and paraphrases are by the author.

Cover by The Word For Today Graphics Department

Cover Photo by David Malin, courtesy of the Anglo-Australian Observatory

THE CREATOR BEYOND TIME AND SPACE
Mark Eastman, Chuck Missler

© 1996, 2002 The Word For Today
Published by The Word For Today
Santa Ana, California 92704

ISBN 0-936728-61-2

All Rights Reserved. No portion of this publication may be reproduced, stored in a retrieval system, or transmitted in any form or by any means, electronic, mechanical, photocopy, recording, or otherwise, without the prior express written consent of The Word For Today Publishers, with the exception of brief excerpts in magazine articles and/or reviews.

Printed in the United States of America.

TABLE OF CONTENTS

PROLOGUE

In the 20th Century, staggering discoveries in physics, astronomy and molecular biology are shaking at the very foundations of secular humanism. Remarkably, this evidence has compelled a number of very prominent scientists to talk about the existence of a Transcendent Creator for the universe and life on earth. Ironically, many of these same discoveries have shown the Bible to be incredibly accurate when it comes to scientific issues. For the first time in history the biblical notion of a finite universe and a Transcendent Creator is now based on solid *scientific* grounds.

At the same time archaeological discoveries of the last two centuries have proven that the Bible is historically accurate and has revealed that its prophetic utterances were not written "after the fact" as alleged by 18th and 19th Century "Higher Critics." Now, with the hindsight of twenty centuries, it is possible to show that the Biblical text is an extraterrestrial, supernaturally designed message system whose origin is from outside our time domain.

The burden of proof for this book is to show the rational, comprehensible evidence for the existence of a Transcendent Creator and the supernatural origin of the Bible's text. This is not meant to be an exhaustive treatment of the subjects. Rather we wish to stimulate the reader to further research.

ACKNOWLEDGEMENTS

The authors would like to thank Pastor Chuck Smith for his tremendous example as a man of God and for his outstanding teaching of the Word of God. Thanks to Al and Cindy Brisendine for your technical and editorial expertise. To Lucky Jonker, Gian Minardi, Carol Kurzman and Gary Kanter for reviewing the manuscript. And to Bob Sneidar for your help and expertise. Special thanks to Denise Kramer for your typing and enormous editorial help and expertise.

Finally, thanks to the late professor A. E. Wilder-Smith for his brilliant insights on the origins of life and his steadfast witness for the Gospel of Jesus Christ.

CHAPTER ONE

THE RISE OF THE GOD CALLED "CHANCE"

"For since the creation of the world His invisible attributes are clearly seen, being understood by the things that are made, even His eternal power and Godhead, so that they are without excuse"

Romans 1:20

As we approach the end of the twentieth century, we leave behind a time of unparalleled accomplishment and turmoil. The achievements of this century are nothing less than staggering. At the beginning of this century most of the world still traveled at the speed of horseback. At the end we routinely travel at the speed of sound and communicate at the speed of light. But the twentieth-century has also provided one of the greatest paradoxes in history.

At the dawn of this century the western world was dominated by a theistic, predominantly Judeo-Christian world view. Universities such as Oxford and Harvard even required courses in theology for graduation. At the end of the twentieth century our public educational institutions and the national media expound primarily an atheistic or agnostic world view which is founded on Darwinian evolutionary theory. In the 1960's this dramatic shift in world view reached its zenith with the declaration that "God is dead!"

This incredible paradigm shift, accomplished in about

1

one hundred years, is unparalleled in history. There is however, a puzzling and paradoxical aspect of this dramatic shift in world view. While the twentieth-century intelligentsia confidently declared that God was dead, more evidence had accumulated for His existence than at anytime in history!

THEN CAME THE TWENTIETH CENTURY

For thousands of years atheistic philosophers rested comfortably on the belief that the universe was eternal and, therefore, "uncaused." In the twentieth century astonishing discoveries in astronomy and physics have, however, destroyed the notion of an eternal universe. The implications of these discoveries are so staggering that many physicists and astronomers have recently asserted that the report of God's death was apparently premature! More than anytime in history, the scientific evidence available to us today demands a Transcendent Creator for this universe.

The Theory of Evolution, popularized in 1859 by Charles Darwin's book, *Origin of Species*, is one of the pillars upon which the atheistic world view rests. The idea of evolution from lower life forms, however, was not conceived by Darwin himself. This belief has been around since the time of the Greek philosopher Anaximander in the sixth-century B.C. Darwin's major contribution was to propose a mechanism through which evolution might have occurred. Darwin's theories brought a measure of scientific respectability and a boost to the proponents of the materialistic world view.[1]

Darwin's theory maintains that we are the product of billions of years of random "fortuitous occurrences" as opposed to intelligent design. Chance chemistry, combined with long time periods, is advanced as the cause for all life on earth. Through the process of "descent with modification," Darwinian theory asserts that all life on earth descended from a common single-celled ancestor which arose in the primordial ooze some 3.5 billion years ago. Consequently, in the evolutionary scenario, humankind is viewed as merely another animal species—an "accident" in the spectrum of life on earth. In the evolutionary paradigm, the Creator-God of the Bible is replaced by the god called "Chance."

By the middle of the twentieth century Darwinian evolutionary theory had become the accepted world view among western universities. However, in the last four decades, evidence has slowly accumulated in the fields of molecular biology and information theory that, according to many devoted evolutionists, has fatally crippled the theory. These discoveries have forced many prominent scientists to admit that without the insertion of information or biochemical know-how onto matter, the origin and evolution of life is impossible. However, to apply information or biochemical know-how onto matter for the purpose of creating life in the universe also demands the involvement of a transcendent intelligence or "mind!"

THE "AGING" WORLD VIEW

For the evolutionary paradigm to take root it was necessary to discredit the established Judeo-Christian world view that was the very foundation of early American society. In the nineteenth century, while evolutionary theory was sweeping through Europe and the United States, the field of "biblical higher criticism" was growing in its attempt to discredit the Bible and the "aging world view" of biblical creation. With the growing acceptance of evolutionary theory and biblical higher criticism, the almost universal acceptance of the divine inspiration and authority of the Bible was replaced with widespread skepticism.

Currently, in nearly all of our public universities students are taught that the Bible is a scientifically inaccurate book composed primarily of myths, legends, mingled with a bit of history. What was once the most revered book in the land, the first textbook in the first public school in

America, has become an object of ridicule and contempt for the intellectual elite, the mass media, and the "politically correct."

Ironically, while the intelligentsia in the western world confidently asserted that God is dead and the Bible is unreliable, astonishing evidence has gradually accumulated in the fields of archaeology, astronomy, geology, physics, and biology which confirms the scientific and historical accuracy of the Bible as well as the supernatural origin of its text.

In the pages that follow we will examine numerous recent scientific discoveries regarding the nature of the universe, the laws of physics, the biological sciences and much more, that were anticipated by passages in the Bible thousands of years before their modern discovery.

Furthermore, we intend to demonstrate, through a careful examination of fulfilled biblical prophecy and the design of its text, that the Bible, which consists of sixty-six books penned by over forty authors, is an integrated message system whose source is an intelligent, extra-dimensional, supernatural Being outside our space-time domain.

Finally, in the last section of this book we will introduce the reader to the Transcendent One who spoke the universe into existence, the One who created life from the dust and the One who authored the biblical text—*The Creator Beyond Time and Space!*

---

1 Materialism (Atheism) is the belief that the universe is a self-existent, "closed system." The existence of a supernatural realm or a Supreme Being is denied by materialism. In this book we use the term scientific materialist as a synonym for atheist and non-theist.

CHAPTER TWO

THE ORIGIN OF THE UNIVERSE

"The heavens declare the glory of God; and the firmament shows His handiwork."

Psalm 19:1

"The Cosmos is all that is, or ever was, or ever will be."[2]

Carl Sagan, Evolutionist

For thousands of years philosophers, theologians and scientists have debated the question of the origin of the universe. From the time of the early Greek philosophers this debate has revolved around two basic questions. First, is the universe eternal and therefore "uncaused," or did the universe have a beginning in time and space? Second, if the universe did begin at a finite point in time and space, was it created by an outside cause, or did it create itself? If the universe was "caused to exist" by an outside intelligence then there are enormous philosophical and religious implications for us as inhabitants of the cosmos.

Throughout history there have been strong proponents on each side of these questions. In the fourth century B.C. Plato and Aristotle popularized the belief that the universe is eternal. The universe was viewed as being infinite in both time and space. For the next 2,300 years this was the predominating model for the universe among scientists and philosophers.

5

During the same time period most theologians argued
that the universe was caused to exist at a finite point in
time. This argument reached its fruition in what is commonly called *The Cosmological Argument* for God.[3] Al-
Ghazali, a Muslim (A.D. 1058–1111), and Thomas
Aquinas, a Christian (A.D. 1225–74), are credited with
fully developing this argument for the existence of God.

Al-Ghazali's cosmological argument is summarized by
the statement:

> "Every being which begins has a cause for its beginning;
> now the world is a being which begins; therefore, it pos-
> sesses a cause for its beginning."[4]

In support of his premise that the universe began at a
finite point in time, Al-Ghazali argues that an infinite
regression of events backward in time is impossible. If the
series of past events is infinite then they could not come to
an end in the present because the infinite cannot come to
an end.[5]

Regarding Al-Ghazali's cosmological argument,
William Lane Craig points out:

> "Ghazali's point may be that if the series [of events] is
> infinite going back into the past, then how could the
> present moment arrive? For it is impossible to cross the
> infinite to get to today. So today could never arrive,
> which is absurd, for here we are!"[6]

Consequently, Al-Ghazali argued, since an infinite
regress of time was impossible, time had a beginning and
therefore, the universe is finite!

Thomas Aquinas' cosmological argument attempts to
prove the existence of an "Unmoved Mover" and an
"Uncaused Cause" for the universe.

Aquinas' proof for an "Unmoved Mover" is based on
motion. All things in motion were caused to move by
something else. All objects have the potential to move, but
they cannot initiate their own movement. Therefore,
since the universe is in motion it must have been moved

by something outside the universe—the "Unmoved Mover".

In a similar manner, Aquinas argued that since all effects in the universe require a cause, there must be a "First Cause" that accomplished the first effect—the creation of the universe.

As logical as the cosmological argument may seem, it is based on the belief that the universe is finite. Through the ages non-theists have attempted to get around this argument by simply stating that the universe is eternal and uncaused.

The one factor missing in the debate over the eternal or finite universe was objective, scientific evidence. Without such evidence both sides were, in effect, required to take a position of faith.

THE NEW PARADIGM: A FINITE UNIVERSE!

In the twentieth century staggering scientific discoveries have led astronomers to conclude that the universe began at a finite point in time and space and that it is not eternal. To the dismay of many scientific materialists, these discoveries strongly support the notion that the universe was caused to exist by an extra-dimensional, Transcendent Creator. In 1978, NASA astronomer Robert Jastrow, a self-described agnostic, stated in his book *God and the Astronomers:*

> "I am fascinated by some strange developments going on in astronomy—partly because of their religious implications and partly because of the peculiar reactions of my colleagues. The essence of the strange developments is that the universe had, in some sense, a beginning—that it began at a certain moment in time!"[7]

In 1989, in his book *Journey to the Stars*, Jastrow notes that the twentieth-century evidence for a finite universe was anticipated by the Bible thousands of years before modern cosmologists discovered this fact:

"Most remarkable of all, astronomers have found proof
that the universe sprang into existence abruptly, in a
sudden moment of creation, *as the Bible said it did.*"[8]
(emphasis added)

Prior to the twentieth century, the belief that the universe was eternal was almost unquestioned by
astronomers. However, as Jastrow points out, this view of
an eternal universe has been severely disrupted by
"strange developments going on in astronomy"—discoveries which Jastrow states carry "religious implications."
Belief in God has always required a measure of faith, but
this belief is now founded on solid scientific evidence!

THE NEW PHYSICS

In 1887, two American physicists, Albert Michelson
and Edward Morley, made an observation about the speed
of light that was the seed of a revolutionary change in the
way scientists viewed the universe. After making measurements of the speed of light, they determined that it was
constant in all circumstances. The speed of light did not
vary even if the observer was rapidly moving away from or
moving toward the source of the light.[9,10]

In 1905 Albert Einstein drew on this information
when he shocked the scientific world with his Special
Theory of Relativity. Einstein's theory expanded upon the
observations made by Michelson and Morley and showed
that measurements of length, mass, velocity, and time are
relative to the velocity of two or more observers.[11]

An example will help us to understand the implications of Einstein's theory on the flow of time. Twin brothers agree to test the Theory of Relativity. One brother
stays on earth and the other agrees to fly in a space ship
at close to the speed of light to a nearby star. The space
traveling twin doesn't notice anything different as he travels at 99% of the speed of light. When he returns, he
checks his calendar and notes that he has experienced a
few years of time passage. When he tries to find his twin,

to his dismay, he finds his twin is long since dead, having experienced centuries of time passage! The space traveler's time has been "dilated" by his incredible velocity. What was perceived as a time period of a few years in space, was on earth several centuries of time passage.

This notion that measurements of time, space, and mass are relative to the observer shocked the scientific community. The view of a predictable, mechanistic universe as described by Isaac Newton centuries earlier had been destroyed with a single theory.

THE EXPANDING UNIVERSE

In 1913 astronomer Vesto Slipher published evidence that indicated that about a dozen galaxies in our vicinity were racing away from us at enormous speeds of up to two million miles per hour. This discovery was a surprise to the scientific community since, prior to that time, astronomers believed that galaxies were fixed and merely rotating in place. He reported his findings at the Proceedings of the American Astronomical Society in 1914.[12]

In 1915 Albert Einstein published his second theory called The General Theory of Relativity. In this theory Einstein extended his Theory of Relativity to include measurements of time, space, matter, and length for accelerating bodies.

Among the many outcomes of Einstein's General Theory of Relativity was the prediction that space is expanding and that all the matter in the universe is moving away from an apparent point of origin. Einstein, however, did not initially recognize this prediction. Astronomer Willem de Sitter found that Einstein had made a mathematical error. When corrected, de Sitter found the mathematical prediction that the universe was apparently expanding away from its point of origin. This mathematical observation explained what Slipher had observed with his telescope in 1914. Einstein's theory and the discoveries that followed, forever changed the way astronomers viewed the universe. Einstein's theories provided the seed for numerous discoveries that point to a finite universe.[13]

With this new evidence at hand, the astronomical community concluded that the universe must have begun at a single point in space, at a definite moment in time, in a sudden burst of light, heat, and energy! This was a radical new model in cosmology (the study of the universe as a whole). This sudden, finite birth of the universe was eventually dubbed the "Big Bang"

BEFORE THE BEGINNING OF TIME THERE WAS NO TIME!!

One of the most remarkable outcomes of Einstein's theories was the discovery that time itself is a physical property of the universe. In fact, it turns out that space and time are so tightly coupled to each other that one cannot exist without the other. Because of this coupling physicists now speak of "space-time."

Nearly seven decades after Einstein published his equations on General Relativity, three British astrophysicists, Steven Hawking, George Ellis, and Roger Penrose turned their attention to the Theory of Relativity and its implications regarding our notions of time. In 1968 and 1970 they published papers in which they extended Einstein's Theory of General Relativity to include measurements of time and space. According to their calculations, time and space had a finite beginning that corresponded to the origin of matter and energy.[14,15] Remarkably, they concluded that prior to that moment, space and time did not exist!

SCIENTISTS REACT TO THE EVIDENCE

The evidence for a finite, expanding universe was not greeted with universal acceptance by the world's astronomers and cosmologists. Einstein reacted angrily at first, but finally conceded to his mathematical error and the evidence for a finite, expanding universe. NASA scientist Robert Jastrow records Einstein's reaction:

> "This circumstance of an expanding universe irritates me.... To admit such possibilities seems senseless."[16]

Einstein realized that if the universe is expanding away from a point, then it had a beginning at that point. If the universe had a beginning, then it must have had a "Beginner," he surmised. This discovery disturbed Einstein so much that for a time he included an imaginary mathematical "cosmological constant" to his formulas. He did this to make the effect of the expanding universe go away. He later admitted that this was the biggest error of his career.

Einstein was not the only scientist to react angrily to the evidence of a finite, expanding universe. Jastrow records that many astronomers and cosmologists were dismayed by the evidence:

> "Theologians generally are delighted with the proof that the universe had a beginning, but astronomers are curiously upset. It turns out that the scientist behaves the way the rest of us do when our beliefs are in conflict with the evidence."[17]

The implications of this new evidence were obvious, and they posed a threat to a purely materialistic world view.

COSMIC EGG OR COSMIC CHICKEN: WHICH CAME FIRST?

After these disquieting discoveries were made, astronomers began to speculate about where the matter came from that exploded in the Big Bang. The book of Genesis states that the matter in our universe arose from an act of a Transcendent Creator at a finite point in time.[18] However, the materialistic world view has no room for a Creator. So an alternate explanation needed to be found.

The fact that matter now exists must somehow be explained. The majority of cosmologists believe that all the matter in the universe came from an infinitely dense, infinitely hot, ball of matter some twelve to twenty billion years ago. This ball of matter has been dubbed "the cosmic egg." The origin of the cosmic egg is a point of enormous dispute.

Whether the universe arose from a cosmic egg or not makes little difference. When all the arguments are distilled down we find that there are really only two options.

1) The matter in our universe is either infinitely old; or

2) The matter in our universe appeared out of nothing at a finite point in the past.

There is no third option.

In the pages that follow, we will examine evidence from physics and thermodynamics that specifically rejects the notion that matter is eternal. Secondly, we will show that if the universe began as a "cosmic egg," there must be a "Cosmic Chicken" as well.

PROTON DECAY

As we have seen, the belief that matter is eternal has been a common explanation put forth by materialistic philosophers to get around an *ex nihilo* (out of nothing) creation. Until the twentieth century, however, there has been no scientific evidence to verify or nullify this claim. In the last 100 years a growing body of scientific evidence has accumulated that has convinced the physics community that matter is not eternal. The first part of this evidence is proton decay.

Protons are positively charged particles which reside in the nucleus of every atom. Each proton consists of at least three quarks. For decades it was assumed that protons were eternally stable. However, physicists now believe that quarks decay irreversibly into antiquarks, pions and positive electrons, and electromagnetic radiation.[19] This decay process occurs at a rate of only once per proton per 1032 years. Consequently, since this process is irreversible, all the atoms in the universe will eventually decay into irretrievable matter and energy. Even though this process of decay will take an enormously long period of time, it is not infinite.

THE LAWS OF THERMODYNAMICS

The Laws of Thermodynamics have been described comprehensively in the last 125 years and provide some of the strongest evidence for a finite universe. For our purposes we will discuss only the First and Second Laws of Thermodynamics.

THE FIRST LAW OF THERMODYNAMICS

The First Law of Thermodynamics asserts that matter or its energy equivalent can neither be created nor destroyed under *natural circumstances*.[20] One of the logical outcomes of this law is that there is no new matter or energy appearing anywhere in the universe, nor is there any matter being annihilated. All matter and energy in the universe is conserved. Consequently, this law is often referred to as the Law of Conservation of Mass and Energy. Although matter can neither be created nor destroyed, it can be converted from one state to another, i.e. from a liquid to gas, liquid to solid, solid to gas. The overwhelming experience of experimental physics confirms this First Law to be a fact. As we shall see, this law has enormous implications regarding the origin of the matter in our universe.

THE SECOND LAW OF THERMODYNAMICS

The Second Law of Thermodynamics deals with the overall order and energy in the universe. In effect, this law asserts that as time advances the universe progresses from a state of order to a state of greater disorder.[21] This law also declares that the energy available to perform work in the universe decreases with the advance of time. This increase in disorder and decrease in usable energy is called the development of "entropy." Therefore, when applied to the universe, the Second Law predicts that the orderliness of the universe is steadily decreasing and it is cooling off.[22] A couple of illustrations will help you to fully understand this law.

If you take a new deck of cards in bridge order[23] and begin to shuffle them, you will notice that the orderly arrangement of the cards will quickly become random and disordered. Common sense tells us that it would never go the other way. In fact, the Second Law is so certain, that if you did observe a random deck of cards go into bridge order with shuffling, you could be certain that you were experiencing a time reversal!

Consider the example of a clock spring. In order to wind up a clock spring, we must apply outside energy with our hands to tighten it. The moment we let go the energy stored in the wound-up spring is gradually converted to heat and work is performed as it moves the various parts of the clock. This winding down of the clock spring can and will run in only one direction—"downhill." Everyone knows that a clock spring can never wind itself, no matter how long we wait. Such an occurrence is forbidden by the Second Law.

In recent times astronomers have compared the universe to a giant clock spring that was wound up at the beginning of creation. At the very point of creation, the total available energy and orderliness in the universe was at its highest point. As galaxies and stars burn out, the available energy for work in the universe is gradually decreasing. Likewise, the degree of order in the universe is constantly decreasing. As stars and galaxies burn out, their mass is converted into energy. With the advance of time, this radiant energy cools to the point of maximum entropy (a measure of disorder). In like manner to the clock spring, as time advances the total available energy in the universe is converted to heat and work. Eventually, the universe will be fully "unwound." When the universe reaches the point of maximum disorder (entropy) and no energy is left to accomplish any work, the universe will have died a "heat death."

Again, Robert Jastrow:

> "The Second Law of Thermodynamics, applied to the cosmos, indicates the universe is running down like a clock. If it is running down, there must have been a time when it was fully wound up...if our views are right, somewhere between the beginning of time and the present day we must place the winding up of the universe."[24]

Here Jastrow agrees that a universe which is currently "running down" must have, at one time, been fully "wound up." The Second Law dictates that matter cannot energize or "wind up" itself. Consequently, a source for the "winding up" must be found. It is simply not possible for matter to energize and order itself of its own accord.

COSMIC EVOLUTION AND THE FIRST LAW

Skeptics often scoff at the biblical creation account because it invokes a supernatural event for the origin of time, space, and matter. Yet, if we search the field of cosmology in the last one hundred years we find that theories on the "natural" (as opposed to supernatural) origin of matter are few and far between. As mentioned before, there are only two options for the origin of matter: it is either eternal or it appeared at a finite point in the past. With the elucidation of the First Law of Thermodynamics the implications of this debate, as we will see, have been clearly defined.

Faced with the evidence of a finite, expanding universe, cosmologists began to look for a way to salvage the existence of an eternal universe. In the 1940's Hermann Bondi, Thomas Gold and Fred Hoyle proposed a mechanism that would allow the *expanding* universe to still be infinitely old.[25,26] This model for the universe, called the "Steady State Model" asserts that as the universe expands, hydrogen atoms arise spontaneously *from nothing* in the deep recesses of space. The result is that the universe appears about the same (in a "steady state") in all ages.

In the last forty years this model for the universe has been discredited by a number of scientific discoveries. The first of these has to do with the age of galaxies. If the universe is infinitely old then we should expect to find galaxies of all ages. However, decades of observations reveal that all the visible galaxies in our universe are "middle aged." Secondly, there is no physical (natural) mechanism for the spontaneous origin of hydrogen atoms. In fact, hydrogen atoms have never been observed to appear spontaneously anywhere in the universe.[27] Thirdly, Isaac Newton's Law of Inertia declares that a body at rest will remain at rest unless acted upon by an outside force. In the "Steady State Model" there is no mechanism to explain the motion of the galaxies.

The First Law of Thermodynamics is called a "law" because within the bounds of scientific observation it has been proven true beyond all reasonable doubt. In effect, the First Law states that you and I can neither create nor destroy matter. Therefore, it follows that if something which exists (you and I) cannot create matter, then something which doesn't exist cannot create it either!

Matter cannot create itself and, in the real world, cannot arise from nothing. Within the bounds of natural law all effects must have a cause.[28] Because of this fact, the spontaneous appearance of hydrogen atoms out of nothing (*ex nihilo* creation) is a definite breach of the First Law of Thermodynamics which asserts that matter, under *natural* circumstances, can neither be created nor destroyed. Therefore, since it is not a natural event, it is by definition a supernatural event—a miracle! This is, we believe, a rather weak starting point for a materialistic scenario to begin.

To avoid this conclusion, a number of physicists have proposed that the laws of physics are different elsewhere in the universe.[29] However, this assertion is not supported by even a shred of scientific evidence. Such appeals reveal the lengths that some will go to avoid a finite beginning for the universe.

Since matter is not eternal, we are left with only one option—it arose out of nothing at a finite point in the past! Ironically, the scientific materialist who argues that all the matter in the universe arose out of nothing is in agreement with the biblical creationist. However, biblical creationists readily admit that the appearance of matter out of nothing was a miracle, performed by a "First Cause" that transcends the physical universe. The scientific materialist, who believes, as Carl Sagan did, that "the Cosmos is all that is, or ever was, or ever will be," is forced to conclude that the cosmic egg arose from nothingness quite apart from any causal agent.

The atheist immediately protests, "If God made the universe then who made God?" The Bible indicates that God is an eternal, transcendent Spirit independent of the space-time domain.[30] Consequently, because time is itself a physical property of the universe which God created, then questions about God's origin are meaningless. This is because God existed before time and He is, therefore, not subject to time-bound concepts such as birth and death. He is outside of time!

Furthermore, because God existed prior to the creation of the universe and the laws by which it is governed, He is not subject to them either—He *supersedes* them. This means that God was never "young" nor is He aging as dictated by the Second Law. He is outside of our space-time domain and outside of the aging effects of time altogether.

At the beginning of the atheist's scenario, there is an equally difficult question. "Who or what made that ball of matter that exploded in the Big Bang?" Their answer is that the cosmic egg made itself! But according to natural law—the first law of thermodynamics—matter can neither be created nor destroyed by natural processes. Therefore, since the question of the origin of the universe (space-time and matter) cannot be explained by natural law, the mystery of it's origin supersedes natural law and is by definition supernatural!

So at the beginning of each model of origins we have unanswerable questions. Atheists may then argue that they are equal starting points. But are they?

The creationist's model begins with an infinitely intelligent, omnipotent, Transcendent Creator who used intelligent design, expertise or know-how to create everything from the sub-atomic particles to giant redwood trees. Was it a miracle? Absolutely!

The atheist's model begins with an even more impressive miracle—the appearance of all the matter in the universe from nothing, by no one, and for no reason. A supernatural event. A miracle! However, the atheist does not believe in the outside or transcendent "First Cause" we call God. Therefore, the atheist has no "natural explanation" and no "supernatural explanation" for the origin of space-time and matter. Consequently, the atheistic scenario on the origin of the universe leaves us hanging in a totally dissatisfying position. He begins his model for the universe with a supernatural event. This supernatural event, however, is accomplished without a supernatural agent to perform it.

COSMIC EVOLUTION AND THE SECOND LAW

If all the matter in the universe could arise by itself out of nothing, the next problem is to explain how the universe developed into highly organized, non-random structures like galaxies, solar systems, and living creatures without the introduction of energy, information or know-how from outside the system.

The Second Law demands that the overall orderliness

of the universe must steadily decrease as time advances. Therefore, if the universe came from a cosmic egg, then the moment it was created it was at its point of maximum order and energy.[31] From that moment in time, the matter within the cosmic egg began decaying as it also cooled off. With the passage of time the Second Law dictates that the universe will eventually die a heat death as it becomes more and more disorderly.

A major problem for any materialistic theory on the origin of the universe is to explain how the early universe became ordered and energized in the first place. Just as a clock spring cannot wind itself up, the Second Law in effect, asserts that the cosmic egg cannot order and energize itself either.

Some have proposed that the cosmic egg sat in space for an almost infinite length of time and then exploded to create the universe. However, the Second Law demands that even the cosmic egg cannot sit unchanging in space forever. The Second Law, which is universal and absolute, demands that even the cosmic egg must cool off, become disordered, and die a heat death within a finite time span. It cannot sit unchanging in space for eternity.[32] Therefore, if it ever existed, even the cosmic egg had a beginning!

The implications of the Second Law have not gone unnoticed by the world's cosmologists. A universe that is aging and wearing out was at one time young and fully "wound up." How it became energized or "wound up" is one of the greatest dilemmas facing the materialist.

Again, NASA scientist Robert Jastrow:

> "Now three lines of evidence—the motions of the galaxies, the laws of Thermodynamics, and the life story of the stars—pointed to one conclusion; all indicated that the universe had a beginning."[33]

Some cosmologists have asserted that the Second Law does not apply to the universe as a whole. However, there is not one shred of evidence for such a claim. In fact, the evidence from decaying stars (novae and supernovae[34]) indicates just the opposite. The universe is wearing out and winding down!

Materialist and science fiction writer Isaac Asimov confirmed that the Second Law applies to the universe as a whole:

> "Another way of stating what the Second Law is, the universe is constantly getting more disorderly.... In fact, all we have to do is nothing, and everything deteriorates, collapses, breaks down, wears out, all by itself— and that's what the Second Law is all about."[35]

The absolute certainty of the Second Law has also been declared by Sir Arthur Eddington, professor of astronomy at Cambridge University in England:

> "The law that entropy always increases (the Second Law of Thermodynamics) holds, I think, the supreme position among the laws of nature. If someone points out to you that your pet theory of the universe is in disagreement with Maxwell's equations [on electricity], then so much the worse for Maxwell's equations.... But if your theory is found to be against the Second Law of Thermodynamics, I can give you no hope: There is nothing for it but to collapse in deepest humiliation."[36]

In this remarkable statement, Eddington asserts that any theory of the universe that denies the Second Law is doomed.

The dilemma of an orderly, aging universe was also recognized in 1983 by Pennsylvania State University physicist Don Page. Writing in the British journal, *Nature*, Page stated:

> "The time asymmetry of the universe is expressed by the Second Law of Thermodynamics, that entropy (randomness) increases with time as order is transformed into disorder. The mystery is not that an ordered state should become disordered but that the early universe was in a highly ordered state...."[37]

In his book, *The Mysterious Universe*, Cambridge University astronomer, Sir James Jeans declares that the orderly state of the universe requires a "creation" event at a finite time in the past:

> "A scientific study of the universe has suggested a conclusion that may be summed up...in the statement that the universe appears to have been designed by a pure mathematician.... The more orthodox scientific view is that the entropy (randomness or disorder) of the universe must forever increase to its final value. It has not yet reached this: we should not be thinking about it if it had. It [entropy or randomness] is still increasing rapidly...there must have been what we may describe as 'creation' at a time not infinitely remote."[38]

The implications of the great "mystery" of an orderly, decaying universe were squarely addressed by materialist and physicist H. J. Lipson when he wrote:

> "I think, however, that we must go further than this and admit that the only accepted explanation is Creation. I know that this is anathema to physicists, as indeed it is to me, but we must not reject a theory that we do not like if the experimental evidence supports it."[39]

Finally, consider this provocative quote by Gordon Van Wylen in his book, *Thermodynamics*:

> "A final point to be made is that the Second Law of Thermodynamics and the principle of increase in entropy have great philosophical implications. The question that arises is how did the universe get into a state of reduced entropy [highly organized, non-random] in the first place, since all natural processes known to us tend to increase entropy [disorder]? The author has found that the Second Law tends to increase his conviction that there is a Creator who has the answer for the future destiny of man and the universe."[40]

The dilemma imposed by a decaying universe, as we can see, has not gone unnoticed by scientists in the twentieth century. Since the universe began in a state of maximum energy and order, the materialist finds himself in the predicament of explaining how such order developed without an outside cause. Robert Jastrow recognized that the universe, like the spring of a clock, needed to be "wound up" at creation. How then did the universe become "wound up" in the first place? Again, when all the theories are broken down, we see that there are only two options:

    1) The universe was either energized ("wound up") and ordered by an outside agent; or

    2) It energized ("wound up") and ordered itself.

There is no third option.

If we propose that the universe ordered and energized itself, are we not, in effect, proposing that giant clocks can wind their own springs? According to natural law, all closed systems (which the universe certainly is according to natural law) tend toward disorder as time advances. Therefore, the proposal that the universe wound up itself is an appeal to something outside the bounds of natural law. That is, a supernatural event—a miracle! Consequently, as in the case of the First Law of Thermodynamics the materialist is forced to invoke another supernatural event (the "winding up" of the universe) without a supernatural agent to perform the task!

Likewise, the proposal that a Transcendent Creator ordered and energized the universe is admittedly an appeal to a supernatural event as well. However, as in the case of the First Law, this model for the origin of the universe *does* possess a causal agent.

SCIENTISTS SCRAMBLE FOR AN ALTERNATIVE

The scientific evidence examined so far demonstrates that the universe's three components: time, space, and matter appeared at a finite point in time. However, since the scientific evidence does not provide a naturalistic explanation for the origin of matter and the "winding up" of the universe, the materialist is forced to appeal to what is, in effect, a supernatural event. Obviously for the materialist, this simply will not do. In order to get around a beginning, an enormous amount of energy has been expended in the search for a loophole. With the "Steady State" (continuous creation) model refuted, a more acceptable alternative has been sought.

THE OSCILLATING UNIVERSE MODEL

There have been several variations of the Big Bang theory proposed during the past several decades. Each variation of the Big Bang has been proposed, in part, to explain away the fact that the universe had a beginning. The most popular and enduring attempt to get around a beginning is the "Oscillating Universe Model."

The "Oscillation Model" proposes that the universe is in a state of endless expansion and contraction events (Big Bangs). Each cycle of explosion, expansion and contraction is believed to take between fifty and one-hundred billion years. This model takes the old assumption that matter is eternal and combines it with the evidence that the universe is expanding. There are, however, fatal flaws to this theory.

The first problem for the "Oscillation Model" is that there is not enough mass in the universe to cause it to re-collapse. As the mass of the universe moves rapidly away from its point of origin, the force of gravity acts upon it to pull it back together. The "Oscillation Model" proposes that all the mass in the universe will eventually be forced to re-collapse into another cosmic egg which explodes again. However, even the most optimistic calculations show there is not enough mass in the universe to both reverse the expansion and accomplish a re-collapse.

Robert Jastrow notes that, under the force of gravity, in order for the universe to collapse back on itself, it would need to have an average density of at least one hydrogen atom in a volume of ten cubic feet. According to Jastrow, the known amount of matter in the universe is *1000 times too small* to reverse the expansion. Consequently, for decades cosmologists have speculated that there is an enormous amount of invisible "dark matter" that is acted on by gravity which would help to accomplish a re-collapse of the universe. Recently, indirect evidence for such matter has been found. However, even if we assume that 99% of the matter in the universe is non-visible, cold-dark matter, there is still not enough by a factor of ten.

Again, Robert Jastrow:

> "Yet, although the estimated density of matter in the universe is greatly increased as a result of this determination (adding cold dark matter), it is still more than ten times too small to bring the expansion of the universe to a halt.... Thus, the facts indicate that the universe will expand forever!"[41]

Even if sufficient dark matter could be found, the Second Law of Thermodynamics poses another insurmountable problem for the Oscillation Model. Applied to the cosmos, the Second Law demands that the total available energy in the universe will diminish as time progresses. Without a doubt, the expansion of all the mass in the universe requires the expenditure of an enormous amount of energy. The Second Law assures that energy expended to expand the universe in one Big Bang is never recycled for the next Big Bang or expansion event. It is dissipated as unreclaimable heat. Therefore, all the energy in the universe will eventually be lost in unreclaimable form.

The example of a bouncing ball will help to illustrate this point. When a ball is dropped on the ground, we notice that it never bounces back as high as when it was first dropped. This is because when the ball hits the ground, under the influence of the force of gravity, energy is lost in the form of heat. Therefore, less energy is available to push the ball back up into the air, just as the Second Law predicts. After each successive bounce, the ball goes up less and less until all the energy used to raise the ball in the first place is dissipated as heat. The Oscillation Model, in effect, proposes that a dropped ball would continue to bounce forever.

Even if the universe could expand and contract numerous times, there would still be a net loss of energy as dictated by the Second Law. Therefore, there could be only a limited number of Big Bangs. A never-ending succession of expansions and contractions would be forbidden by the Second Law. Since there can only be a limited number of expansion and contraction events, the materialist must still explain who or what wound up and ordered the universe for its *first* expansion event.

BIBLICAL COSMOLOGY

The fact that the universe is expanding, finite, and decaying irreversibly, is a concept that surely surprised twentieth-century cosmologists. The notion that space and time had a beginning is an idea that our three dimensional, finite minds have a difficult time grasping. Yet, according to the theories of Einstein, Hawking, Penrose, and Ellis, time and space did not exist before the moment of creation! As bizarre as these concepts may seem, the Bible has clearly taught these facts in its text for 3,500 years! Written over a period of over 1,500 years, by over forty authors, the Bible dared to claim that time, space, and matter were created at a finite moment in the history of the universe.

It has become fashionable to ridicule the Bible as scientifically inaccurate and outdated. However, as we will see, there are dozens of passages in the Bible which demonstrate tremendous scientific foreknowledge. In fact, there are verses that read like a contemporary astrophysics textbook!

"STRETCH OUT THE HEAVENS"

The notion that space itself is expanding is a concept which is difficult for most of us to fathom. Nevertheless, while other cultures taught that the earth rested on the backs of elephants, turtles, or the Greek god Atlas, the writers of the Bible proclaimed the concept of a finite, expanding universe!

In the Old Testament numerous allusions are made to the concept of an expanding universe. In the book of Psalms, written seven to ten centuries B.C., we find an interesting verse:

> "Bless the LORD, O my soul! O LORD my God, You are very great: You are clothed with honor and majesty, Who cover Yourself with light as with a garment, *Who stretch out the heavens like a curtain.*" Psalm 104:1–2

In the eighth century B.C. the prophet Isaiah also alludes to the stretching forth, or expanding of the universe by God.

> "Thus says God the LORD, Who created the heavens and *stretched them out,* Who spread forth the earth and that which comes from it, Who gives breath to the people on it, and spirit to those who walk on it." Isaiah 42:5 (NKJV)

> "I have made the earth, and created man on it. It was I—*My hands that stretched out the heavens,* and all their host I have commanded." Isaiah 45:12 (NKJV)

According to these verses, when the universe was created, space was literally expanded or stretched out from its point of origin. The psalmist in the verse above also describes the heavens as being laid out like "a curtain." It is interesting to note that in 1991 astronomers discovered a vast "curtain" or "wall" of galaxies hundreds of millions of light years across!

Now the skeptic might argue that the biblical authors were lucky. They just happened to describe the creation of the universe in a fashion which is in complete agreement with twentieth-century cosmology! However, as we will see, there are dozens of additional Bible verses that anticipate contemporary scientific knowledge.

"IN THE BEGINNING"

As we saw earlier, the theories of Albert Einstein provided the seed for the surprising discovery that time is also finite. This concept has been clearly delineated in the pages of the Bible for over 3,000 years.

In the book of Genesis (the book of Beginnings) we are told:

> "In the beginning God created the heavens and the earth." Genesis 1:1

The Hebrew word for create, *bara*, literally means to create matter from nothing. The word "beginning" has been understood by the rabbis to mean "at the beginning of time." So a literal rendering of Genesis 1:1 reads, "At the beginning of time, God created from nothing the heavens (space) and the earth (matter)."

The notion of time having a beginning is also found in the New Testament. In second Timothy 1:9 we read:

> "Having saved us and called us with a holy calling, not according to our works, but according to His own purpose and grace which was given to us in Christ Jesus *before time began.*"

Talk about contemporary scientific foreknowledge! This verse not only indicates that time had a beginning, it also implies that the God of the Bible transcends time and space. That is, He is able to manifest Himself through cause and effect both outside and inside the dimensions of our space-time domain.

THERMODYNAMICS AND THE BIBLE

The concepts contained within the First and Second Laws of Thermodynamics, though relatively "recent" discoveries, have been unequivocally proclaimed in the Bible for thousands of years.

As we have seen, the First Law of Thermodynamics states that the sum total of the mass and energy in the universe is conserved. In effect, this law asserts that there is no matter being created nor destroyed anywhere in the universe. This fact has been clearly described in the Bible for over 3,500 years. In Genesis 2:2–3 we are told:

> "And on the seventh day God *ended* his work which he had made."

Other references on the completed work of God are found throughout the Bible:[42]

> *"The works were finished from the foundation of the world.* For he spake in a certain place of the seventh day on this wise, and God did rest the seventh day from all his works." Hebrews 4:3–4 (KJV)

The fact that matter and energy are nowhere being annihilated is also taught in Nehemiah 9:6 (NKJV):

> "You have made heaven, the heaven of heavens, with all their host, the earth, and all the things that are on it, the seas and all that is in them, and *You preserve them all.* The host of heaven worships You."

The fascinating thing about all these references is that they speak in the *past tense* about the creation. Nowhere in the Bible does it speak of creation still going on. A small point maybe, but still amazing when you consider the Bible was written by over forty authors, from such varied backgrounds, thousands of years before the laws of thermodynamics were conceived.

As we have seen, the contemporary belief that the universe is "wearing out" is something predicted by the Second Law of Thermodynamics. For thousands of years this was denied by scientists. Aristotle believed that the universe was static, eternal, and would never wear out. Even Isaac Newton, a Christian, believed in an eternal, static universe. And yet, if these men had carefully examined the biblical text, they would have found the concept of a decaying universe clearly described.

The Second Law of Thermodynamics, the law of decay,

seems obvious to us as we see examples of decay all of our lives. However, the Bible applies the Second Law in ways that are surprising and yet totally consistent with twentieth-century cosmology. Let's look at a few examples.[43]

> "Of old you laid the foundation of the earth, and the heavens are the work of Your hands. *They will perish, but you will endure. Yes, all of them will grow old like a garment:* Like a cloak you will change them, and they will be changed." Psalm 102:25–26 (NKJV)

> *"For the heavens shall vanish away like smoke, the earth will grow old like a garment,* and those who dwell in it will die in like manner." Isaiah 51:6 (NKJV)

> *"Heaven and earth will pass away,* but my words shall not pass away." Matthew 24:35 (NKJV)

It is fascinating to find such accurate scientific descriptions of the universe. Prior to the twentieth century, the notion that the universe is "wearing out" or "passing away" was foreign to the minds of most scientists and philosophers. Such scientific foreknowledge could not have been derived from observation or intuition. When the Bible was being penned there was no observable evidence that the universe was wearing out. In fact, the consensus of the world's scientists and philosophers was that it *was not* decaying.

Nearly 2,000 years after the final biblical writer penned the radical notion of a finite, decaying universe, those very same concepts were finally "discovered" by modern cosmologists. The fact that the Bible contains such uncanny scientific foreknowledge has not gone unnoticed by the scientific establishment.

In a speech to Washington National Cathedral in 1990, Harvard University astronomer, Owen Gingerich Ph.D., noted the remarkable correlation between biblical and scientific cosmology when he stated:

> "Both the contemporary scientific account and the age old biblical account assume a beginning.... And its

essential framework, of everything springing up from that blinding flash, bears striking resonance with those succinct words of Genesis 1:3: 'And God said, let there be light.' "

Finally, in a startling admission, NASA astronomer Robert Jastrow confirmed this claim when he said:

"Now we see how the astronomical evidence leads to a *biblical view* of the origin of the world: the chain of events leading to man commenced suddenly and sharply at a definite moment in time, in a flash of light and energy!"[44] (Emphasis added)

For centuries the biblical teaching of a finite universe was ridiculed by skeptics. Then came Einstein, Slipher, de Sitter, Hawking, Penrose and Ellis. They aren't laughing any more!

TALK ABOUT GOD!

Lest the skeptic think that we are stretching our interpretation of the cosmological discoveries in this century, consider the fact that in the last quarter-century a number of astrophysicists and cosmologists have begun to talk about God. The evidence for a finite, decaying, and finely-tuned universe has led many to conclude that there must be a Mind behind it all. Remarkably, many of these men are professed atheists who have been forced by the weight of twentieth-century discoveries in astronomy and physics to concede the existence of an intelligent Designer behind the creation of the universe.

After examining the incredible evidence for design in living systems and the cosmos, Sir Fred Hoyle, a well known antagonist to Christianity, stated that:

"a super intellect has monkeyed with physics, as well as with chemistry and biology."[45]

Paul Davies, once a champion of the atheistic, materialistic world view, recently stated:

"[There] is for me powerful evidence that there is something going on-behind it all.... *It seems as though somebody has fine-tuned nature's numbers to make the Universe....* The impression of design is overwhelming."[46] (Emphasis added)

In 1988 astronomer George Greenstein stated in his book *The Symbiotic Universe:*

"As we survey all the evidence, the thought insistently arises that some supernatural agency—or, rather, Agency—must be involved. *Is it possible that suddenly, without intending to, we have stumbled upon scientific proof of the existence of a Supreme Being?* Was it God who stepped in and so providentially crafted the cosmos for our benefit?"[47] (Emphasis added)

In 1987 theoretical physicist Tony Rothman made this remarkable statement in *Discover*:

"The medieval theologian who gazed at the night sky through the eyes of Aristotle and saw angels moving the spheres in harmony has become the modern cosmologist who gazes at the same sky through the eyes of Einstein and sees the hand of God not in angels but in the constants of nature.... When confronted with the order and beauty of the universe and the strange coincidences of nature, it's very tempting to take the leap of faith from science into religion. I am sure many physicists want to. I only wish they would admit it."[48]

Physicist and Nobel Laureate Arno Penzias stated in 1992:

"Astronomy leads us to a unique event, a universe which was created out of nothing, one with the very delicate balance needed to provide exactly the conditions required to permit life, and one which has an underlying (one might say 'supernatural') plan."[49]

Finally, at the end of his book, NASA astronomer Robert Jastrow, a professed agnostic, eloquently expresses the implications of the cosmological discoveries of this century:

"For the scientist who has lived by his faith in the power of reason, the story ends like a bad dream. He has scaled the mountains of ignorance; he is about to conquer the highest peak; as he pulls himself over the final rock, he is greeted by a band of theologians who have been sitting there for centuries."[50]

The fact that so many prominent scientists have gone against the tide to make such statements should force even the most devout materialists to stop and take notice. The evidence is so compelling that the materialistic world view is now seen by these men as the scientifically untenable one. Something or Someone, has set into motion and tinkered with this universe!

AQUINAS, AL-GHAZALI REVISITED

Our search for the cause of this universe has brought us to a remarkable conclusion. The evidence for an expanding universe, the laws of thermodynamics and the inevitable decay of matter confirm that the universe is not eternal—that it began at a certain point in time. Ironically, the twentieth-century quest for the secrets of the universe has also confirmed the cosmological arguments of Aquinas and Al-Ghazali.

The cosmological argument for God, as formulated by Aquinas and Al-Ghazali, asserts that everything that begins to exist must have a cause for its existence. Since the universe had a beginning to its existence (a fact verified by twentieth-century science), then the universe must have a cause for its existence.

Put another way, since time is not eternal, there cannot be an infinite regression of beings nor an infinite regression of universes. Since the First Law of Thermodynamics demands that matter cannot create itself, then there must have been a cause for time, space, and matter. Secondly, since the Second Law of Thermodynamics asserts that the universe cannot order and energize itself, there must have been an "Unmoved

Mover" who wound up and ordered the universe "at a time not infinitely remote."[51] Such an event is outside the bounds of natural law, i.e. a supernatural event.

Prior to the twentieth century, scientific materialists circumvented the cosmological argument for God by simply asserting that the universe was eternal. At the end of this century, faced with overwhelming evidence that the universe is finite, an altogether different tactic is employed to get around the simple logic of the cosmological argument.

First, to explain the origin of matter, it is simply assumed that matter arose from nothing. This of course is in defiance of the First Law of Thermodynamics. Secondly, the incredible balance and order of the universe is assumed to have arisen from non-order, on a massive scale, in defiance of the Second Law. Both of these events, if they could occur, are outside the bounds of natural law— that is, supernatural events. These are poor starting places for a materialistic universe where supernatural events are not allowed to operate.

Because each model (theistic and non-theistic) for the origin of the universe begins with what are, in effect, supernatural events, we must ask ourselves, "which of the two models is most reasonable?" The belief that a transcendent "First Cause," who devised the concept, the blueprints, and the reason for making the universe, created and ordered the physical universe; or, the scientific materialist's model, where no "First Cause" is allowed to operate—where matter arose from nothingness then ordered and energized itself! Considering the two options, both supernatural events, inexplicable by natural law, isn't it more logical to believe that the miraculous appearance of the universe was the result of a "First Cause," i.e., God?

So it comes down to which of the miracles you will believe—the materialist's view of the universe, which begins with two supernatural events without a supernatural agent to perform them, or the miraculous appearance of the universe performed by an intelligent, Transcendent Being. Each of these requires a step of faith. However, believing in a miraculous effect (the origin of the universe) where no miraculous cause exists requires even more faith than simply believing that, "In the beginning God created the heavens and the earth."

THE COSMIC CHICKEN!

Since the universe cannot be self-caused, we are forced to conclude, on logical grounds, that a "First Cause" for the universe must exist. Compelled by the weight of twentieth-century physics, many prominent scientists have come to this same conclusion. Even Albert Einstein is said to have declared that "God does not play dice."

In the 1930's, British physicist Sir James Jeans made this startling admission regarding the existence and attributes of a Transcendent Creator for this universe:

"Nature seems very conversant with the rules of pure mathematics.... In the same way, a scientific study of the action of the universe has suggested a conclusion which may be summed up...in the statement that the universe appears to have been designed by a pure mathematician...the universe can be best pictured, although still very imperfectly and inadequately, as consisting of pure thought.... If the universe is a universe of thought, then its creation must have been an act of thought. Indeed the finiteness of time and space almost compels us, of ourselves, to picture the creation as an act of thought.... *Modern scientific theory compels us to think of the creator as working outside time and space, which are part of his creation, just as the artist is outside his canvas.*"[52] (Emphasis added)

The existence of such an "Unmoved Mover" or "Uncaused Cause" is very difficult for us to conceive. However, we are in a position to speculate about some of the attributes He must possess. Sir James Jeans' illustration of an artist and his canvas, although simple, is a good starting point to understand the attributes of such a Creator.

First, in order to create the universe, the Creator would need to possess enormous power and scientific know-how. Second, He would unquestionably need to exist outside the "canvas," and yet third, be able to simultaneously enter the "canvas" and act unencumbered within it. This ability to simultaneously facilitate causes and effects both inside and outside the dimensions of our universe is called "transcendence," and is absolutely vital to the creation of the universe.

Possessing a transcendent nature allows the Creator to, in effect, "fax" His scientific know-how into our space-time domain and use this knowledge and power to carefully craft and "wind up" the material universe. A transcendent nature also places the Creator outside the time dimension, allowing Him, in effect, to see the beginning from the end.

The existence of a Creator with the attributes of incredible power, intelligence and transcendence is something the Bible has proclaimed for millennia. In fact, the Bible is the only "holy book" on earth that proclaims a fully Transcendent Creator who existed before creation and is now capable of acting, unencumbered, within the three dimensions of the universe He created. As we will see, the Bible not only proclaims such a Creator, it also proves His existence by demonstrating that the biblical text came from an extra-dimensional, transcendent, supernatural source beyond time and space. No other "holy book" on planet earth can demonstrate such an origin.

So the One that "wound up" the universe, the "Cosmic Chicken" and the "Uncaused Cause" are one and the same. He is the God of the Bible—the Creator who exists beyond time and space!

2 Carl Sagan, *Cosmos*, Random House, New York. (1980), pg. 4.

3 William Lane Craig, *Apologetics; An Introduction*. Chapter 3. (Moody Press, 1984).

4 Al-Ghazali, *Kitab al-Iqtisad fi'l-I'tiqad*, pg. 203.

5 This section adapted from William Lane Craig, *Apologetics; An Introduction*. p.63, (Moody Press, 1984)

6 *Ibid*. pg. 63.

7 Robert Jastrow, *God and the Astronomers*, (W.W. Norton & Co., New York, 1978), pg. 11.

8 Robert Jastrow, *Journey to the Stars*, (Bantam Books, 1989), pg. 43.

9 The speed of light is approximately 186,000 miles per second. Traveling at 5 miles per second in a space ship with headlights on, an observer in front of you would measure the speed of light from your headlights to be 186,000 miles per second and not 186,005 miles per second.

10 Robert M. Eisberg, *Fundamentals of Modern Physics*. New York: John Wiley and Sons, 1961, pp. 7-9.

11 Albert Einstein, *The Principle of Relativity* in Annals of Physics, 17:891-921, 1905), also *Relativity* by Albert Einstein.

12 Jastrow, *God and the Astronomers*, pg. 23.

13 We recognize that a small minority of scientists, both evolutionists and creationists, reject the theories of Einstein. This is, however, a small minority opinion. There is observational evidence which demonstrates that Einstein's theories are accurate to five decimal points.

14 Steven W. Hawking, George F.R. Ellis, "The Cosmic Black-Body Radiation and the Existence of Singularities in our Universe," *Astrophysical Journal*, 152. (1968), pp. 25-36.

15 Steven W. Hawking and Roger Penrose, "The Singularities of Gravitational Collapse and Cosmology," *Proceedings of the Royal Society of London*, series A, 314 (1970) pp. 529-548.

16 Jastrow, *God and the Astronomers*., pg. 27.

17 Jastrow, *God and the Astronomers*, pg. 16.

18 A Transcendent Creator would have the remarkable capability of simultaneously acting and existing both inside and outside our space-time domain. He could transcend or cross the dimensions of timeless eternity and manifest himself in our dimensions of space-time as well.

19 James S. Treifel, *The Moment of Creation*, Scribner's and Sons, pp. 141-142.

20 As opposed to supernatural circumstances.

21 The Second Law applies to both closed and open systems. A

closed system is an environment in which no matter, energy, or information can enter or escape under *natural* (as opposed to supernatural) circumstances. Our universe is, by this definition, a closed system.

22 As time goes forward, in a closed system, randomness always increases. An apparent exception is seen in living systems where energy is "captured" by metabolic machines and then applied to raw materials which are then ordered in a preprogrammed manner. Machines, however, are not randomly produced entities. They are the result of intelligent, purposeful design (*telos* or purposefulness). Such purposefulness is never the result of chance. It is the result of a mind.

23 A new deck of cards is always arranged in bridge order. In bridge order the cards are arranged in order from aces, kings, queens, jacks, etc...down to the two cards from top to bottom.

24 Jastrow, *God and the Astronomers*, pg. 48.

25 H. Bondi and T. Gold, "The Steady State Theory of the Expanding Universe," *Monthly Notices of the Royal Astronomical Society*, 108:252-270 (1948).

26 Fred Hoyle, "A New Model for the Expanding Universe," *Monthly Notices of the Royal Astronomical Society*, 108:372-382 (1948).

27 For a detailed discussion see Gerald Schroeder, *Genesis and the Big Bang*, Chapter 4. Bantam Books, 1990.

28 In the realm of quantum mechanics some particles have *apparently* arisen spontaneously as a result of a "quantum fluctuation." However, they quickly annihilate themselves.

29 Fred Hoyle proposed that the continuous creation of matter be considered a natural law itself. He included a creation constant in Einstein's theory of relativity.

30 We will develop this further in later chapters.

31 As is the case with all matter, the moment the cosmic egg was created, according to the Second Law, would have been its moment of lowest entropy. From that moment, with the advance of time, the cosmic egg would begin to decay and cool off until a state of maximum entropy or heat death is reached.

32 Some physicists have argued that the cosmic egg was not subject to the Second Law because the laws of physics were not created yet. However, this is an appeal to something outside the known natural laws of the universe and is, therefore, an appeal to the supernatural.

33 Jastrow, *God and the Astronomers*, pg. 111.

34 A nova is an exploding star.

35 Taken from the video, *The Evolution Conspiracy*, Jeremiah Films.

36 Roy Peacock, *A Brief History of Eternity*, (Good News Publishers, Wheaton, Ill.), pg. 75.

37 Don Page, *Nature*, July, (1983) Volume 304:39-40.

38 Sir James Jeans, *The Mysterious Universe,* Cambridge University Press, pg. 181.

39 *Physics Bulletin* Vol. 31, (1980), pg. 138.

40 Gordon Van Wylen, *Thermodynamics*, New York: John Wiley & Sons, (1959), pg. 169.

41 Jastrow, *God and the Astronomers*, pg. 125.

42 Also see Psalm 148:6, Isaiah 40:26, II Peter 3:7, Hebrews 4:10

43 Also see Romans 8:20-22, I John 2:17, Hebrews 12:27.

44 Jastrow, *God and the Astronomers*, pg. 14.

45 Sir Fred Hoyle, "The Universe, Past and Present Reflection," *Annual Reviews of Astronomy and Astrophysics*, 20:16 (1982).

46 Paul Davies, *The Cosmic Blueprint* (New York: Simon & Schuster, 1988), pg. 203; Paul Davies, "The Anthropic Principle," *Science Digest* 191, no. 10 (October 1983), pg. 24.

47 George Greenstein, *The Symbiotic Universe* (New York: William Morrow, 1988), pg. 27.

48 Tony Rothman, "A 'What You See Is What You Beget' Theory," *Discover*, May 1987), pg. 99.

49 Henry Margenau and Roy Varghese, ed., *Cosmos, Bios, and Theos*, (La Salle, IL: Open Court, 1992), pg. 83.

50 Jastrow, *God and the Astronomers*, pg. 116.

51 Sir James Jeans, *The Mysterious Universe*. (Macmillan Co. 1930) pg. 146.

52 Jeans, *op. cit.*, pgs. 138-39, 146, 154.

CHAPTER THREE

THE ORIGIN OF LIFE–
THE "HARDWARE"

"And the LORD God formed man of the dust of the ground and breathed into his nostrils the breath of life; and man became a living being."

Genesis 2:7

From early childhood, humans develop a fascination with things that crawl, slither, walk, swim and fly. Eventually, we all ponder the question of our own origin. Since the time of the early Greeks, the debate has raged regarding the cause of life on earth. Scientific materialists assert that life was caused by the interplay of time and natural laws (chance chemistry) acting on non-living matter. As some have put it, "the fortuitous occurrence of accidental circumstances." On the other hand, creationists view the origin of life as the product of intelligent design by a Creator who transcends our space-time domain. This Creator pierced the veil of our four-dimensional universe, then applied information or biochemical "know-how" onto matter at the time of creation. Consequently, incredibly complex mechanisms such as brains, kidneys, eyes, hearts, and lungs are viewed as either the result of careful design and forethought, or the products of blind, undirected, chance chemistry. Intelligent design or chance chemistry? When all the frills are stripped away, this is the fundamental question in the debate on the origin of life.[53]

In the fourth century B.C. Aristotle argued that the design we see in living systems is evidence for a divine designer. In the thirteenth century A.D., Thomas Aquinas included the design principle (called the teleological argument) among his four arguments for the existence of God. In modern times the assertion that design in biology requires a designer was presented in its classical form by William Paley; in his watchmaker argument.[54]

Paley pointed out the many parallels between machines and the structures found in living systems. He argued that if we were to find a watch on the ground we would never conclude that it simply arose by a chance combining of atoms. The various gears, springs, and mechanisms in the watch obviously require a designer. Paley argued that since life on earth has every appearance of contrivance or machine-like design, there must have been a designer for such life.

David Hume attacked this long-accepted argument for design head on. Hume argued that the complex, machine-like structures found in living plants and animals have only the "appearance" of design. According to Hume, they were only superficially like machines, but natural in essence.[55] These "non-machines," he argued, were "natural" and therefore needed no designer-creator. Hume argued that the teleological argument for God would only hold true if organisms were deeply analogous—at the molecular level—to machines as we know them.

Since the molecular structure of living systems was not known at the time of Hume and Paley, there was no way to verify Paley's claim that living systems were, in fact, machines. Consequently, for nearly two centuries, scientific materialists and philosophers have maintained that Paley's argument is not valid and the God hypothesis is superfluous.

However, in the last half of the twentieth century, astonishing discoveries regarding the molecular structure and function of living systems have brought the materialistic, random-chance origin of life scenario into serious question. In the field of molecular biology, discovery after discovery has revealed that living systems contain structures which conform in every way to the modern definition of a machine. In fact, the parallel between machines and living systems has now been shown to extend all the way to the molecular level.

Molecular biologist Michael Denton stated in 1986:

> "Although the tiniest bacterial cells are incredibly small, weighing less than 10^{-12} grams, each is in effect a veritable micro-miniaturized factory containing thousands of exquisitely designed pieces *of intricate molecular machinery,* made up altogether of one hundred thousand million atoms, far more complicated than any machine built by man and absolutely without parallel in the non-living world."[56] (Emphasis added)

According to Nobel Laureate Jacques Monod, machines are purposeful (teleonomic) aggregates of matter that use energy to perform work.[57] Clocks, gasoline powered engines, refrigerators, etc., are all machines. And the sum total of experimental science and engineering knowledge confirms that *all* machines are the result of purposeful design by an intelligent source. The theory of evolution asserts that inanimate matter, which possesses no concepts, know-how, or purposefulness, developed into machines by chance! In no field of science—except neo-Darwinian biology—is it believed that machines can arise by chance.

THE SCOPE OF THE PROBLEM

For over one hundred years the primary focus on the question of life's origin has been to explain the origin of the incredibly complex molecules which accomplish the reproduction, repair, and metabolism of living things.[58] Any viable theory on the random-chance origin of life *must* explain the origin of this chemical "hardware." However, the question of life's origin is much more complex than just explaining the origin of the molecular machinery found in living cells.

Like a computer, living systems require much more than just "hardware" to function. They also require "software" or coded instructions to direct the activities of the cellular "hardware." Like a computer, this "software" needs to reside within each living system. Unlike a computer, living systems also possess the marvelous ability to reproduce and pass to the next generation both the "hardware" and the "software."

During the time of Charles Darwin, scientists suspected that such "software" or coded instructions must exist in living systems. However, the actual structure of the cellular "hardware" and the source of the cellular instructions were not known. When the structure of the DNA molecule was deciphered by James Watson and Francis Crick in 1953, a revolution in our understanding of cellular growth and metabolism began.[59] Since that time, molecular biologists have conclusively demonstrated that the growth and metabolism of all life on earth is carefully controlled by a language convention (or system) called "the Genetic Code" which is "carried" by the DNA molecule.[60]

Like all language conventions, the genetic code has rules and regulations which govern the actions of the cellular hardware. The question is where did this code and the rules by which it is governed come from? In the last fifty years the field of information theory has shed a great deal of light on the nature of codes and programs. It turns out that one of the basic tenets of information theory is that *all* language conventions are the result of intelligent forethought or design. Consequently, random chance, which is the antithesis of intelligent design, will never generate a code or a language convention—including the genetic code. This fact poses a serious threat to the materialistic scenario on the origin of life.

The enormous task faced by the materialist is this:

any theory which attempts to explain the origin of life in the absence of a Creator, *must* be able to explain the origin of the machine-like molecular "hardware," as well as the enormously complex, coded information found in all living systems without the introduction of know-how, concepts, contrivance or intelligent design. As we will see, this task has proven so formidable that it has led some molecular biologists to despair, some to absurdity, and some to a Divine Creator for the solution to the problem.

SPONTANEOUS GENERATION

The atheist's scenario on the origin of life proposes that some four billion years ago, inanimate chemicals developed by chance into highly complex, living, single-celled organisms. It is generally believed to have occurred somewhere in a "primordial ooze," near deep hot oceanic vents or in a shallow tidal pool.

This process has been dubbed "Spontaneous Generation." According to evolutionary theory, this single-celled organism then evolved into all the complex life forms on earth in a relentless struggle for resources. Darwin called this process "descent with modification."

The evolutionary development of life on earth is commonly depicted in biology textbooks as an "evolutionary tree." If life did arise spontaneously and then evolve into increasingly complex life forms, then spontaneous generation represents the *trunk* of that evolutionary tree and the branches are the various species that evolved from these earlier forms. If the origin of life cannot be shown to be plausible by the interaction of matter, random-chance, energy and time alone, then the existence of an evolutionary tree is a dubious proposition at best. Without a trunk there can be no tree. Invoking any metaphysical (miraculous) events into the scenario violates evolution in its purest form.

FROM MUD TO MAN?

The notion that life could arise from inanimate, non-living matter is not a recent idea. This idea was seriously proposed in the sixth century B.C. by the Greek philosopher, Anaximander. He argued that life arose from mud when it was exposed to sunlight, and that it subsequently evolved into all life forms, including man.

During the dark ages people speculated that rats and flies arose spontaneously from garbage because they mysteriously appeared when garbage was left out. Others had noticed that when meat and broths were left exposed they became covered with maggots and microorganisms. These observations led some to believe that these life forms arose suddenly and spontaneously from non-living, inanimate matter. However, by the late 1700's many scientists began to question the idea of spontaneous generation.

Many, including Charles Darwin's grandfather, Erasmus Darwin, felt that the difference between the living and the non-living world was the presence of some "life force." In fact, many thought that it was the mere presence of electricity in living matter that separated it from non-living matter. Many experiments were done with electricity to try to create life spontaneously from non-living broths. This fascination led to the Frankenstein story of the late 1800's.

Louis Pasteur entered the debate in 1862 when he published the results of his experiments on the spontaneous generation of microorganisms in broths. Using swan-necked glass flasks, Pasteur showed that previously boiled broths remained uncontaminated with microorganisms unless the neck of the flask was broken. Broken flasks quickly teemed with life as the broths became cloudy. The work of Louis Pasteur seemingly ended the debate on the question of the sudden, spontaneous origin of life.

By the end of the nineteenth century, the majority of scientists believed that spontaneous generation was not possible. Loyal Darwinists, however, insisted on spontaneous generation, recognizing that it was the foundation upon which pure evolutionary theory rests. Ernst Haeckel stated in 1876:

> "If we do not accept the hypothesis of spontaneous generation, then at this one point in the history of evolution we must have recourse to the miracle of a supernatural creation."[61]

THE NEW PARADIGM

The spontaneous generation debate heated up again in 1924 when Russian biochemist I. A. Oparin proposed that life had arisen from simpler molecules on the lifeless earth under much different atmospheric conditions than exist today.[62] However, instead of life arising suddenly, as previous spontaneous-generation theories proposed, Oparin believed that it occurred over a very long period of time.

In 1929 English biologist J. B. S. Haldane published a paper in which he proposed that ultraviolet light, acting on a primitive atmosphere, containing water, ammonia and methane, produced oceans with the consistency of a "hot dilute soup" containing the building blocks of life.[63]

Ernst Haeckel one of the chief proponents of Darwinism in the nineteenth century, had argued that although spontaneous generation was not observable under the current conditions on earth, it did take place in the past under unknown chemical conditions. Oparin and Haldane made the first serious proposals regarding those conditions.

In 1952 Harold Urey noted that most of the planets in our solar system, except earth, have an atmosphere which contains little or no free oxygen.[64] Furthermore, Urey knew that the building blocks of life are quickly destroyed if they are exposed to an environment containing oxygen.[65] Therefore, he concluded that spontaneous generation must have occurred on the early earth with an atmosphere consisting mainly of hydrogen, ammonia, methane, water vapor, but little or no molecular oxygen. Lightning, volcanic eruptions, sunlight, and deep-oceanic volcanic vents are among the energy sources proposed to "finance" the necessary chemical reactions. It was presumed that the building blocks of life were made in the atmosphere and then gradually fell to earth eventually accumulating in the primeval ocean.

Despite absolutely no geological evidence for the existence of this "primeval soup," the Oparin-Haldane-Urey theories became scientific dogma. These foundational assumptions have provided the framework for the modern theory of chemical evolution in the last forty years.

STANLEY MILLER'S BOMBSHELL

In 1953 a graduate student named Stanley Miller set out to verify the Oparin-Haldane-Urey hypothesis with a simple but elegant experiment.[66] The results of this experiment have been taught to every high school and college biology student for nearly four decades.

Using a system of glass flasks, Miller attempted to simulate the early atmospheric conditions. He passed a mixture of boiling water, ammonia, methane and hydrogen through an electrical spark discharge. At the bottom of the apparatus was a trap to capture any molecules made by the reaction. This trap prevented the newly-formed chemicals from being destroyed by the next spark. Eventually, Miller was able to produce a mixture containing very simple amino acids, the building blocks of proteins.

Miller drew on decades of knowledge of organic chemistry in setting up his experiment. The proportions of the various gases used, the actual apparatus, the intensity of the spark and the chemical trap, were all carefully adjusted to create maximum yield from the experiment.

On the first attempt, after a week of electrical discharges in the reaction chamber, the sides of the chamber turned black and the liquid mixture turned a cloudy red.

The predominant product was a gummy black substance made up of billions of carbon atoms strung together in what was essentially tar, a common nuisance in organic reactions.[67] However, no amino acids used by living systems, or other building blocks of life, were produced on the first attempt.

After rearranging the apparatus, the experiment produced two amino acids, glycine and alanine, the simplest amino acids found in living systems. If we search the remaining products, we find a number of simple amino acids, but in yields so low that their concentrations would be insignificant in a body of water (Table 1).

Regarding the products of the Miller-Urey experiment, evolutionist Robert Shapiro stated:

> "Let us sum up. The experiment performed by Miller yielded tar as its most abundant product.... There are about fifty small organic compounds that are called 'building blocks'.... Only two of these fifty occurred among the preferential Miller-Urey products."[68]

TABLE 1. THE PRODUCTS OF THE MILLER EXPERIMENT

Tar	85%
Carboxylic acids not important to life	13.0%
Glycine	1.05%
Alanine	0.85%
Glutamic acid	trace
Aspartic acid	trace
Valine	trace
Leucine	trace
Proline	trace
Serine	trace
Treonine	trace

In the past forty years, many scientists have repeated the work of Miller and Urey. Electrical sparks, heat, ultraviolet radiation, light, shock waves, and high energy chemical catalysts have been used in an attempt to create the building blocks of life.[69] In general, when amino acids have been made, they occur in approximately the same proportion, with glycine and alanine predominating, as in the Miller's experiment.

THE CASE OF THE MISSING LETTERS

In the English language convention there are twenty-six letters that are used to write sentences, paragraphs, chapters, and books. These letters are strung together according to hundreds of predetermined rules. Anyone with a knowledge of those rules can understand the information conveyed by the sequence of letters.

In all living systems there are a special set of four chemical "letters," called nucleotides, which are used to "write" the information stored by the code of life, the Genetic Code. Millions of these nucleotides are strung together, end to end, in long chains, thus forming the DNA molecule (Figure 1). The instructions necessary to produce all the living structures on earth are "written" by the rules of the genetic code and carried by these chains of chemical letters. These chemical letters represent only a tiny part of the "hardware" that must arise by chance in order for spontaneous generation to occur. However, nucleotides are much more complex than the simple amino acids made by Miller and Urey, and would require much more chemical expertise to produce.

Many claims have been made that nucleotides of DNA have been produced in such "spark and soup" experiments. However, after a careful review of the scientific literature, evolutionist Robert Shapiro stated that the nucleotides of DNA and RNA,

> "...have never been reported in any amount in such sources, yet a mythology has emerged that maintains

the opposite.... I have seen several statements in scientific sources which claim that proteins and nucleic acids themselves have been prepared.... These errors reflect the operation of an entire belief system.... The facts do not support this belief.... Such thoughts may be comforting, but they run far ahead of any experimental validation."[70] (Emphasis added).

After nearly four decades of trying, with the best equipment and the best minds in chemistry, not even the "letters" of the genetic code have been produced by random chemical processes. If the letters cannot be produced by doctorate-level chemists, how can we logically assume that they arose by chance in a chemical quagmire?

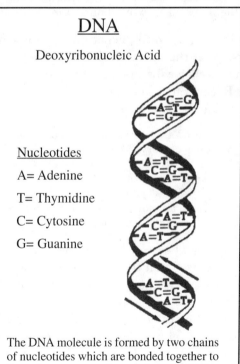

DNA

Deoxyribonucleic Acid

Nucleotides

A= Adenine

T= Thymidine

C= Cytosine

G= Guanine

The DNA molecule is formed by two chains of nucleotides which are bonded together to form the structure of a spiral double helix, somewhat like a ladder which is twisted from the top down.

Figure 1.

A TROUBLED PARADIGM

Stanley Miller's experiment was seen by believers as virtual proof that organic chemicals, and ultimately life, could be produced by chance chemistry. It brought a greater measure of scientific respectability to the theory of spontaneous generation and evolutionary thought. Evolution, according to the purists, could now be taught as a virtual certainty. The impact of this experiment on the scientific community is expressed by evolutionist and astronomer Carl Sagan:

> "The Miller-Urey experiment is now recognized as the single most significant step in convincing many scientists that life is likely to be abundant in the cosmos."[71]

This opinion, however, is not universally held by evolutionists. With the advantage of three decades of hindsight, and extensive discoveries in molecular biology, evolutionist Robert Shapiro comments on the significance of the Miller-Urey experiments:

> "The very best Miller-Urey chemistry, as we have seen, does not take us very far along the path to a living organism. A mixture of simple chemicals, even one enriched in a few amino acids, no more resembles a bacterium than a small pile of real and nonsense words, each written on an individual scrap of paper, resembles the complete works of Shakespeare."[72]

After a careful examination of the Miller experiment, Shapiro recognized that the simple chemicals he produced are a far cry from the incredible complexity of a living cell.

In the last 20 years a number of scientists have spoken out regarding the problems with the Haldane-Oparin paradigm. Most of the assumptions of the primordial atmosphere, even the existence of the "primordial soup," have been seriously questioned by origins researchers. Carl Woese, of the University of Illinois expressed the inadequacy of the Oparin thesis:

"The Oparin thesis has long ceased to be a productive paradigm: it no longer generates novel approaches to the problem.... These symptoms suggest a paradigm whose course is run, one that is no longer a valid model of the true state of affairs."[73]

Let's look at some of the evidence that has threatened the Oparin-Haldane-Miller thesis.

THE MYTH OF THE PRE-BIOTIC ATMOSPHERE: THE OXYGEN PROBLEM

The atmospheric conditions proposed by Oparin, Haldane and Urey were radically different from what presently exists. Because oxygen destroys the chemical building blocks of life, they speculated that the early earth had an oxygen-free atmosphere. However, in the last twenty years, evidence has surfaced that has convinced most atmospheric scientists that the early atmosphere contained abundant oxygen.

In the 1970's Apollo 16 astronauts discovered that water is broken down into oxygen and hydrogen gas in the upper atmosphere when it is bombarded by ultraviolet radiation. This process, called photo dissociation, is an efficient process which would have resulted in the production of large quantities of oxygen in a relatively short time. Studies by the astronauts revealed that this process is probably a major source of oxygen in our current atmosphere.

$2 H_2O + uv$ Radiation $\rightarrow H_2$ (hydrogen gas) $+ O_2$ (oxygen gas)

The assumption of an oxygen-free atmosphere has also been rejected on theoretical grounds. The ozone layer around planet earth consists of a thin but critical blanket of oxygen gas in the upper atmosphere. This layer of oxygen gas blocks deadly levels of ultraviolet radiation from the sun.[74] Without oxygen in the early atmosphere, there could have been no ozone layer over the early earth. Without an ozone layer, all life on the surface of planet earth would face certain death from exposure to intense ultraviolet radiation. Furthermore, the chemical building blocks of proteins, RNA and DNA, would be quickly annihilated because ultraviolet radiation destroys their chemical bonds.[75] It doesn't matter if these newly formed building blocks are in the atmosphere, on dry ground, or under water.[76,77,78]

So we have a major dilemma. The products of the Miller-Urey experiments would be destroyed if oxygen was present, and they would be destroyed if it wasn't! This "catch 22" has been noted by evolutionist and molecular biologist Michael Denton:

> "What we have then is a sort of 'Catch 22' situation. If we have oxygen we have no organic compounds, but if we don't we have none either."[79]

Even if the building blocks of life could survive the effects of intense ultraviolet radiation and form life spontaneously, the survival of any subsequent life forms would be very doubtful in the presence of such heavy ultraviolet light. Ozone must be present to protect any surface life from the deadly effects of ultraviolet radiation from the sun.

Finally, the assumption that there was no oxygen in the early atmosphere is not borne out by the geologic evidence. Geologists have discovered evidence of abundant oxygen content in the oldest known rocks on earth. Again, Michael Denton:

> "Ominously, for believers in the traditional organic soup scenario, there is no clear geochemical evidence to exclude the possibility that oxygen was present in the Earth's atmosphere soon after the formation of its crust."[80]

All of this evidence supports the fact that there was abundant oxygen on the early earth.

AMMONIA AND METHANE SHORT-LIVED

The assumption of an atmosphere consisting mainly of

ammonia, methane, and hydrogen, has also been seriously questioned. In the 1970's scientists concluded that
ultraviolet radiation from the sun, as well as simple "rainout," would eliminate ammonia and methane from the
upper atmosphere in a very short time.[81] In 1981, atmospheric scientists from NASA concluded that:

> "the methane and ammonia-dominated atmosphere
> would have been very short lived, if it ever existed at
> all."[82]

THE MYTH OF THE PRE-BIOTIC SOUP

During the last two decades, the notion of a primordial
soup has not fared too well either. Studies of the atmosphere, ultraviolet radiation, and the dilutional effect of a
large body of water, have convinced many scientists that
the ocean could not have developed into the "hot dilute
soup" that was envisioned by Darwin, Oparin, and
Haldane.

Oparin envisioned the production of cellular building
blocks in the atmosphere as a result of lightning or ultraviolet radiation. Stanley Miller's experiment attempted to
validate this concept. Once produced, these chemicals
would theoretically build up in the primordial oceans and
combine to form the first living systems. However, since
Miller's experiments in 1953, it has been estimated that it
would take up to two years for amino acids to fall from the
atmosphere into the ocean.[83] This is a problem because
even small amounts of ultraviolet radiation would destroy
the building blocks before they reached the oceans.
Furthermore, as we saw earlier, lack of ozone would further expedite this destruction.[84]

SAVED BY THE TRAP!

A problem seldom noted by textbooks is that the chemical reactions that produced the amino acids in Miller's
experiments are reversible. That is, the same energy
sources that cause the formation of the building blocks of
life will also destroy those same building blocks unless

they are removed from the environment where they were created. In fact, the building blocks of life are *destroyed* even more efficiently than they are created. This was foreseen by Miller and Urey, so they included a chemical trap to remove the newly formed chemicals before the next spark. Of course, this luxury would not be available on the early earth.

These problems have convinced many origins researchers that the idea of a primordial soup is quite unlikely. Michael Denton comments on the lack of evidence for the primordial soup:

> "Rocks of great antiquity have been examined over the past two decades and in none of them has any trace of abiotically produced organic compounds been found.... Considering the way the pre-biotic soup is referred to in so many discussions of the origin of life as an already established reality, it comes as something of a shock to realize that *there is absolutely no positive evidence for its existence.*"[85] (Emphasis added)

THE ORIGIN OF DNA AND PROTEINS

Up to this point we've discussed the origin of just the building blocks of living cells. The destructive effect of oxygen, ultraviolet radiation from the sun and the short duration of an optimal atmosphere for their production, makes it unlikely that significant quantities of viable nucleotides and amino acids could ever accumulate in the primitive ocean. However, even if they did accumulate in sufficient quantities, the next step is to explain how they combined to form the self-duplicating DNA molecule and the thousands of proteins found in the simplest living cells. For the materialistic scenario to be taken seriously, it must provide a plausible explanation for the origin of these enormous molecules without the introduction of biochemical know-how.

THE PROBLEM OF CHIRALITY

One of the most difficult problems for the materialistic

scenario on the origin of life is something called molecular chirality. The building blocks of DNA and proteins are molecules which can exist in both right and left-handed mirror-image forms (Figure 2). This "handedness" is called "chirality."[86,87] These mirror-image chemicals are referred to as dextrorotary (dextro-form) and levorotary (levo-form).[88]

In all living systems the building blocks of the DNA and RNA exist exclusively in the right-handed form, while the amino acids in virtually all proteins in living systems, with very rare exception, occur only in the left-handed form.[89]

The dilemma for materialists is that *all* "spark and soup-like" experiments produce a mixture of 50% left (levo) and 50% right-handed (dextro) products.[90,91]

Such a mixture of dextro and levo amino acids is called a *"racemic* mixture." Unfortunately, such mixtures are completely useless for the spontaneous generation of life.[92]

Complex molecules such as DNA and proteins are built by adding one building block at a time onto an ever-growing chain. In a "primordial soup" made up of equal proportions of right and left-handed building blocks, there is an equal probability at each step of adding either a

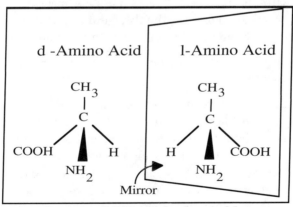

Levo and Dextro Amino Acids

Figure 2.

right or left-handed building block.[93,94] Consequently, it is a mathematical absurdity to propose that only right-handed nucleotides would be added time after time without a single left-handed one being added to a growing DNA molecule. Sooner or later an incorrect, left-handed nucleotide will be added. The same goes for proteins. Every time another amino acid is added to the growing chain of amino acids the chances are virtually certain that both right and left-handed amino acids will be added.

With *unguided or undirected* chemistry, a primordial ooze consisting of right and left-handed building blocks can only result in the production of DNA and proteins composed of a mixture of right and left-handed building blocks.

This dilemma has enormous implications for the materialistic scenario.[95] For a living cell to function properly, it is absolutely necessary for it to contain the correct three-dimensional structure in its DNA and proteins.

This correct three-dimensional structure is in turn dependent upon proteins built from a pure mixture of left-handed amino acids and DNA built from right-handed nucleotides. Consequently, if even one nucleotide or amino acid with the incorrect "handedness" is inserted into a DNA or protein molecule, the three-dimensional structure will be annihilated and it will cease to function normally.

ENZYMES: THE CELL'S MINIATURE FACTORIES

The importance of the three-dimensional structure of proteins can best be illustrated by the function of enzymes. Virtually all of the complex chemical reactions in living cells involve special proteins called enzymes. Enzymes act to speed up (catalyze) chemical reactions in biological systems. Enzymes are employed in the production of DNA, RNA, proteins, and nearly every chemical reaction in the cell. Digestion, thought, sight, and the function of nerves and muscles all require the use of enzymes. In fact, these activities would be impossible without them.

Enzymatic reactions occur like "lock and key" mechanisms. An enzyme (the lock) has a highly specific three-dimensional shape which will only allow chemicals with the correct three-dimensional fit (the key) to bind and result in a chemical reaction (Figure 3).

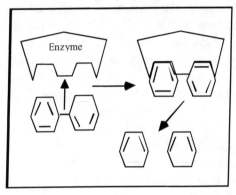

In this illustration the enzyme breaks the bond that holds two sugar molecules together releasing two unbonded sugars.

Figure 3.

The three-dimensional structure of these protein enzymes (which is determined by the sequence of pure l-amino acids) *must* be preserved within a narrow range or these "lock and key" chemical reactions *cannot* occur. Consequently, a primordial soup consisting of equal portions of left and right-handed amino acids, which will only result in proteins containing equal portions of left and right-handed amino acids, is incapable of forming enzymes with the correct three-dimensional shapes and precise "lock and key" mechanisms. Therefore, a primordial soup of left and right-handed building blocks is completely incapable of forming life.

Since all spark and soup experiments produce a 50/50 mix of right and left-handed amino acids, chemists have tried to decipher how only left-handed amino acids became integrated into the proteins of living systems. For decades chemists have attempted to separate out a pure mixture of left-handed amino acids from a racemic mix by chance chemistry alone. Chance, or *undirected* chemistry, has however, consistently proven to be an inadequate mechanism for the separation of the right and left-handed amino acid forms.[96] So, how did it happen? Mathematically, random-chance would never select such an unlikely pure molecule out of a racemic primordial soup.

The solution is simple, yet it has profound implications. To separate the two amino acid forms requires the introduction of *biochemical expertise* or *know-how*, which is the very antithesis of chance! However, biochemical expertise or know-how comes *only* from a mind. Without such know-how or intelligent guidance, the right and left-handed building blocks of life *will never* separate. Consequently, enzymes, with their lock and key mechanisms, and ultimately, life, are impossible![97]

However, the existence of a mind or a Creator involved in the creation of life is anathema to the atheist's scenario. But the volume of biochemical knowledge supports this fact: To produce pure mixtures of left-handed amino acids and right-handed nucleotides requires intelligent guidance. And since no human chemists were around before the origin of life on earth, the source of this intelligent guidance must have been extraterrestrial!

TOXIC WASTE WIPES OUT SPONTANEOUS GENERATION

The major products made in Miller's experiment were a mixture of tar and thousands of organic acids. This "chemical junk," which comprised 98% of the material produced by Miller, is very similar to the chemical waste that the U.S. government is spending billions of dollars to remove from neighborhoods all around the country. Why are they removing these chemicals? Because they are toxic to humans.

Organic acids, such as those produced by Miller, can damage DNA, causing cancer and other diseases. They also poison our enzymes by irreversibly binding to them.[98] Any primordial soup would be filled with these toxic products and would quickly and efficiently prevent the functioning of DNA, RNA, and proteins. The result: death! In fact, it is unlikely that any currently living cell on earth could survive in the chemical environment produced by Miller's experiment.[99] Considering the toxicity of the primordial soup, it is perhaps the last place on earth that life might arise.[100]

H_2O "WASHES UP" SPONTANEOUS GENERATION

We noted previously that DNA and proteins are built by adding one building block at a time onto an ever-lengthening chain. With the addition of each amino acid or nucleotide, a molecule of water is released. This is called a condensation reaction and is fully reversible, i.e., it can proceed in either direction as indicated by the arrows in figure 4.

Reversible Condensation Reaction

Amino Acid + Amino Acid $\rightleftharpoons$ Protein + H_2O

Nucleotide + Nucleotide $\rightleftharpoons$ DNA + H_2O

Figure 4.

In previous sections we have seen that neither air nor land are safe havens for the newly formed building blocks of life because of their certain destruction by oxygen or intense UV radiation. So believers in spontaneous genera-

tion have concluded that the first life forms may have aris-
en near a deep sea volcanic vent, safe from oxygen and UV
radiation. Although a water environment may seem like a
safe place for the formation of life, it is the release of a
water molecule in the above reaction that creates one of
the most difficult problems for the theory of spontaneous
generation.

Every first-year chemistry student is taught that
reversible chemical reactions will *never* proceed in a direction that produces a product that is already present in
excess amounts in the reaction vessel.[101] The production
of DNA and proteins from their building blocks results in
the production of a large number of water molecules. A
problem for the oceanic vent theory (or any water based
primordial soup theory) is that there is already an abundance of water. Consequently, the reaction above will
never proceed in a direction which produces more water.
In fact, the laws of chemistry and thermodynamics
demand that the reaction go in the opposite direction!
Therefore, in a watery solution containing the building
blocks of life, the overwhelming majority of these building
blocks would be unbonded. As a result, a watery environment is perhaps the last place that long chains of amino
acids or nucleotides would form.[102]

EQUILIBRIUM—THE VILLAIN OF THE PLOT

There is one final hurdle that must be successfully
cleared if the materialist's scenario on the origin of life is to
have credibility. This is the problem of chemical equilibrium. The notion of equilibrium is one with which you are all
familiar, even if you've never taken a chemistry course. In
any broth or solution we notice that there is the tendency
for the materials to become evenly distributed with time.
This tendency is called the development of equilibrium.[103]

A simple example will help us to understand. If a drop
of red dye is put into a container of water the dye particles
gradually disperse throughout the solution until the

entire solution turns a dilute red color. The larger the volume of the solvent (i.e., the water in our dye experiment), the more dilute will be the solution once the dye particles have become evenly distributed. This dilutional effect is irreversibly tied to the arrow of time. As time advances, as predicted by the Second Law, the dye particles become evenly distributed until the solution reaches a state of chemical equilibrium.[104]

As we saw previously, the chemical reactions leading to the formation of DNA and proteins are reversible. This means that the building blocks of DNA and proteins are broken off of the chain just as easily as they are added. Consequently, the building blocks of life, if they survived the effects of oxygen and UV radiation, would constantly be combining and coming apart in the primordial soup. This combining and coming apart of chemical building blocks proceeds until a state of equilibrium is reached. In the case of amino acids and nucleotides, the building blocks of DNA and proteins will be predominantly unbonded when the solution is at equilibrium.[105,106]

Since the natural tendency for the building blocks of life is to disperse and remain un-bonded, the question materialists must answer is how did the building blocks of life become bonded and stay bonded in a primordial soup which is steadily progressing towards equilibrium?

In living systems enzymes are "programmed" to accomplish this feat by extracting and utilizing energy from the environment to synthesize and preserve DNA and proteins.[107] Consequently, in this capacity enzymes fulfill the definition of a machine or an engine, as defined by Nobel Laureate Jacques Monod—a purposeful (teleonomic) aggregate of matter that uses energy to perform work.

In the absence of such molecular machinery (i.e., enzymes), the reversibility of these chemical reactions *ensures* that any building blocks which may have become bonded will rapidly become unbonded in a watery environment unless they are removed from the solution in equilibrium.[108,109] However, removing the building blocks from equilibrium requires a mechanism or a metabolic machine (which *do not* arise by chance).

Harold Blum dealt with this very dilemma. He recognized that the production of proteins or DNA from a solution of unbonded building blocks required a "mechanism" or metabolic "motor" that can capture free energy from the environment, then use it to remove the building blocks from equilibrium, i.e. keep them bonded:

> "...If proteins were reproduced as they must have been, if living systems were to evolve—free energy has to be supplied. The source of this free energy is a fundamental problem we must eventually face...the fact remains that no appreciable amounts of polypeptides [proteins] would form unless there were some factor which altered the equilibrium greatly in their favor."[110]

By altering "the equilibrium greatly in their favor," Blum means allowing them to stay bonded. However, inanimate matter contains no "mechanism," "machines," or "biochemical know-how" that can extract free energy from the environment and store or preserve the bonded building blocks before they break down again.

Therefore, the dilemma for the materialist is explaining the origin of the first such metabolic "machine" by chance. In practice and in theory, machines are never the result of chance. They are the result of design.[111,112] This fact is not only intuitive, but it has been verified by the overwhelming body of experimental science.

A. E. Wilder-Smith addresses this problem of the origin of the first metabolic motor:

> "What Dr. Blum is saying is: how was the motor to extract the energy from the environment built before life processes had arisen to build it? Once a motor (enzyme metabolic system) is present, it can easily supply the free energy necessary to build more and more

motors, that is, to reproduce. But the basic problem is: How do we account for the building of the first complex enzymatic protein metabolic motor to supply energy for reproduction and other cell needs.... The Creationist believes that God synthesized non-living matter into living organisms and thus provided the motors which were then capable of immediately extracting energy from their environment to build more motors for reproduction. This view is thus perfectly sound scientifically and avoids the hopeless impasse of the materialistic Darwinists in trying to account for the design and building of the first necessarily highly complex metabolic motors by random processes. Once the motor has been designed, fabricated, and is running, the life processes work perfectly well on the principles of the known laws of thermodynamics...."[113]

So the net of this dilemma is that *intelligent guidance* is required to create a metabolic motor which will synthesize and preserve the chains of DNA and proteins. Such guidance comes only from a mind, and not from inanimate inorganic matter!

TIME: THE UNLIKELY VILLAIN

When confronted with the problem of equilibrium, most scientific materialists will appeal to the magic ingredient of time. In chapter one we saw this appeal by Nobel Laureate, George Wald:

"Time is in fact the hero of the plot. Given so much time the impossible becomes possible, the possible probable, and the probable virtually certain. One has only to wait: Time itself performs the miracles."[114]

However, Dr. Blum, who is a materialist, points out that Wald's faith in the miraculous ingredient of time is mere wishful thinking. Prolonged time periods, he asserts, actually worsen the dilemma:

"I think if I were rewriting this chapter [on the origin of life] completely, I should want to change the emphasis somewhat. I should want to play down still more the importance of the great amount of time available for highly improbable events to occur. *One may take the view that the greater the time elapsed the greater should be the approach to equilibrium,* the most probable state, and it seems that this ought to take precedence in our thinking over the idea that time provides the possibility for the occurrence of the highly improbable.[115] (Emphasis added)

According to Dr. Blum, the magic bullet of time does not increase the likelihood that chains of DNA or proteins will form by chance chemistry. In fact, according to Dr. Blum, increasing the time factor actually ensures that any primordial soup would consist of predominantly unbonded amino acids and nucleotides!

THE CHICKEN OR THE EGG?

Any discussion of the origin of life would not be complete without a look at the greatest paradox of all: What came first, DNA or the proteins essential for the production of DNA?

Since the structure of DNA was deciphered in 1953, biologists have discovered that the process of duplicating DNA requires as many as twenty specific protein enzymes. These enzymes function to unwind, un-zip, copy, and rewind the DNA molecule. There are even enzymes that screen and correct for copying errors!

The instructions for the production of all proteins, including these enzymes, are in turn stored on the DNA molecule. So which came first: The DNA molecule or the proteins necessary to make DNA? You can't make DNA without highly specific proteins. But you can't make proteins unless you have a system in place to code for and build those proteins in the first place. And that means DNA.

Harold Blum recognized this catch 22 when he stated:

"...The riddle seems to be: How, when no life existed, did substances come into being which, today, are absolutely essential to living systems, yet which can only be formed by those systems? ...A number of major properties are essential to living systems as we see them today, the origin of any of which from a 'random' system is difficult enough to conceive, let alone the simultaneous origin of all."[116]

Robert Shapiro also commented on this dilemma:

"Genes and enzymes are linked together in a living cell—two interlocked systems, each supporting the other. It is difficult to see how either could manage alone. Yet if we are to avoid invoking either a Creator or a very large improbability, we must accept that one occurred before the other in the origin of life. But which one was it? We are left with the ancient riddle: Which came first, the chicken or the egg?"[117]

The simultaneous origin of DNA, RNA, and the proteins necessary to produce them is, according to Blum and Shapiro, very difficult to conceive. In fact, as we will see next, it is a mathematical impossibility.

THE ODDS

During the last several decades a number of prestigious scientists have attempted to calculate the mathematical probability of the random-chance origin of life. The results of their calculations reveal the enormity of the dilemma faced by materialists.

In the 1950's Harold Blum estimated the probability of just a single protein arising spontaneously from a primordial soup. Equilibrium and the reversibility of biochemical reactions eventually led Blum to state:

"The spontaneous formation of a polypeptide of the size of the smallest known proteins seems beyond all probability. This calculation alone presents serious objection to the idea that all living matter and systems are descended from a single protein molecule which was formed as a 'chance' act."[118]

In the 1970's British astronomer Sir Frederick Hoyle set out to calculate the mathematical probability of the

spontaneous origin of life from a primordial soup environment. Applying the laws of chemistry, mathematical probability and thermodynamics, he calculated the odds of the
spontaneous generation of the simplest known free-living
life form on earth—a bacterium.

Hoyle and his associates knew that the smallest con-
ceivable free-living life form needed at least 2,000 independent functional proteins in order to accomplish cellular
metabolism and reproduction. Starting with the hypothetical primordial soup he calculated the probability of the
spontaneous generation of just the proteins of a single
amoebae.[119] He determined that the probability of such
an event is one chance in ten to the 40 thousandth power,
i.e., 1 in $10^{40,000}$. Prior to this project, Hoyle was a believer in the spontaneous generation of life. This project, however, apparently changed his opinion 180 degrees.

Mathematicians tell us that if an event has a probability which is less likely than one chance in 10^{50}, then
that event is mathematically impossible. Such an event, if
it were to occur, would be considered a miracle.

Consider this. To win a state lottery you have about 1
chance in ten million (10^7). The odds of winning the state
lottery every single week of your life from age 18 to age 99
is 1 chance in 4.6 x10^{29}.[120] Therefore, the odds of winning the state lottery every week consecutively for eighty
years is more likely than the spontaneous generation of
just the proteins of an amoebae!

In his calculations Hoyle assumed that the primordial
soup consisted only of left-handed amino acids. As we
noted before, spark and soup-type experiments always
yield a 50/50 mix of left and right-handed building blocks.
Hoyle knew that if the soup consisted of equal portions of
right and left-handed amino acids then mathematical
probability of the origin of pure left-handed proteins
would be exactly zero!

After completing his research, Hoyle stated that the
probability of the spontaneous generation of a single bac-

teria, "is about the same as the probability that a tornado sweeping through a junk yard could assemble a 747 from the contents therein."[120]

Hoyle also stated:

> "The likelihood of the formation of life from inanimate matter is one to a number with 40 thousand naughts [zeros] after it. It is enough to bury Darwin and the whole theory of evolution. There was no primeval soup, neither on this planet nor on any other, *and if the beginnings of life were not random they must therefore have been the product of purposeful intelligence.*"[121] (Emphasis added)

Hoyle's calculations may seem impressive, but they don't even begin to approximate the difficulty of the task. He only calculated the probability of the spontaneous generation of the proteins in the cell. He did not calculate the chance formation of the DNA, RNA, nor the cell wall that holds the contents of the cell together.

A more realistic estimate for spontaneous generation has been made by Harold Morowitz, a Yale University physicist.[122] Morowitz imagined a broth of living bacteria that were super-heated so that all the complex chemicals were broken down into their basic building blocks. After cooling the mixture, he concluded that the odds of a single bacterium re-assembling by chance is one in $10^{100,000,000,000}$. This number is so large that it would require several thousand blank books just to write it out. To put this number into perspective, it is more likely that you and your entire extended family would win the state lottery every week for a million years than for a bacterium to form by chance!

In his book, *Origins—A Skeptics Guide to the Creation of Life on Earth*, Robert Shapiro gives a very realistic illustration of how one might estimate the odds of the spontaneous generation of life. Shapiro begins by allowing one billion years (5×10^{14} minutes) for spontaneous biogenesis. Next he notes that a simple bacterium can make a copy of itself in twenty minutes, but he assumes that the first life was much simpler. So he allows each trial assembly to last one minute, thus providing 5×10^{14} trial assemblies in 1 billion years to make a living bacterium. Next he allows the entire ocean to be used as the reaction chamber. If the entire ocean volume on planet earth were divided into reaction flasks the size of a bacterium we would have 10^{36} separate reaction flasks. He allows each reaction flask to be filled with all the necessary building blocks of life. Finally, each reaction chamber is allowed to proceed through one-minute trial assemblies for one billion years. The result is that there would be 10^{51} tries available in 1 billion years. According to Morowitz we need $10^{100,000,000,000}$ trial assemblies!

Regarding the probabilities calculated by Morowitz, Robert Shapiro wrote:

> "The improbability involved in generating even one bacterium is so large that it reduces all considerations of time and space to nothingness. Given such odds, the time until the black holes evaporate and the space to the ends of the universe would make no difference at all. If we were to wait, we would truly be waiting for a miracle."[123]

Regarding the origin of life Francis Crick, winner of the Nobel Prize in biology, stated in 1982:

> "An honest man, armed with all the knowledge available to us now, could only state that in some sense, the origin of life appears at the moment to be almost a miracle, so many are the conditions which would have had to have been satisfied to get it going."[124]

Regarding the probability of spontaneous generation, Harvard University biochemist and Nobel Laureate, George Wald stated in 1954:

> "One has to only contemplate the magnitude of this task to concede that the spontaneous generation of a living organism is impossible. Yet we are here—as a result, I believe, of spontaneous generation."[125]

In this incredible statement by Wald we see that his adherence to the materialist's paradigm is independent of the evidence. Wald's belief in the "impossible" can only be explained by faith: "...the substance of things hoped for, the evidence of things not seen."[126]

Despite these incredible odds, and the seemingly insurmountable problems we have discussed, spontaneous generation is taught as a fact from grammar school to university. In fact, NASA scientists reported to the press in 1991 their opinion that life arose spontaneously not once, but multiple times, because previous attempts were wiped out by cosmic catastrophes!

The reason for this fanatical adherence to spontaneous generation is eloquently pointed out by George Wald:

> "When it comes to the origin of life there are only two possibilities: Creation or spontaneous generation. There is no third way. Spontaneous generation was disproved one hundred years ago, but that leads us to only one other conclusion, that of supernatural creation. *We cannot accept that on philosophical grounds;* therefore, we choose to believe the impossible: That life arose spontaneously by chance!"[127] (Emphasis added)

According to Wald, it's not a matter of the evidence, it's a matter of philosophy! Like George Wald, many people do not like, and cannot accept the alternative: that all life on earth was created by a Transcendent Creator. So, as Wald said, they are willing to "believe the impossible," in order to cling to their belief that the universe is a closed system. A system that has no room for such a Creator.

MAN A MACHINE!! PALEY VINDICATED

When William Paley put forth his watchmaker argument in 1818, the force of his argument was weakened by David Hume's assertion that the "machine" analogy was only superficial. Hume argued that the analogy between machines and living systems could not be shown to extend to the "deepest" (molecular) level. Therefore, according to

Hume, the analogy was invalid and there was no need for a designer of biological systems.

During the time of Darwin and Hume the living cell was viewed as a mere blob of amorphous unorganized protoplasm. Consequently, Hume's assertion that the cell was not "machine-like" seemed reasonable. For nearly 150 years Paley's watchmaker argument was felt to be fatally weakened by the reasoning of Hume.

However, the astonishing discoveries in molecular biology during the last 40 years have finally and unequivocally demonstrated that living systems are, in fact, machines—even to the deepest, molecular level! From the tiniest enzyme to the most complex organ systems found in man, Paley's machine analogy is confirmed.

At the enzymatic level we see an eerie resemblance to the design and operation of chemical factories. At the organ level we find "hardware" of an unimaginable complexity and ingenuity. In our five senses we find sensory receivers made of multiple components, each machine-like, the operation of which is absolutely necessary for each sense (taste, sight, smell, hearing, touch) to function properly. In the function of the human heart we see an incredibly efficient and durable hydraulic pump, the likes of which no engineer has imagined. Finally, in the structure of the human brain we find a computer 1000 times faster than a Cray supercomputer with more connections than all the computers, phone systems and electronic appliances on planet earth!

In each of these systems, at every level, we find machine-like structures which are truly "teleonomic" (purposeful) aggregates of matter, each executing its role in a pre-programmed manner.

In 1985 evolutionist Michael Denton made this astonishing admission regarding Paley's machine analogy:

> "It has only been over the past twenty years with the molecular biological revolution and with the advances in cybernetic and computer technology that *Hume's crit-*

*icism has been finally invalidated and the analogy
between organisms and machines has at last become
convincing....* In every direction the biochemist gazes,
as he journeys through this weird molecular labyrinth,
he sees devices and appliances reminiscent of our own
twentieth-century world of advanced technology. In the
atomic fabric of life we have found a reflection of our
own technology. We have seen a world as artificial as
our own and as familiar as if we had held up a mirror to
our own machines.... *Paley was not only right in asserting the existence of an analogy between life and
machines, but was also remarkably prophetic in guess-
ing that the technological ingenuity realized in living
systems is vastly in excess of anything yet accomplished
by man.*"[128] (Emphasis added)

The implication of vindicating Paley's machine analogy were also noted by Denton:

"If we are to assume that living things are machines for
the purposes of description, research and analysis, and
for the purposes of rational and objective debate, as
argued by Michael Polyani and Monod among many others, there can be nothing logically inconsistent, as Paley
would have argued, in extending the usefulness of the
analogy to include an explanation for their origin."[129]

Since machines need a designer and since living systems possess "appliances reminiscent of our own twentieth-century world of advanced technology" it is "logically"
consistent to assert that such appliances (the mechanisms
in living systems) must, according to Denton, require a
designer as well!

Consequently, according to Denton:

"The conclusion may have religious implication."[130]

Finally, consider this provocative statement by Hoyle
and Wickramasinghe:

"The speculations of *The Origin of Species* turned out to
be wrong.... It is ironic that the scientific facts throw
Darwin out, but leave William Paley, a figure of fun to

the scientific world for more than a century, still in the tournament with a chance of being the ultimate winner."[131]

If the most knowledgeable chemists using the most up to date equipment cannot create machines as complex as a single amoebae, is it credible to assert that chance, which is the antithesis of intelligence or know-how could do so? I think not.

The Emperor is naked—and many in the scientific establishment are beginning to suspect!

---

53 Of necessity this chapter is somewhat technical. A knowledge of chemistry is not, however, necessary to grasp the major points. After this chapter it's "down hill."

54 William Paley, *Natural Theology on Evidences and Attributes of the Deity*, 18 ed., Lackington, Allen and Co. (1818).

55 David Hume, *Dialogues Concerning Natural Religion*, Fontana Library Ed. Collins, (1779).

56 Michael Denton, *Evolution: A Theory in Crisis*, Adler and Adler, 1986, 250.

57 For a detailed discussion on Jacques Monod's theories see Wilder-Smith, A. E., *The Natural Sciences Know Nothing of Evolution*, The Word for Today Publishers, Costa Mesa CA. 1981. 1-800-272-WORD.

58 These chemicals include DNA (Deoxyribonucleic Acid), RNA (Ribonucleic Acid), proteins, fats, sugars, vitamins and many others. Altogether, there are about fifty organic molecules required to manufacture the simplest living cells.

59 J. D. Watson, and F. H. C. Crick, "Structure of Deoxyribose Nucleic Acid." *Nature* (1953) 171:737-738.

60 This code or language convention is the same for all life on earth, whether a bacterium, a man, or a blue whale. The difference between a man and a whale is the "software" programs that are written by that code of life which is mutual to them both. To put it another way, the English language convention is common to both novels and short poems. The difference between the two forms of writing is how the

English language convention is applied to each style.

61 Ernst Haekel, *The History of Creation*. vol 1:348. New York, Appleton.

62 I. A. Oparin, 1924. *Proiskhozhdenie Zhizni* , Izd. Moskovski Rabochi, Moskow. Reproduced in English in *Origins of Life-The Central Concepts*. Edited by Deamer and Fleischaker, Jones and Bartlett Publishers, Boston, 1994.

63 J. B. S. Haldane, *Rationalist Annual*, 148:3-10, (1929).

64 Free oxygen refers to molecular oxygen in the form of O_2 or O_3.

65 Harold C. Urey, *The Planets, Their Origin and Development*, (Yale University Press, 1952).

66 Stanley Miller, *Science*, Vol 117, (1953), pp. 528-529.

67 The remaining 15% of the reaction products consisted of thirteen organic chemicals in concentrations ranging from .25% to 4%. All of the thirteen products were in a class of chemicals known as carboxylic acids. Amino acids, the building blocks of proteins are one type of carboxylic acid. There are an unlimited number of carboxylic acids that could be made. The smallest carboxylic acid possible is formic acid, with only one carbon atom, and in fact, was the most prominent carboxylic acid made with a yield of 4%. This acid is unimportant in most life forms, although it is found in ant venom! Three other carboxylic acids, with three carbon atoms, but unimportant to life, were made with a yield of 2.7%.

68 Robert Shapiro, *Origins-A Skeptics Guide to the Creation of Life on Earth*, (1986), pg. 105.

69 This body of work is detailed in the book *The Mystery of Life's Origin*. C. Thaxton, W. Bradley, R. Olsen , Chapter 3.

70 Shapiro, *op. cit.*, 108-109.

71 Shapiro, *op cit.*, 99.

72 Shapiro, *op. cit.*, 116.

73 Shapiro, *op. cit.*, 114.

74 Ozone, which consists of three oxygen atoms bonded together, is made when oxygen in the atmosphere interacts with ultraviolet radiation from the sun. O_2 + Ultraviolet Light » Ozone (O_3).

75 Eventually, exposure to ultraviolet radiation will break down amino acids into tar, water, methane, and ammonia.

76 Ultraviolet radiation of this intensity would wipe out all newly formed building blocks even to a depth of ten meters under the water.

77 It has been estimated that in order to form an effective ozone layer, the atmospheric oxygen content would need to be at

least 10% of the amount in our current atmosphere. However, this same concentration of oxygen is also enough to quickly and effectively wipe out those same building blocks. Ultraviolet light breaks the chemical bonds of complex molecules such as amino acids and nucleotides, making them useless for the spontaneous generation of life.

78 C. Thaxton, W. Bradley, R. Olsen, *The Mystery of Life's Origin*; Chapter 3.

79 Denton, *op. cit.*, 262.

80 Denton, *op. cit.*, 261.

81 Rainout means the effect that simple rain would have on the concentrations of atmospheric methane and ammonia. In a very short time, rain alone would eliminate most of these substances from the early atmosphere.

82 Joel Levine, and Tommy Augustson, *The Pre-biological Paleoatmosphere: Stability and Composition.* Presented at the 6th College Park Colloquium, October 1981. See *Origins of Life*, Volume 12 (1982), pp. 245-259.

83 Organic building blocks would be destroyed even if it took only a few minutes for them to fall from the atmosphere to the ocean. Once in the ocean, the intense ultraviolet radiation would destroy them up to a depth of ten meters.

84 Upon reaching the water, chemicals produced in the atmosphere would need to combine to form DNA, RNA, and proteins. To form the first cell, these chemicals would need to be concentrated and then covered by the protective covering called the cell wall. A serious problem for such a scenario is the normal dilutional effect of water. Chemicals tend to disperse, causing watery solutions to become very diluted with the progression of time. The rate of destruction of unprotected building blocks, combined with this dilutional effect, would greatly decrease the concentration of the "soup" envisioned by Oparin and Haldane.

85 Denton, *op. cit.*, pg. 261.

86 Molecular chirality results when a carbon atom is attached to four different chemical groups or substituents. The result is molecules that are mirror images of one another, just as our two hands are mirror images of one another.

87 The amino acids made by Miller's experiment were among the simplest in nature, containing only one asymmetric carbon. More complex molecules, such as nucleotides, may contain more than one asymmetric carbon. With the addition of each asymmetric carbon the number of possible molecules (called isomers) doubles.

88 The terms dextrorotory and levorotary refer to the direction these chemicals rotate the plane of polarized light. A solution of dextrorotory amino acids rotates the plane of polarized light to the right while levorotary solutions to the left.

89 The Penicillin fungus makes d-amino acids to poison potential bacterial invaders. Strychnine, an obvious poison, is also a d-amino acid and is toxic to cellular enzymes.

90 For 80 years chemists have been trying to synthesize optically pure mixtures of amino acids in the lab using stochastic chemical processes. However, this has never been accomplished. According to physical chemists, it is impossible because the two isomers have identical entropy states.

91 Miller and Urey acknowledged that the chemical makeup of their experiment consisted of *equal portions* of left-handed and right-handed amino acids.

92 Racemates are not optically active and in the laboratory always result in proteins which contain a 50/50 mix of levo and dextro amino acids or nucleotides.

93 In practice, laboratory experiments have shown that right-handed building blocks have a slightly greater affinity, or attraction, for other right-handed building blocks. Therefore, at each step in the addition of another building block, there is a 3/7 chance that the next one added will be the same optical isomer as the one previously added.

94 The smallest known free living life forms, bacteria, have about 12,000,000 nucleotides in their DNA. If we were to calculate the odds of adding twelve million successive right-handed nucleotides to the growing chain, without a single left handed one being added, it would be .5 raised to the 12 millionth power, $(.5^{12,000,000})$!

95 The materialist is left with a limited number of options. Either the first life forms had a mix of right and left-handed building blocks in their DNA and proteins, or a racemic primordial soup (which always results from Miller-Urey type experiments), somehow defied the laws of mathematics and gave rise to pure mixtures of left-handed amino acids and right handed nucleotides. The first option (racemic life) is impossible because a three-dimensional structure of enzymes and proper functioning is not possible with a mix of dextro and levo amino acids. The second option is a mathematical absurdity.

96 Some have suggested that certain clay or crystal surfaces might "select" one isomer over another and, therefore, purify a mixture of like-handed (optically pure) molecules.

However, this argument ignores the fact that the entropy states of the two isomers are identical and are very difficult to separate. Secondly, experimental chemistry shows that it is impossible to get pure mixtures of one or the other isomer this way. Irregularities in the structure of the clay or crystal surfaces would result in the accumulation of both isomers, i.e., contaminants. Since this is so, if even one incorrect isomer gets integrated into a protein or nucleic acid, its 3-D structure would be destroyed.

97 A minority of chemists have suggested that perhaps life started out with racemic proteins and later only the levo amino acids were selected out. However, there is no known mechanism whereby chance chemistry can accomplish such a "selection" process. Furthermore, the structure of proteins is so tightly coupled to function that the intermediates between the racemic proteins and the optically pure proteins (consisting of only levo amino acids) would not be functional. In fact, the removal of even one amino acid often destroys the structure and function of a protein. To change from a racemic protein to an optically pure one would mean the substitution of 50% of the amino acid residues.

98 Most chemicals that are poisonous to plants, animals or humans kill their victims by binding specifically and irreversibly to the active site of metabolic enzymes.

99 Another devastating fact regarding the "toxic waste" produced by "spark and soup" experiments is that these chemicals, composed mainly of carboxylic acids, bind to amino acids far more readily than amino acids bind to each other! Therefore, it is incredulous to conclude that pure, uncontaminated mixtures of amino acids or nucleotides could combine, or be selected out by chance, from such a mixture of "chemical junk."

100 Anyone that has worked in a biochemistry lab knows that the smallest amount of impurity in the reaction vessels will halt the activity and efficiency of enzymes. In fact, the presence of common ocean water is "dirty" enough to halt the function of free enzymes in such an experiment. Therefore, even the ocean is an unlikely place for enzymes and life to evolve.

101 This is called the law of mass action.

102 Recognizing the dilemma that these reversible condensation reactions pose, some have proposed that the origin of life occurred near super hot oceanic volcanic vents. Next to such vents the temperatures can reach thousands of degrees,

thus causing a relative decrease in the amount of water. This would theoretically drive the condensation reaction toward the production of "post-cursors" or proteins. The flaw in this argument is that heat (110 degrees Fahrenheit or greater) quickly and efficiently breaks down (denatures) proteins rendering them structurally and functionally incompetent.

103 A solution is said to be at equilibrium when it reaches a state of greatest entropy and lowest energy state.

104 In a solution that is in equilibrium there will always be local areas where the dissolved particles may, for a transient period, not be evenly distributed. That is, there will be areas of decreased entropy (increased order). These exceptions are transient since they are in equilibrium with the surrounding particles.

105 The Second Law, coupled with the fact that these condensation reactions are reversible, drives the solution in the net direction of a mixture containing predominantly unbonded building blocks. According to thermodynamic calculations by Harold Blum (Time's Arrow and Evolution), in a watery solution about 1% of amino acids will exist as dipeptides (two bonded amino acids), .001% as tripeptides and less than one in 10-20 will exist in a chain of ten amino acids. Those that do bond will be quickly unbonded when a collision with water occurs unless these unlikely, reduced entropy molecules are stored and kept away from the solution in equilibrium.

106 In a primordial soup, random molecular movement would cause the building blocks of life to diffuse away from their site of origin. Just as concentrated red dye will disperse when dropped into water, the building blocks of DNA and protein will also diffuse until equilibrium is reached. At this point there would be billions of water molecules for every unbonded building block. This process, along with the rapid breakdown of nucleotides and amino acids by oxygen and UV radiation, makes it almost impossible to imagine how, in a watery environment, biochemical precursors could combine, stay combined and continue to build upon each other in the face of the concept of chemical equilibrium.

107 Enzymes are able to function as metabolic machines which extract free energy from the environment (e.g. photosynthesis) and use this energy to overcome the effect of equilibrium in the synthesis and preservation of DNA and proteins. During the synthesis of proteins, enzymes first "activate" or

energize amino acids (using ATP) and allow them to bond and stay bonded. This enormously complex process requires a specific transfer RNA molecule for the activation and bonding of each of the twenty amino acids used in living systems. This energy is then used to overcome the effect of equilibrium in the preservation of DNA and proteins in a state of increased order. In effect, enzymes capture the building blocks, bind them together, essentially removing them from the solution, and then preserve them in their bonded state. However, these cellular machines or mechanisms (enzymes) are designed to store and maintain these deviations from equilibrium. The problem for the materialist is to explain how such deviations from equilibrium were stored in the absence of any mechanism or system capable of doing this. Inorganic matter possesses neither the know-how nor the mechanism to store the decreased entropy found in the chains of DNA and protein.

108 To overcome the effect of equilibrium, many scientists will unwittingly assert that the addition of enough energy into a thermodynamically open system (such as the earth) will cause the system to stray from equilibrium and allow the accumulation or storage of "corners" of increased order (or negative entropy). It is true that the introduction of more energy causes an increase in the number of chemical collisions and a corresponding increase in the number of unlikely polymers (consisting of two, three, four or more bonded building blocks). However, in order for DNA or protein synthesis to occur, these deviations from equilibrium must be stored or preserved. If they (the polymers) are not stored, then collisions with water, which are constantly occurring, will just as easily break down the randomly-formed polymers. Furthermore, the addition of long time periods simply acts to drive even localized "corners" of decreased entropy to a state of equilibrium, i.e. predominantly unbonded building blocks.

109 Crystals are often presented as examples of structures that display reduced entropy, and yet are at equilibrium. However, the order that we see in a crystal is a secondary order which is dependent upon the order already present in the atoms.

110 Harold F. Blum, *Time's Arrow and Evolution*. (2d ed., Princeton, N.J. Princeton University Press, 1955).

111 Machines result when information (know-how) is intelligently and deliberately combined with the natural law in

matter for the purpose of creating a purposeful mechanism.

112 For a detailed discussion on the origin of machines see *The Scientific Alternative to Neo-Darwinian Evolutionary Theory: Information Sources and Structures.* A. E. Wilder-SmithWilder-Smith, The Word for Today Publishers, Costa Mesa, Ca. 92628 (Phone 1-800-272-WORD).

113 A. E. Wilder-SmithWilder-Smith, *Man's Origin Man's Destiny*, (1993 English ed.) The Word for Today Publishers, (Phone 1-800-272-WORD), pp. 45-46.

114 George Wald, "The Origin of Life", *Scientific American* 191:48 (May 1954).

115 Blum, *op. cit.*, 178a.

116 Blum, *op. cit.* 17.

117 Shapiro, *op. cit.* 135.

118 Harold F. Blum, *Time's Arrow and Evolution* (2d ed., Princeton, N.J. Princeton University Press, 1955).

119 In Hoyle's experiment he assumed a primordial soup that contained all of the twenty essential amino acids.

120 *Nature*, vol. 294:105, November 12, 1981.

121 *Nature*, vol. 294:105, November 12, 1981.

122 Harold Morowitz, *Energy Flow in Biology* (New York; Academic Press, 1968).

123 Shapiro, *op. cit.*, 128.

124 Francis Crick, *Life Itself-Its Origin and Nature*, Futura, London, (1982).

125 George Wald, "The Origin of Life", *Scientific American* 191:48 (May 1954).

126 See the New Testament, Hebrews 11:1.

127 George Wald, "The Origin of Life", *Scientific American* (May 1954).

128 Denton, *op cit.*, pg. 340.

129 *Ibid.*, 341.

130 *Ibid.*, 341.

131 Sir Fred Hoyle and Chandra Wickramasinghe, *Evolution from Space: A Theory of Cosmic Creationism* (New York: Simon and Schuster, 1981), pp. 96-97.

CHAPTER FOUR

THE ORIGIN OF LIFE—
THE "SOFTWARE"

"And God said, Let the earth bring forth grass, the herb
yielding seed, and the fruit tree yielding fruit after his
kind, whose seed is in itself, upon the earth: and it was
so."

Genesis 1:11 (KJV)

When George Wald and Francis Crick stated that
the spontaneous origin of life was "impossible,"
they were speaking primarily about the origin of
the cellular "hardware." Indeed, when we consider the
effect of equilibrium, the reversibility of biochemical reactions in water and the fact that the building blocks of life
are not safe in the air or on the land,[132] spontaneous biogenesis stands shoulder to shoulder with raising the dead
and walking on water—events which also defy the Second
Law of Thermodynamics and the Law of Chemical
Equilibrium—something which cannot be explained by
natural law. However, for the purpose of this chapter we
will allow that sometime on the early earth the oceans
became filled with spontaneously derived DNA.

The question we must now answer is this: Would a
DNA molecule that arose by chance possess any information, codes, programs, or instructions? To put it another
way—can information, codes, or programs arise by
chance? In the last half of the twentieth century, evidence
has accumulated which has decisively answered this ques-

tion. The answer profoundly impacts the debate on the existence of God.

ENCYCLOPEDIA ON A PINHEAD: CHANCE OR DESIGN

At the moment of conception, a fertilized human egg is about the size of a pin head. Yet, it contains information equivalent to about six billion "chemical letters." This is enough information to fill 1000 books, 500 pages thick with print so small you would need a microscope to read it! If all the DNA chemical "letters" in the human body were printed in books, it is estimated they would fill the Grand Canyon *fifty times!* The source of this information (the "software") is at the very core of the debate on the origin of life.

When Carl Sagan said, "The cosmos is all that is, or ever was, or ever will be," he was expressing the materialists' position that the universe is a closed system.[133] That is, they believe that no information or matter can be inserted into our universe from outside our space-time domain. Consequently, with no intelligent source, materialists are forced to conclude that the sum total of the information on the DNA molecule arose by chance.

On the other hand, creationists believe that a Transcendent Creator pierced the veil of our universe and infused information and order onto the chains of the DNA molecule. Again we see that the debate boils down to chance or design. To settle this debate we must look at the nature of information as defined in the field of information science.

THE NATURE OF INFORMATION

The modern field of information science has revolutionized our daily lives in the last four decades. Computers, fax machines, cellular phones and many other daily conveniences would not have been possible without the rapid advances in the field of information theory.

In recent years information engineers have examined the nature of the genetic code and concluded that it is an error-correcting digital coding system. While digital coding systems can be very complex, error-correcting digital codes are much less common and much more complex. Furthermore, the DNA molecule has built-in redundancy. That is, the same packet of information (called a gene) is often located in more than one place in the organism's DNA. Consequently, if one gene becomes corrupted with informational errors, the backup gene will take over the function of that gene! This level of complexity is found in only the most sophisticated computer systems.

The DNA coding system can be compared to that of a compact disc. The music on a compact disc is stored in a digital fashion and can only be appreciated if you have a knowledge of the language convention used to create the information on the disc. Appropriate machinery, which functions to translate that code into music, is also required for the music to be played. In a compact disc player this decoding process involves dozens of electronic and moving parts.

It isn't much different in the living cell. The information carried by the DNA molecule contains the instructions for all the structures and functions of the human body. Within each cell resides all the necessary hardware to decode and utilize that information.

When we look at a compact disc, we see no evidence of the musical information stored on the disc's surface. We see only the rainbow effect on the surface of the disc. Without the knowledge of the language convention used to create the disc and the machinery to translate it, we must simply be content with the colorful surface. This is exactly the same dilemma we face with spontaneously derived DNA or any information storage system.[134]

If we examine the sequence of nucleotides on the DNA molecule, they simply have the appearance of a long chain of chemicals and not the appearance of a message system or a code. It is only when one possesses a knowledge of the language convention (the genetic code) and the appropriate machinery to translate the coded information on the DNA molecule, that the nucleotide sequence becomes understandable. Without such knowledge and machinery, the sequences on a spontaneously derived DNA molecule are meaningless.

Consequently, the enormous challenge facing the scientific materialist is to explain how a language convention (the genetic code) and the necessary cellular machinery to translate the information stored on the DNA molecule arose independently without intelligent guidance.

This chicken-or-egg dilemma has confounded scientists for decades. Chemist John Walton noted the dilemma in 1977 when he stated:

> "The origin of the genetic code presents formidable unsolved problems. The coded information in the nucleotide sequence is meaningless without the translation machinery, but the specification for this machinery is itself coded in the DNA. Thus without the machinery the information is meaningless, but without the coded information the machinery cannot be produced. This presents a paradox of the 'chicken and egg' variety, and attempts to solve it have so far been sterile."[135]

By allowing the spontaneous generation of long chains of DNA, what would you have? Do those chains of nucleotides possess a code or a program? Of course not. What you have is an admittedly complex chemical which has the *potential* of carrying a code or information. However, there is no inherent information on such spontaneously generated DNA unless a system of interpreting those sequences exists first. A couple of simple examples will help us to understand the nature of this dilemma.

"SAVE OUR SOULS!"

If I were to show you a sign which had painted on it the sequence, dot, dot, dot, dash, dash, dash, dot, dot, dot, and if you were knowledgeable in Morse code you would know that this means S-O-S, and that I am in trouble. However, if I take that same sign to an isolated tribe of South American Indians, they will see the unlikely arrangement of dots and dashes, but there will be no information content transmitted to them without the knowledge of the language convention we call Morse code.

THE ENGLISH LANGUAGE

Similarly, if I take a book written in English and hand it to an Australian Bushman, it will make absolutely no sense without a *prior* knowledge of the English language convention. Just like the dots and dashes, the 26 letters of the English language have no inherent information in them. Their shapes have the appearance of order (reduced entropy) but by themselves they are meaningless. It is when you "shepherd" or gather the letters into *specific sequences*, as determined by the rules of the previously existent language convention, that their arrangement begins to have meaning. Unless the language convention and the hardware (the human brain) to interpret it exists first, the arrangement of the letters can transmit no meaning.

PRIMORDIAL DISK SOUP

The magnetic disks used to store and retrieve information in computers provides another fascinating analogy to the DNA molecule. When I purchase a blank computer disk, have I purchased a code or program? No. I have only purchased a chemical medium which has the *potential* to carry a code or a program. However, to possess real information the blank disk must be formatted and programmed by a computer which was in turn built for this purpose.

While the disk is being formatted a "program" is placed on it from an intelligent source (the computer) that exists outside and separate from the disk. This is accomplished by arranging the iron atoms on the disk in a pre-determined fashion according to the rules of the computer's language convention. Once the disk is formatted and imputed with information, it weighs no more than it did before this procedure was done. This is because information has no mass or weight.

As in the case of the 26 letters of the English alphabet, the structure or shape of the iron atoms on the disk does not convey or possess any information in and of itself. Rather, information (a code or program) is *conveyed* by the orderly arrangement of the iron atoms. This arrangement of atoms is then interpreted by the computer's hardware according to the predetermined rules of its language convention. Without the hardware and the pre-existent language convention, the arrangement of the iron atoms is meaningless.

Does the computer create its own language convention? Obviously not. Just as the hardware requires intelligent design, so does the computer's language convention require an intelligent source—a computer programmer.

By allowing an ocean of spontaneously derived DNA, I have given you the equivalent of an ocean full of blank floppy disks! In order for the DNA molecule to carry information, its molecules need to be arranged in a specific sequence as predetermined by the chemical code or language convention. But the language convention *must* exist first. According to the principles of modern information theory, language conventions come only from an intelligent source—a mind!

Miller and Urey were able to produce the unlikely, ordered building blocks of proteins. In the future someone may even produce nucleotides by chance chemical processes. However, without a pre-existent language convention, these chemical letters will be no more effective in transmitting information than a *random* sequence of beads on a string, iron atoms in a disc, or letters on a page.

CODES BY CHANCE?

In the twentieth century, theories on the origin of the chemical hardware in living systems have come and gone with each generation.[136] However, theories on the origin of codes and programs are few and far between. The claim by creationists that codes, programs and language conventions, such as the genetic code, arise only from intelligent sources is often protested by scientific materialists (although most information engineers have no problem with this statement). Yet no one has come up with a rational theory on how true information, which is the antithesis of chance, can arise by random chance processes. As we will see, however, this problem has led to some irrational solutions.

One of the most celebrated theories on the origin of information by chance comes from materialist Manfried Eigen. In his book *Das Spiel*, Eigen attempts to show how a code or program might develop by chance. Eigen argues that if the letters of the genetic code can arise by chance, then why not the words, the sentences, the paragraphs and the entire book?

Eigen envisions a machine that possesses the remarkable ability to generate, by chance, the letters of the English language and then randomly shuffle and combine those letters for millions of years. After examining the volumes of randomly generated letters we find some rather amazing combinations. The machine has generated "AND," "MAN," "DOG," "CAT," "The Lord is my shepherd, I shall not want...." We stand back and see that, indeed, this machine has generated meaningful sentences. Eigen argues that this is proof of the random chance production of information. Is this true?

In his book, *The Natural Sciences Know Nothing of Evolution*, A. E. Wilder-Smith demonstrates the fallacy of Eigen's argument. Wilder-Smith invites a non-English speaking friend from Switzerland to examine the output of the machine. Again the machine puts out the random sequences such as "HAT," "FISH," "BOY," etc. His Swiss friend stares at the machine with a blank look, quite unlike the smile an Englishman might carry. While the Englishman stands amazed at the randomly generated information, our Swiss friend points out that the sequences have no meaning to him at all because he has no knowledge of the English language convention.

Eigen's argument that "true information" has been generated by chance, is erroneous because he interprets his sequences by the rules of a previously existing language convention we call the English language. But where did the rules of English come from?

Wilder-Smith points out that the sequence of letters has meaning only when we "hang" the rules and the conventions of the English language on the sequences themselves. Just as dots and dashes are meaningless without a knowledge of the Morse Code, so too are the random arrangements of any letters, chemicals, beads, or magnetic medium meaningless without rules and conventions by which we interpret the sequences. But the rules of any language system are themselves arbitrary (i.e. man-made), abstract agreements between at least two intelligences which declare that a specific sequence of letters has a certain meaning.[137] Put another way, the rules of any language system are neither a part of nor conveyed by any natural laws of nature. Therefore, a language convention, with its rules and regulations, must be devised first.

Information engineers know that language conventions *will not, cannot,* and *do not* arise by chance. Every information engineer or computer programmer knows that chance must be eliminated if one is to successfully write a code or program. In fact, chance is the very antithesis of information.

If Bill Gates of Microsoft Corporation commissioned you to write a new software program and you simply began to type randomly on your computer with the hope that a new language or program might result, you would likely be assisted to a psychiatric facility for an extended medical leave of absence. We know intuitively that this method will never result in the generation of new information.

Yet, according to evolutionary dogma, the random shuffling of nucleotides for millions of years supposedly produced not only the DNA molecule but the code which governs the storage and retrieval of the information it carries as well. If we make such a claim, are we not, in effect, asserting that formatted computer floppy disks, which are filled with millions of bits of information, can arise by the random combining of iron oxide and plastic rather than being the product of an intelligent source which is outside and separate from the floppy disk?

THE MONKEY AND THE TYPEWRITER

For centuries scientists have suspected that living systems contain a mechanism for the storage and retrieval of information used for cellular metabolism and reproduction. With the elucidation of the structure of DNA in 1953 and the subsequent deciphering of the genetic code in the 1960's this was finally confirmed. However, the debate on the origin of this cellular information predates the actual discovery of the DNA molecule by at least 100 years.

As in the case of the cellular "hardware," evolutionists have also appealed to the magic ingredient of time to explain the origin of the information, the "software," stored by living systems. Since the 1700's scientific materialists have argued that, given enough time, anything was possible, even the origin of the complex programs necessary for the production of life. Creationists, on the other hand, have argued that where there is design there must be a designer and where there are codes or language conventions there must be an architect for such information.

On June 30, 1860, at the Oxford Union in England, this was the very topic in the "Great Debate" between the Anglican Archbishop of Oxford University, Samuel

Wilberforce and evolutionist and agnostic, Thomas Huxley.

Bishop Wilberforce, a Professor of Theology and Mathematics at Oxford University, applied the logic of the teleological argument for God. He argued, as did William Paley, that the design we see in nature required a Designer. Therefore, the information (an evidence for design) found in living systems could not arise by chance.

Huxley, on the other hand, declared that given enough time all the possible combinations of matter, including those necessary to produce a man, will eventually occur by chance molecular movement. To prove his point Huxley asked Wilberforce to allow him the service of six monkeys that would live forever, six typewriters that would never wear out and an unlimited supply of paper and ink. He then argued that given an infinite amount of time these monkeys would eventually type all of the books in the British Library including the Bible and the works of Shakespeare!

Applying the mathematical laws of probability, Huxley showed that if time (t) is infinite, then the probability (P) of an event happening is equal to one, i.e., one hundred percent.[138] Consequently, he argued that with an infinite amount of time any and all combinations of letters, including the necessary chemical combinations to produce life, will eventually be typed out purely by chance, without the necessity of a Creator.

Bishop Wilberforce, a skilled mathematician, was forced to concede the truth of Huxley's point. To this very day the Monkey-Typewriter argument is frequently applied by evolutionists when confronted with the question of the origin of life.

Bishop Wilberforce lost the debate because he was unable to see the flaw in Huxley's argument. At the time of this debate the nature of biochemical reactions and the genetic code was not understood. Consequently, Huxley's argument seemed reasonable. When time is infinite the probability formula does indeed predict that all possible combinations of letters will occur. However, with the revolutionary discoveries in molecular biology and information science in the last four decades, Huxley's use of a typewriter to simulate the chemical reactions in living systems has, in fact, been shown to be erroneous.

In the last chapter we saw that the chemical reactions in living systems, such as the combining of amino acids and nucleotides, are reversible. The reversibility of these chemical reactions is quite unlike those simulated by Huxley's typewriter.

A century after the "Great Debate," Professor A. E. Wilder-Smith, who also studied at Oxford University, demonstrated the fallacy of Huxley's argument. Wilder-Smith points out that because the chemical reactions upon which our bodies run are reversible, for Huxley's argument to be valid, his monkeys would need to use typewriters which also type reversibly![139] With each key stroke such a typewriter places the ink on the paper, and when the key is released the ink jumps back onto the hammer of the typewriter leaving the paper reversibly without a trace!

This is, in fact, a more accurate demonstration of what happens in biological reactions. The building blocks of life continually combine ("type in") and come apart ("type out") as the solution approaches a state of equilibrium. With a typewriter that types reversibly—typing in (bonding) and typing out (uncombining)—we will have typed as much in one minute as we would have in 5 billion years![140]

Huxley's argument is invalidated by the fact that the building blocks in biological reactions do not stay combined. The building blocks of DNA and proteins are driven (by the Second Law and chemical equilibrium) to *break down* (come apart) in the watery environment in which they supposedly arose.

On the other hand, the hypothetical books typed by

Huxley's monkeys are stable end products. They do not decompose (come apart) into their individual letters as do the building blocks of life. Therefore, Huxley's illustration is an erroneous and inaccurate representation of biological systems.

Finally, we saw that Stanley Miller's spark and soup experiment generated 50% right-handed and 50% left-handed amino acids. We saw that right-handed amino acids are, in many cases, poisonous to enzymes and living cells. Consequently, if the keys in Huxley's typewriter represent a true primordial soup, every other key stroke would be potentially lethal! How far do you think the monkeys would get toward typing the genetic code with such odds?

In his characteristic style, Sir Fred Hoyle comments on the improbability that Huxley's monkeys might type the genetic code:

> "No matter how large the environment one considers, life cannot have had a random beginning. Troops of monkeys thundering away at random on typewriters could not produce the works of Shakespeare, for the practical reason that the whole observable universe is not large enough to contain the necessary monkey hordes, the necessary typewriters, and certainly the waste paper baskets required for the deposition of wrong attempts. The same is true for living material."[141]

TIME: MAGIC BULLET OR UNLIKELY VILLAIN

When confronted with the many evidences against the spontaneous origin of life, the scientific materialist will inevitably and repeatedly appeal to the magic ingredient of prolonged time periods to accomplish biochemical impossibilities. However, as in the case of the chemical "hardware," the addition of prolonged time periods does not increase the likelihood of spontaneously-derived information.

In the previous chapter on the origin of the cellular "hardware," we saw that the laws of thermodynamics and chemical equilibrium demand that all systems tend toward disorder with the advance of time. In the field of information science, these laws have enormous implications as well.

When applied to the field of information science, the Second Law demands that the total amount of information in a closed system *decreases* as time advances.[142] Put another way, as time advances the sum total of the information stored on magnetic tape, the pages of a book, or the sequences of a DNA molecule always degrades. This is, in fact, exactly what we observe with these media. As time advances, DNA molecules collect informational errors (mutations) and the organism eventually dies. Ancient scrolls lose their ink. Old recordings become filled with informational noise. In each case the result is always the same—loss of information.

The Theory of Evolution demands that just the opposite occurs. To change an amoebae into a human being requires a million-fold increase in the information stored in the DNA of each cell. According to evolutionary theory, this increase in information must also occur without any intelligent guidance. Such an occurrence would not only breach a foundational truth of information theory—that *true* information comes only from a mind—it would also defy the Second Law of Thermodynamics which demands that the information stored on the DNA molecule must degrade and not increase.[143]

In their book *Evolution From Space*, Sir Fred Hoyle and Chandra Wickramasinge address the problem of the origin of the information carried on the DNA molecule:

> "From the beginning of this book we have emphasized the enormous information content of even the simplest living systems. *The information cannot in our view be generated by what are often called 'natural' processes,* as for instance through meteorological and chemical

> processes occurring at the surface of a lifeless planet. As
> well as a suitable physical and chemical environment, a
> large initial store of information was also needed [for
> the origin of life]. *We have argued that the requisite
> information came from an 'intelligence'....*"[144]
> (Emphasis added)

In this remarkable statement, Hoyle and
Wickramasinghe admit that living systems require "enormous" amounts of information for their construction. This
information, they conclude, cannot be generated by "natural" or random chemical processes. Consequently, they
assert that the source of the information is from an "intelligence."

The implications of this admission by Hoyle and
Wickramasinghe are mind boggling. Since, in their opinion, chance "chemical processes occurring at the surface of
a lifeless planet [earth]" cannot create new information,
then the source of information found in living systems
must have been of extraterrestrial origin!

ET: THE SOWER OF LIFE?

By the end of the 1960's the evidence from thermodynamics, mathematical probability and information theory
were taking their toll on the Oparin-Haldane-Miller paradigm. With each new discovery in molecular biology the
concept of spontaneous generation gradually took on the
appearance of a miracle, rather than an unlikely accident
of chemistry.

In the 1970's speculation on the origin of life took an
unexpected and bizarre turn. Because the laws of chemistry, physics and mathematical probability so mitigate
against the possibility of spontaneous generation, scientists began to look for an extraterrestrial source for the
origin of life!

Francis Crick, co-discoverer of DNA, and one of the
most respected molecular biologists in the world, has conceded that the spontaneous origin of life on earth is "almost

a miracle." Consequently, since life could not have arisen by chance, he proposed that the first life forms on earth were single-celled "spores" delivered here from interstellar space![145,146] This theory, called "Directed Panspermia" then asserts that these "interstellar spores" subsequently evolved into all the life forms on earth. Similar conclusions were drawn by Hoyle in his book *Evolution From Space*.[147]

These men recognized that something beyond the bounds of planet earth was required to generate the information and complexity found within living systems.

Scientists recognize that there are only two options for the origin of life: intelligent design or spontaneous biogenesis. Faced with the apparent impossibility of spontaneous biogenesis on earth, one might have suspected that these men would invoke a supernatural, extra-dimensional, intelligent Creator for the origin of life. However, this was not the case. Crick, and others, have concluded that since life could not have arisen by chance on planet earth, the laws of chemistry and physics must, therefore, be more favorable elsewhere in the cosmos and that life arose there first and was later delivered to earth.

Michael Denton comments on this bizarre twist:

> "Nothing illustrates more clearly just how intractable a problem the origin of life has become than the fact that world authorities can seriously toy with the idea of panspermia."[148]

The dramatic shift from a theistic, Judeo-Christian world view to a secularized, neo-Darwinian "age of reason" was accomplished, in part, by those who desired to explain away the biblical miracle of creation. It is ironic, therefore, that as we approach the end of the twentieth century some of the world's most prominent scientists are forced to conclude that life on earth had an extraterrestrial origin. This is, in theory, exactly what the Bible has said all along. However, the "Extraterrestrial" the Bible speaks of is not just from beyond earth, but from beyond time and space as well!

The assertion that elsewhere in the universe the laws of physics and chemistry are more favorable for the origin of life is not supported by even a shred of scientific evidence. To invoke such an explanation is, in effect, an appeal to something outside the bounds of natural laws, i.e., a metaphysical, supernatural cause.

In 1981 Sir Fred Hoyle commented on this appeal to metaphysics:

> "I don't know how long it is going to be before astronomers generally recognize that the combinatorial arrangement of *not even one* among the many thousands of biopolymers [DNA, RNA, proteins] on which life depends could have been arrived at by natural processes here on the Earth. Astronomers will have a little difficulty at understanding this because they will be assured by biologists that this is not so, the biologists having been assured in their turn by others that it is not so. *The 'others' are a group of persons who believe, quite openly, in mathematical miracles.* They advocate the belief that tucked away in nature, outside of normal physics, there is a law that performs miracles (provided the miracles are in the aid of biology). This curious situation sits oddly on a profession that for long has been dedicated to coming up with logical explanations of biblical miracles."[149] (Emphasis added)

If we are to assume that the laws of physics and chemistry are essentially uniform throughout the physical universe, then we must logically conclude that life could not have arisen by chance *anywhere* in the universe.

Even if the laws of physics were found to be more favorable in a distant corner of the universe, there would still be no explanation for the coded information (which does not arise by chance) that is carried by the DNA molecule.

Consequently, the source of the cellular "hardware" as well as the information carried by the DNA molecule must have been an intelligent, extra-dimensional one—beyond the bounds of space and time.

"OF THE DUST OF THE GROUND"

The evidence presented thus far has brought us to a remarkable conclusion. As we have seen, the order and complexity in the universe is well beyond the reach of chance. We have seen that to "wind up" and order the physical universe requires the introduction of energy and intelligent guidance from a source outside the bounds of the space-time domain. Furthermore, the enormous complexity of living systems and the nature of the information on the DNA molecule cannot be explained by natural laws within the dimension of our universe.

Surely, at the dawn of the twentieth century, few scientists would have anticipated that their quest to explain the existence of the universe on natural grounds would have brought us to the point where their own discoveries now demand the existence of the very Creator they were trying to explain away! And yet, this is exactly what has occurred.

To create the universe and its life forms the Creator must, of necessity, be transcendent. To create the universe in the first place He must have preceded it. Secondly, to order and establish the matter within galaxies, solar systems and living beings, He would need to "enter," in effect, the arena of space-time that He created. This ability to simultaneously exist inside and outside the dimensions of the universe demands a transcendent, supernatural Creator.

To many, invoking a supernatural cause for the origin of the universe is abhorrent. However, to invoke the god called "chance" is, according to many, a belief in "mathematical miracles." So we must choose between mathematical miracles, without a supernatural agent to perform them, or a Transcendent Creator—the "First Cause," who ordered and established the universe and its life forms. The god called "chance" or intelligent design? You must choose.

For thousands of years the Bible has revealed a

Transcendent Creator who acted prior to the origin of our space-time domain.[150] To create the universe and life on earth, He transcended time and space, then inserted information or know-how onto matter. The result was the birth of an ordered, energized universe filled with information and every appearance of contrivance and design.

The Bible declares that this same Creator entered time and space physically in the person of Jesus Christ. Finally, the Bible authenticates the authority of its message by demonstrating that its text came from a transcendent, supernatural Being who exists beyond time and space.

Proving these facts is the remaining burden of this book.

---

132 Due to the destructive effects of oxygen and UV radiation.

133 Carl Sagan, *Cosmos*, Random House, New York, 1980, pg. 4.

134 During the time of recorded history there have been dozens of information storage and retrieval systems developed by man. The use of clay tablets, ink on paper, beads on a string and modern computers have all been used to store and retrieve information. No matter what medium mankind has used, all of these systems share two vital elements. Each of the systems uses a material medium (air molecules to carry voice, clay tablets, beads, etc...) to carry the information. Secondly, each of the systems employs the use of specific rules and regulations which determine the meaning of the arrangement of the letters on a page, beads on a string or impressions on a tablet. Consequently, the information in the Encyclopedia Britannica can just as surely be stored by beads on a rope as it can with a compact disc.

135 John Walton, "Organization and the Origin of Life" *Origins*, Vol. 4, No. 1, 1977, pp. 30-31.

136 In the last decade a number of scientists have proposed that RNA and not DNA was the first self duplicating molecule upon which life arose. The function of information storage

was later transferred to DNA which evolved later. However, RNA is even more unstable in water. Its chemical bonds are even more sensitive to the destructive effects of equilibrium in a watery environment. All of the processes that are destructive to DNA are even more destructive to RNA. Furthermore, spontaneously derived RNA would also contain NO information. Others have claimed that the first life forms were clay based self reproducing systems (See Shapiro). However, no rational system of converting silica or clay based life to carbon based life is imaginable. Further, where did the information for reproduction, growth, metabolism and repair come from in clay based systems?

137 This is one of the fascinating evidences that God exists in at least two personages.

138 According to the probability formula $Pt=1-(1-P1)t$, when time (t) is infinity then the probability of any event happening Pt approaches 100%.

139 A. E. Wilder-Smith, *The Natural Sciences Know Nothing of Evolution*, The Word for Today, Costa Mesa, Ca.

140 The problem is even worse for biological systems. Because of the Second Law of Thermodynamics and Law of Mass Action, amino acids and nucleotides "type out" far more readily than they "type in" in a watery environment.

141 Sir Fred Hoyle and Chandra Wickramasinghe, *Evolution from Space: A Theory of Cosmic Creationism* (New York: Simon and Schuster, 1981), pgs 148.

142 In the field of information science, this is actually a corollary to the Second Law. Applied to information storage and retrieval systems the Second Law demands that the net amount of information in a closed system always decreases as time advances. A closed system is an environment in which no information, matter or energy can be added or removed from beyond its boundaries. Applied to biology, the sum total of genetic information within an interbreeding pool of genes will degrade with the advance of time. This is the very cause of extinction in biological systems. In breeding situations bringing in "new blood" (new alleles) into an isolated breeding population has the effect of stabilizing the population and delaying the inevitable extinction. In this situation new information is "injected" into a gene pool that was, in effect, previously a closed system.

143 The Second Law, applied to information theory, demands that in order for the information in a system to increase it must be inserted from outside the system from an intelligent

source. Since the net amount of information in a closed system decreases with the advance of time and since, according to materialists, our universe is a closed system, then at the beginning of time, the total amount of information in the universe was at a maximum. Since information does not arise by chance, the challenge for the materialist is to determine where it came from in the first place?

144 Hoyle and Wickramasinghe, *op. cit.*, pg. 150.
145 Francis Crick, *Life Itself,* Simon and Schuster, New York, 1981.
146 Francis Crick and Leslie Orgel, "Directed Panspermia", *Icarus*, 19:341-46.
147 Fred Hoyle, *Evolution from Space*; 1981.
148 Michael Denton, *Evolution: A Theory in Crisis*, pg. 271, Adler and Adler, 1986.
149 Hoyle, Sir Fred, "The Big Bang in Astronomy," *New Scientist*, 19 November 1981, p. 526.
150 II Timothy 1:9 "who has saved us and called us with a holy calling, not according to our works, but according to His own purpose and grace which was given to us in Christ Jesus before time began." Also, Ephesians 1:4 "just as He chose us in Him before the foundation of the world, that we should be holy and without blame before Him in love."

CHAPTER FIVE

THE BIBLE: FROM
BEYOND TIME AND SPACE

"Remember the former things of old, for I am God, and
there is no other; I am God, and there is none like Me,
declaring the end from the beginning, and from ancient
times things that are not yet done, saying, 'My counsel
shall stand, and I will do all My pleasure,'"

Isaiah 46:9–10

For centuries scientific rationalists have maintained
that believing in a Supreme Being or Creator-God is
akin to committing intellectual suicide. However,
the twentieth century has supplied an abundance of scientific discoveries which point to a Transcendent Creator
who ordered and energized the universe. This evidence is
so powerful that numerous prominent scientists have
begun to speak openly about the existence of just such a
Being.

Because a Transcendent Creator possesses the sufficient means to act in our space-time domain, He also has
the capability to make contact with us! There are many
ways that this could be accomplished. The Creator could
split the sky in each generation and visibly demonstrate
His presence. He could write His name in the sky as a
reminder that we are not alone. He could manifest in a
body, walk among us and demonstrate His deity by con-
trolling the forces of nature. Or, He could simply speak to
us in written form. Whatever the method, if the Creator

has the technology to create us, He certainly has the technology to get a message to us.

The Bible not only claims to be that message, it also declares (in both testaments) that the very Creator of the universe has manifested Himself in a physical, human body and walked among us! In the book of Genesis, chapter 18, God appears to Abraham in the form of a man. Later in Genesis chapter 32, we find the story of God wrestling with Jacob. In the New Testament, Jesus of Nazareth is presented as the Messiah of Israel and God in the flesh.[151] His deity and transcendent nature are proclaimed and authenticated by His miraculous ministry, His command of the forces of nature, and His ability to "materialize" out of nowhere.

Throughout its text, the Bible claims to be the exclusive "Word of God." Statements such as, "Thus says the Lord," or "The Word of the Lord came to me," are commonplace in the Bible. To many, such claims by the writers of the Bible may seem pretentious. However, the Bible authenticates that its text is an extra-dimensional message system from a Transcendent Creator in several ways.

First, because the Bible declares that God is omniscient (all-knowing), He possesses a perfect understanding of the physical universe. Consequently, one of the ways that the Bible authenticates its divine authorship is by revealing an accurate and detailed knowledge of the physical universe. As we will see, throughout the Bible's text there are highly specific and accurate statements regarding the laws of physics, the nature of our solar system, planet earth, and its life forms. What's more, these statements were penned centuries before this scientific knowledge was discovered by any human society. This phenomenon, called scientific foreknowledge, is present throughout the text of the Bible. Furthermore, we find that the scientific statements in the Bible are without error or contradiction.

The second way the Bible demonstrates its divine

authorship is through its supernatural design. As we have said, the Bible consists of sixty-six books, penned by over forty authors, over thousands of years, which despite such varied authorship, in every book, in thousands of different ways, it evidences the "fingerprints" of a supernatural message system. Every number, every place name, every word and every letter is there by supernatural design. In chapter seven we will examine this evidence.

Finally, because the Creator revealed in the Bible exists outside our space-time domain, He is able to "see" the beginning and the end of our time domain simultaneously. Consequently, the Bible authenticates that its message is of extra-dimensional origin through predictive prophecy, i.e., by writing history in advance! In chapter eight we will examine several prophecies that were fulfilled in minute detail centuries after they were written.

No other "holy book" on planet earth authenticates its message in these ways. By doing this the Bible authenticates that it is *the* very Word of God.

---

151 John 1:1.

CHAPTER SIX

SCIENCE AND THE BIBLE

"He stretches out the north over empty space; He hangs the earth on nothing."

Job 26:7

In the twentieth century it is commonly presumed that the Bible is fraught with scientific inaccuracies and misconceptions. Students are often given the impression that numerous scientific fallacies, including a flat earth and a geocentric universe, are contained within the Bible. However, when the biblical text is carefully examined the reader will quickly discover an uncanny scientific accuracy unparalleled by any document of antiquity.

Within the text of the Bible are an extraordinary number of unambiguous statements regarding the creation and design of the universe, planet earth and its life forms. The Bible does not use scientific jargon nor is it a scientific text per se. However, as we will see, the Bible does describe scientific phenomena in common terminology with unmistakable clarity. While it is true that statements about the physical universe are common in ancient religious documents, those found in the Bible are unique. In virtually all ancient religious documents it is common to find scientifically inaccurate myths about the nature of the universe and the life forms on planet earth. Any cursory review of ancient mythology will readily confirm this statement. However, the Bible is unique because of the conspicuous absence of such myths. In fact, throughout the Bible we find scientifically accurate concepts about the physical universe that were not "discovered" by modern scientists until very recent times. This scientific foreknowledge, which was written thousands of years before its modern discovery, is evidence that the men who penned the Bible had "inside information."

We intend to show that the author of life and the physical universe is, in fact, the author of the Bible and the source of that "inside information." In the final analysis, when its text is carefully examined, the reader will discover that where the Bible speaks on scientific issues it is one-hundred percent accurate.

COSMOLOGY

Throughout the Bible we find statements about the origin, design and destiny of the universe. In chapter two we saw the concepts of an expanding, finite, decaying universe clearly elucidated by the biblical authors thousands of years before these facts were discovered by twentieth-century astrophysicists. Moreover, the fact that matter can neither be created nor destroyed (the First Law of Thermodynamics) and the universal law of decay (the Second Law of Thermodynamics) are also clearly taught in the Bible. Beyond this, in the biblical text we find a number of incredibly accurate scientific statements about the nature of the physical universe.

TIME, SPACE AND MATTER

In the very first verse of the Bible we find remarkable evidence of supernatural authorship.

> "In the beginning (time), God created the heavens (space) and the earth (matter)." Genesis 1:1

For thousands of years scientists and philosophers have speculated about the basic components or makeup of the universe. In the twentieth century, physicists have confirmed that the universe, at its foundation, consists of space, time and matter. In fact, space and time are so tightly linked that astrophysicists now speak of space-time. While scientific and philosophical speculations about the basic structure of the universe has varied widely, the fact that the universe consists basically of space, time and matter was clearly foreseen in the very first verse of the Bible.

"THE HOSTS OF HEAVEN"

At the time the Bible was penned (1,500 B.C.–100 A.D.) there were no telescopes to aid in the study of the cosmos. On a clear night, unencumbered by the light of the moon, only about 3,000–4,000 stars could be seen with the unaided eye. Yet in the eighth century B.C. God told the prophet Jeremiah that the number of stars could not be numbered:

> "As the host of heaven cannot be numbered, nor the sand of the sea measured, so will I multiply the descendants of David My servant and the Levites who minister to Me." Jeremiah 33:22 (NKJV)

When Jeremiah wrote this verse there was no way he could have known that the stars were innumerable. In fact, in the eighth-century B.C., astronomers believed that *it was* possible to number the stars. As evidence are the many star charts that were done prior to the advent of the telescope.

Astronomers now estimate that there are at least 100 billion stars in our Milky Way galaxy and 100 billion galaxies in the universe. For anyone to number the "hosts of heaven" (the total number of stars) would be a truly impossible task. Counting at a rate of ten stars per second it would take over 100 trillion years. Surely the host of heaven cannot be numbered!

THE RISING OF THE SUN?

Some of the most accurate scientific statements in the Bible concern the nature of our solar system. Nearly 3000

years ago the psalmist wrote that the sun follows a circuit
or circular path through the universe:

> "Its [the sun's] rising is from one end of heaven, and its
> circuit to the other end; and there is nothing hidden
> from its heat." Psalm 19:6 (NKJV)

For centuries critics argued that the psalmist was
here proclaiming that the sun rotated around the earth.
However, the term "sunrise" is a common phrase used by
all, even astrophysicists, and is not intended to be a scientific declaration.

Secondly, since the advent of powerful telescopes
astronomers have determined that the sun is part of an
enormous spiral galaxy, the Milky Way. We now know that
the sun moves in a "circuit" or circular course, at speeds
approaching 600,000 miles per hour, within one of the spiral arms of the Milky Way galaxy. In turn, the Milky Way
is hurtling through space at an estimated speed of
2,000,000 miles per hour! These facts are remarkably compatible with the psalmist's understanding of our sun's
path through the cosmos! Without "inside information"
from an extraterrestrial source, there is no way that the
writer could have possessed such incredible knowledge.

THE FLAT EARTH?

The belief in a flat earth is often erroneously traced to
the Bible. However, nowhere in its text is a flat earth proclaimed. In fact, the scientific descriptions of the earth are
so accurate they could comfortably fit in the pages of a
contemporary astronomy textbook.

The idea that the Bible teaches a flat earth might be
traced to a verse in Revelation 7:1, where the Apostle John
speaks of the "four corners" of the earth:

> "After these things I saw four angels standing at the
> four corners of the earth, holding the four winds of the
> earth, that the wind should not blow on the earth, on
> the sea, or on any tree." Revelation 7:1 (NKJV)

When the King James Bible was translated in 1610, the Greek words translated to the English, "four corners," were mistranslated. The literal meaning in the original Greek text is the "four quarters" of the earth. Translated correctly, the phrase is representative of the four directions (north, south, east, west) used in standard surveying and mapping today.

Christopher Columbus is often erroneously credited with proving that the earth is spherical with his voyage to North America in 1492. In fact, the Greek mathematician Pythagoras proposed that the earth was a sphere in the sixth century B.C. The Greek philosophers Hipparchus (second century B.C.) and Aristotle also came to the same conclusion. Eratosthenes (third century B.C.) was the first to prove scientifically that the earth was a sphere. At the same time he measured the size of the earth's circumference. Although his measurements were off by about fifteen percent they are impressive considering the information he had to work with. Prior to this time the belief in a flat earth was quite prevalent.

Despite contrary assertions, the fact of a spherical earth was clearly proclaimed in the Bible by the prophet Isaiah nearly twenty-eight centuries ago. In the fortieth chapter of the book of Isaiah we read:

> "It is He who sits above the circle of the earth, and its inhabitants are like grasshoppers, Who stretches out the heavens like a curtain, and spreads them out like a tent to dwell in." Isaiah 40:22 (NKJV)

When Isaiah wrote this verse he used the Hebrew word *khug* to describe the shape of the earth. Although this word is commonly translated into the English word "circle," the literal meaning of this word is "a sphere!"

ATLAS, ELEPHANTS, TURTLES OR JOB?

Throughout the centuries philosophers, theologians and scientists have speculated about the resting place of planet earth. Upon what or whom the earth is resting became an important part of mythology in many ancient cultures. To the ancient Greeks the candidates were Atlas or Hercules. The Hindus believed that elephants or turtles were the pillars upon which the earth rested.

The fact of a free floating earth was apparently foreign to most ancient cultures. In a world where all objects fall rapidly to their destruction, such a suggestion must have been terrifying. However, in the book of Job, commonly believed to be the oldest book in the Bible, we find an astonishing piece of scientific foreknowledge. While speaking of the incredible power of God, Job states of the earth:

> "He stretches out the north over empty space; He hangs the earth on nothing." Job 26:7 (NKJV)

When we consider that twenty-eight centuries ago the prevailing view of the earth was that it was flat and resting on the back of an animal or Greek god, the biblical view of a spherical earth suspended on nothing is astonishing. A good guess? No way. In the book of Job alone there are a mere two dozen disclosures of such scientific foreknowledge.[152] Far from being a scientifically inaccurate book, the Bible exhibits knowledge about the earth and the universe that appears to have come from a being with an extraterrestrial perspective.

PHYSICS

One of the greatest discoveries of the last one hundred years is the elucidation of the structure of the atom. All matter in the universe consists of atoms, or their components parts, protons, neutrons or electrons. These are in turn composed of smaller sub-atomic particles such as quarks, pions, gluons etc.... There is a fascinating verse in the New Testament that seems to anticipate atomic structure:

> "By faith we understand that the worlds were framed by the word of God, so that the things which are seen were not made of things which are visible." Hebrews 11:3

At a time when the basic structure of matter was unknown, nearly two thousand years ago, the author of the book of Hebrews accurately described the fact that the matter we can see is made of particles which are not visible in natural light. It is a fundamental fact of physics that any particle that is smaller than the wavelength of light will in fact be invisible to the naked eye or light microscopes. The atom and its sub-atomic particles, are smaller than the wavelength of visible light and therefore, are invisible!

In the New Testament, 2 Peter 3:10, we find an eerie verse which seems to anticipate another discovery of twentieth-century physics:

> "But the day of the Lord will come as a thief in the night, in which the heavens will pass away with a great noise, and *the elements will melt with fervent heat;* both the earth and the works that are in it will be burned up." 2 Peter 3:10 (NKJV)

Atomic fission, the reaction that occurs in nuclear power plants and certain atomic bombs, occurs when the nucleus of radioactive elements are split with the release of enormous amounts of energy and radioactivity. The result of an atomic explosion is that the elements involved "will melt with fervent heat!" Could it be that the Holy Spirit had the process of atomic fission in mind when Peter wrote this verse?

It is unlikely that a more accurate description of the results of an atomic explosion could be found within the archives of our twentieth-century libraries. When the New Testament was written (circa. A.D. 50–100) the beliefs regarding the nature of matter were very crude. The Greeks, for example, believed that the basic elements of the universe were fire, water and earth. In the face of this view, so dominant during biblical times, it is truly remarkable to find the biblical authors accurately describing aspects of subatomic structure as well as the results of nuclear fission! Could it be that the author of the Bible was also the author and designer of protons, neutrons, electrons, quarks etc...?

OCEANOGRAPHY

In 1855 Matthew Fontaine Maury (1806–1873), the "Father of Oceanography," published a book on his remarkable discovery that the oceans possess predictable currents or paths. He encouraged sailors to use these shipping paths to increase efficiency and decrease the number of accidents. Eventually, Maury was dubbed "Pathfinder of the Seas." In the book, *Matthew Fontaine Maury: Pathfinder of the Seas,* Charles Lewis recounts the entire story.[153] Though Maury's discovery was indeed important to his time, it was hardly a new revelation.

Nearly twenty-eight centuries earlier the psalmist wrote:

> "...The fish of the sea that pass through the paths of the seas." Psalm 8:8 (NKJV)

In the eighth century B.C. the prophet Isaiah echoed this when he wrote:

> "Thus says the LORD, who makes a way in the sea and *a path through the mighty waters,*" Isaiah 43:16

When these verses were written (circa. 1100–703 B.C.) the only seas known to the ancient Hebrews were the Mediterranean and Red Seas, as well as the large inland lakes (The Dead Sea and the Sea of Galilee). None of these bodies of water possess significant observable currents. Furthermore, at that time there was no empirical knowledge of "paths in the seas" or shipping lanes in any sea. Matthew Maury's discovery was based on observational data collected from the fifteenth to nineteenth centuries A.D., thousands of years after that very concept was penned by the psalmist!

THE HYDROLOGIC CYCLE

Nearly 300 years ago European scientists Pierre Perrault and Edme Mariotte collected evidence about the flow of the Seine River that eventually led to an accurate and detailed understanding of the water cycle on planet earth. During the Middle Ages the source of rain water was something of a mystery. The observations of Perrault, Mariotte and others eventually led to the discovery that rain clouds develop from evaporation of ocean water. In the twentieth century the nature of the water cycle is now well understood even by the average grammar school student.

Although their discovery was important to our understanding of global weather, it turns out that they were "scooped" by several thousand years. In the book of Job we find the earth's water cycle accurately described at least four thousand years before the discoveries of Perrault and Mariotte!

"For He draws up drops of water, which distill as rain from the mist, which the clouds drop down and pour abundantly on man." Job 36:27–28(NKJV)

Centuries later King Solomon wrote in the book of Ecclesiastes:

"The wind goes toward the south, and turns around to the north; the wind whirls about continually, and comes again on its circuit. All the rivers run into the sea, yet the sea is not full; to the place from which the rivers come, there they return again." Ecclesiastes 1:6–7

King Solomon lived around three-thousand years ago and yet he had an astonishing understanding of global wind currents and the earth's water cycle. The phrase, "The wind goes toward the south, and turns around to the north; the wind whirls about continually, and comes again on its circuit," is an accurate and astonishing description of the circular flow of air around the earth, called the "jet stream," well known to anyone who watches the evening news and weather reports. This verse also reveals that Solomon understood that the source of river water is the oceans. He states that the "sea" is " the place from which the rivers come, there they return again."

Finally, nearly 2,700 years ago the prophet Amos stated:

> "He...who calls for the waters of the sea, and pours them out on the face of the earth; the LORD is His name." Amos 9:6 (NKJV)

Again we see an uncanny knowledge that the source of rainwater is oceanic evaporation. When we consider that scientists did not discover these facts (oceanic evaporation and the global circular wind currents) until nearly twenty-five hundred years after the prophet Amos penned his book, these biblical passages stand as truly astonishing.[154]

MEDICAL SCIENCE

In the book of Genesis God specifically directed Abraham to circumcise all newborn males on the eighth day (Genesis 17:12). For thousands of years this tradition has been faithfully exercised by Orthodox Jews. Why the eighth day?

A remarkable discovery by twentieth-century scientists has shed light on a possible reason for circumcision on the eighth day. When an infant is born the blood clotting mechanism is immature. Any cut or injury in the first few days of life can result in excessive bleeding. After several days of life, the vitamin K in the infant's diet allows an important blood clotting factor, called prothrombin, to be produced in sufficient amounts to effect efficient clotting of the blood.

Today infants are given an injection of vitamin K at birth. Consequently, efficient blood clotting is established within hours. Without such therapy, it turns out that the prothrombin concentration reaches its peak on the eighth day of life! What a coincidence.

The skeptic might argue that the Jews deciphered the correct day by trial and error. However, there are many cultures that circumcise their young on the first, fourth, sixth, seventh and twentieth days of life. If the Jews determined by trial and error that the eighth day was best, why did these cultures come to such different conclusions? Could it be that Abraham was given "inside information" from the One that created the clotting mechanism in the first place?

There are dozens of additional examples of advanced Bio-medical knowledge in the Bible.

In the book of Deuteronomy 23:12–14, Moses instructed the Israelites to bury human waste products for hygienic purposes. While the merits of this procedure seem obvious to us now, during the Middle Ages Europe was nearly wiped out because they failed to heed this advice. As a direct result of dumping human waste into the streets, millions of people died from the "Black Plague," a disease caused by the microscopic organism Yersinia Pestis. These organisms thrived in the human waste and were carried into the homes by fleas on the backs of rats! Had they simply followed the biblical teaching these horrible plagues would never have occurred.

In Leviticus 17:11 God stated that "...the life of the flesh is in the blood, and I have given it to you upon the altar to make atonement for your souls; for it is the blood that makes atonement for the soul." This statement, "the life of the flesh is in the blood," implies that the blood contains vital ingredients that sustain the life of animals and man.

Though this statement may seem obvious to us now, this has not always been the case. In recent times it was believed that the blood needed to be "let out" when people fell ill. Consequently, for centuries physicians practiced "blood letting" (draining the blood out of an individual) in an attempt to rid the body of unwanted poisons. As you might guess many of these people died from the procedure. In fact, George Washington was a victim of this very procedure at the end of his life!

In the twentieth century, medical science has proven true this statement of Moses. The blood of man and animals carries all of the necessary nutrients for the maintenance and repair of living systems. Without a functioning cardiovascular system and an adequate supply of blood, there can be no life—something that Moses understood nearly 3,500 years ago!

AN AMAZING DISCOVERY!

Imagine yourself on an archaeological expedition in the Dead Sea region of Israel during which an absolutely astonishing discovery is made. In a recently discovered cave you find an ancient papyrus containing a complete set of plans which accurately describes the structure and function of a Boeing 747! Would you be impressed?

You turn the scrolls over to ancient manuscript experts who conclude that the scrolls were written in Hebrew nearly 2,200 years ago! Skeptical, you transfer the plans to the local university radiometric dating lab. The results are the same. The ink and the papyri are found to be from before the time of Christ!

The press immediately reports the story and the academic community begins their analysis. Some assert that an advanced civilization of extraterrestrials took the plans back in time and planted them in the caves. The skeptics assert that the whole thing is an elaborate hoax. However, the evidence is clear. The scrolls are ancient. Still others declare that a supernatural transcendent being gave this twentieth-century scientific knowledge to the ancient scribes who recorded it only to be found centuries later.

Each of these analyses share a common thread. Each theorist knows that ancient scribes could possess no knowledge of 747's unless they were instructed by someone with twentieth-century scientific and engineering know-how.

According to the UFO proponents, this knowledge was transported into the past by extraterrestrial beings which have the ability to transcend time.

On the other hand the skeptic knows that, under *natural circumstances*, such scientific foreknowledge is impossible. Since the skeptic does not believe in the supernatural realm, and since time travel is also, in effect, "supernatural", he is forced to conclude that the scrolls are fraudulent.

To the believer in a Transcendent Being, the answer is obvious. The detailed scientific knowledge required to design and build a 747 was sent back by a Creator, who transcends our time domain, to a time where such knowledge was otherwise unknowable.

This story serves to illustrate the incredible, supernatural nature of the biblical text. The possession of twentieth-century scientific foreknowledge (the 747 plans) by ancient scribes could only have come about through a miraculous disruption of the space-time continuum. Likewise, the scientific foreknowledge within the biblical text must have come from a Being with a transcendent nature as well. This knowledge, while always possessed by the Creator, was "faxed" into our space-time domain to a people and time where such knowledge was, under natural circumstances, impossible.

How are we to interpret such scientific foreknowledge in a non-theistic world view? The skeptic might assert that the biblical writers, though mere mortals, got "lucky." Over thousands of years, from three continents, the forty authors of the Bible just happened to describe, by chance, the nature of our universe, the laws of physics, planet earth and its life forms in a way that is in complete harmony with twentieth-century science. Such an assertion is at best incredulous. Surely no one would contend that the ancient scribes who wrote the plans for a 747 got "lucky" as they doodled on ancient papyri. And yet the scientific foreknowledge in the Bible is also, as we have seen, quite specific and accurate.

What about collusion? Because such scientific foreknowledge is "anticipatory," or ahead of its time, we cannot argue that it was placed in the Bible as a result of collusion. This would be akin to arguing that two ancient scribes, who know nothing about twentieth-century aeronautical engineering, colluded to draw up plans for a 747! When the arguments are broken down we find that the ancient scribes were either incredibly lucky (i.e. chance) or they were guided by an extra dimensional Being with extraordinary "inside information."

In this chapter we have examined only a small number of the many verses in the Bible that reveal an uncanny scientific foreknowledge.[155] This alone is powerful evidence for a supernatural origin. However, in addition to this, though it was written at a time when scientifically inaccurate mythology was rampant, the Bible is remarkably free of such concepts. Far from being an inaccurate book of scientific mythology, the Bible, with its ability to anticipate twentieth-century science, carries the "fingerprints" of a Being with incredible "inside information"— the Being who created the universe in the first place—the Creator beyond time and space!

---

152 See *The Remarkable Record of Job*, by Henry Morris, Masters Books (1988).
153 Lewis, Charles; *Matthew Fontaine Maury: Pathfinder of the Seas*, 1927, (U.S. Naval Institute).
154 See also Ecclesiastes 11:3, Job 26:8.
155 For a much more detailed analysis of this subject see *The Biblical Basis for Modern Science*, by Henry Morris, Masters Books, (1987).

CHAPTER SEVEN

BEYOND COINCIDENCE:
EVIDENCE FOR THE
SUPERNATURAL DESIGN
OF THE BIBLICAL TEXT

"It is the glory of God to conceal a thing: but the honour
of kings is to search out a matter."

Proverbs 25:2 (KJV)

One of the most exciting discoveries a student of the
Bible can make is to find evidence for its supernatural design. There are many aspects of the biblical
text that speak of divine inspiration. The brevity of the
Bible's books, the impartiality of the authors, and the
"matter of fact" way astonishing events are portrayed, are
subtle hints of a supernatural origin of the text. In addition, there are dozens of structural "coincidences" in the
Bible's text which evidence the "fingerprints" of supernatural engineering. In the twentieth century, more than any
time in history, it can be demonstrated that the Bible is a
skillfully designed, integrated message system that evidences supernatural engineering in every detail. Sixty-six
books, penned by over forty authors, over thousands of
years, whose origin you can prove is from beyond our
space-time domain!

In this chapter we'll examine evidence for the supernatural engineering and integrity of the biblical text. In
the next chapter we'll look at evidence that conclusively

proves the Bible's text came from beyond our space-time domain.

"IN BEGINNING ELOHIM"

In the very first book of the Bible, the book of Genesis, there are a number of design characteristics that hint at a supernatural authorship of the text. In fact, in the very first verse, Genesis 1:1 the Jewish rabbis see an early hint of supernatural authorship.

Genesis 1:1

28 letters= 4x7

Seven is the number of *completion*

Four is the number of *creation*

4x7 implies the creation is complete

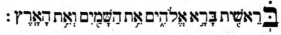

בְּרֵאשִׁית בָּרָא אֱלֹהִים אֵת הַשָּׁמַיִם וְאֵת הָאָרֶץ :

the earth	and	the	God	Created	In
		Heavens	("Elohim")		Beginning

Figure 1.

The first verse of the book of Genesis is a remarkably concise and accurate description of the origin of the space-time domain and its contents. Not only is the universe "an effect," caused to exist by a source outside the space-time domain, i.e. God, this verse in its very structure indicates that the creation was complete, as implied by the mathematical structure 4x7.

The number four is recognized as the number of creation.[156] Seven, the most commonly used number in the Bible, is the biblical number of "completion or perfection." It is often associated with God and spiritual perfection.

Consequently, the number 28 (4x7) represents a "completed or perfect creation!"

It's interesting to note that in the thirteenth century A.D., a Jewish Sage by the name of Nachmanides inferred from the shape of the first letter in Genesis (*Beyth*), that prior to Genesis 1:1, time, space and matter did not exist.[157] Talk about contemporary scientific foreknowledge! Centuries later Einstein came to the same conclusion.

AN AMAZING DISCOVERY IN GENESIS 5

The Jewish rabbis have a belief that we will not understand the Scriptures until the Messiah comes. But when He comes, He will not only interpret each of the passages for us, He will interpret the very words; He will even interpret the very letters themselves; in fact, He will even interpret the *spaces between* the letters. To many, this saying is no more than a quaint expression. However, in the fifth chapter of the book of Genesis we find an astonishing example of the kind of secrets that lay hidden in the biblical text.

As Christians we frequently use the familiar term, "Gospel," or "Good News." Where is the first place it appears in the Bible? The answer may surprise you.

MANY BEGETS

In Genesis chapter 5 we have the genealogy of Adam through Noah. Adam begat Seth; Seth begat Enosh and so on down to Noah. On the surface this is one of those tedious chapters which we often tend to skim over quickly as we pass through. But God always rewards the diligent student. Let's examine this chapter more closely.

A STUDY OF ORIGINAL ROOTS

In our Bible, we read the *Hebrew* names of individuals. What do these names mean in English? In some cases the meaning of proper names can be difficult since a direct translation is often not readily available. A study of the original roots, however, can yield some fascinating insights.[158] Let's take one of them as an example.

THE FLOOD JUDGMENT

Methhuselah comes from *Muth*, a root that means "death"; and from *shalak*, which means "to bring." The name Methuselah means, "his death shall bring."

Methuselah's father was given a prophecy of the coming Great Flood, and was apparently told that as long as his son was alive, the judgment of the flood would be withheld. (Can you imagine raising a kid like that? Every time the boy caught a cold, they must have panicked!). In fact, the very year that Methuselah died, the flood came![159]

It is interesting that Methuselah's life, in effect, was a symbol of God's grace in forestalling the coming judgment of the flood. It is, therefore, fitting that his lifetime is the oldest in the Bible speaking of the abundance of God's grace.

THE OTHER NAMES

If there is such significance in Methuselah's name, let's examine the other names to see what may lie behind them.

Adam's name means "man." As the first Man, that seems straightforward enough.

SETH

Adam's son was named Seth which means "appointed." Eve said, "For God hath appointed me another seed instead of Abel whom Cain slew."[160]

ENOSH

Seth's son was called Enosh, which means "mortal," "frail," or "miserable." It is from the root *anash*, to be incurable, used of a wound, grief, woe, sickness, or wickedness.

It was in the days of Enosh that men began to defile the name of the Living God.[161]

Enosh's son was named Kenan, which can mean "sorrow" or "wandering nomad."[162]

MAHALALEL

Kenan's son was Mahalalel, which means "the Blessed God." Often Hebrew names include El, one of the names of God, as in Daniel, "God is my judge."

JARED

Mahalalel's son was named Jared, from a verb *yaradh*, meaning "shall come down."

ENOCH

Jared's son was named Enoch, which means "teaching." He was the first of four generations of preachers. In fact, the earliest recorded prophecy was by Enoch, which dealt, amazingly enough, with the Second Coming of Christ, (although it is quoted in the book of Jude in the New Testament):

> "Now Enoch, the seventh from Adam, prophesied about these men also, saying, 'Behold, the Lord comes with ten thousands of His saints, to execute judgment on all, to convict all who are ungodly among them of all their ungodly deeds which they have committed in an ungodly way, and of all the harsh things which ungodly sinners have spoken against Him.'" Jude 14–15

METHUSELAH

Enoch was the father of Methuselah, whom we have already mentioned. Enoch walked with God *after* he begat Methuselah.[163] The year that Methuselah died the flood came.

Enoch, of course, never died: he was translated.[164] (If you'll excuse the expression, "raptured.") That's how Methuselah can be the oldest man in the Bible, yet he died "before" his father!

LAMECH

Methuselah's son was named Lamech, which means "despairing." This same root also seems to lie behind our English word, lamentation. While a similar root can mean "strength," this name is linked, through traditional Jewish sources, with the Lamech in Cain's line who, according to tradition, inadvertently killed his son Tubal-Cain in a hunting incident.[165]

NOAH

Lamech, of course, is the father of Noah, which is linked with *nacham*, "to bring relief" or "comfort." This is highlighted in Genesis 5:29.

If we read the meaning of the names in the order they appear an astonishing story of redemption is spelled out! Now let's put it all together: (*see table*)

The Composite List

Hebrew	English
Adam	Man
Seth	Appointed
Enosh	Mortal
Kenan	Sorrow
Mahalalel	The Blessed God
Jared	Shall come down
Enoch	Teaching
Methuselah	His death shall bring
Lamech	The Despairing
Noah	Rest.

That's rather remarkable:

"Man (is) appointed mortal sorrow; (but) the Blessed
God shall come down teaching (that) His death shall bring
(the) despairing rest."

Here's the "Gospel" hidden within a genealogy in
Genesis!

It is hard to imagine Jewish rabbis "conspiring" to
place the "Christian Gospel" right here in their venerated
Torah!

Random chance? Not a chance! The Bible is an integrated message system, the product of supernatural engineering. Every number, every place name, every detail—
every jot and *tittle*—is there for our learning, our discovery, and our amazement. Truly, our God *is* an awesome
God.

THE AKEDAH

In the book of Hosea, God tells the prophet that "I
have spoken by the prophets, and I have multiplied
visions, *and used similitudes*, by the ministry of the
prophets." The term "similitudes" can be understood, in
biblical parlance, as a "type" or in modern terms, a
"model," given as a foreshadow of something yet future. In
the Old Testament there are dozens of stories which are,
in fact, "types" of events that were fulfilled in the birth,
life and ministry of Jesus Christ.[166] Perhaps the most
dramatic example of such a "type" is the "Akedah"—
Abraham's offering of Isaac in Genesis 22.

ABRAHAM'S OFFERING OF ISAAC

Genesis 22 is arguably one of the most dramatic and
challenging stories in the entire Bible. In the text
Abraham is told by God to sacrifice his "only son," Isaac,
on top of a mountain that God would lead him to. With
unimaginable faith Abraham takes Isaac, two young men,
and a donkey, and travels three days to Mount Moriah to
kill his son as a sacrifice to the Lord.

Upon arrival Abraham leaves the donkey and the two

young men at the base of the mount and takes Isaac to the top where he prepares to offer him as a sacrifice for sin. At the final moment, an angel interrupts the proceedings and a ram is substituted for Isaac.

But what's the real point of this famous event?

SOME OBSERVATIONS

It is important to note that Isaac was not the "only son" of Abraham. Abraham had another son, Ishmael, who was born out of an adulterous relationship with Hagar, the handmaiden of Abraham's wife, Sarah. So, calling Isaac the "only son" of Abraham was, in fact, an "error" in the text of Genesis! But, stay tuned.

Secondly, we need to recognize Abraham's assumptions. He knew that Isaac would be *resurrected* if killed: God had promised Abraham that Isaac would have children.[167] It was God's problem, not Abraham's. (Abraham had learned a lot about faith by the time he gets to chapter 22!)

Also, Abraham *knew* that he was acting out a *prophecy*! He named the location, "In the mount of the Lord it shall be seen."[168]

With this in mind, let's re-examine some of the details.

As they leave the two young men at the base of the hill, Abraham indicates that they *both* will return.[169]

As Abraham and Isaac climb the hill, Isaac is carrying the wood on his back, and asks, "Where is the lamb?" Good question!

Abraham answers, "God will provide (who?) *himself* a lamb...."

How long was Isaac "dead" to Abraham? He was, in traditional Jewish style, "dead" to Abraham as soon as the commandment came.[170] When the angel intervened, in the heart and mind of Abraham, Isaac was, in effect, miraculously "resurrected" to life *three days* later! At this point in the story we can see a number of parallels or "types."

In the New Testament, Jesus of Nazareth is presented as the Son of God Who is sacrificed by crucifixion for
the sins of the world. After being tried by the Jewish
Sanhedrin and the Roman procurator, Pontius Pilate,
Jesus carried a Roman cross on His back up a hill to the
place of the skull, called Golgotha. Though He had done
no wrong, Jesus (the Son) willingly submitted to the
Father and allowed Himself to be sacrificed for the sins of
many. Three days later Jesus resurrected from the dead.
He now awaits the time when He will be united with His
bride—the Church. The parallels between Abraham's
offering of Isaac and God's offering of His only Son are
astonishing.

In the Genesis 22 story Abraham is a "type" of the
Father and Isaac is a "type" of the Son. In the mind of
Abraham his son was as good as dead *three days* before he
was miraculously resurrected. In Genesis 22:6 we are told
that Abraham put the wood for the sacrifice "on Isaac." It
seems logical therefore, that Isaac carried the wood on *his
back* as he ascended the mountain. Furthermore, although
he was a full grown man at the time, Isaac willingly submitted to his father and laid down on the altar to give his
life for the purpose. Finally, Abraham was told to go to the
mountain called "Moriah." It is reasonable to assume that
Abraham understood this to mean the top of the mountain.

The entire episode was played out in an anticipation of
a New Testament event—the crucifixion of the Son of God
as a sacrifice for sins. But there's more.

THE TOPOLOGY OF MT. MORIAH

If we examine the topology of Mount Moriah, we find
it is a ridge system between the Mount of Olives and
Mount Zion. It is bordered by the Kidron Valley on the
east, the Hinnom Valley on the south, and the Tyropoean
Valley on the west.

If we approach the Mount as Abraham did, from

Beersheba to the south, we begin at about 600 meters above sea level, and climb to its peak, about 777 meters above sea level. What a coincidence!

THE TEMPLE

Many years later, King David would purchase the threshing floor of Araunah where Solomon would eventually build the Temple.[171] A threshing floor was located where a prevailing wind would facilitate the separation of the grain from the chaff. In this case, it was at about 741 meters above sea level, but just below the peak. (See the topological map on page 135.)

THE OFFERING SITE

The peak of the Mount is at a place just outside the city wall to the north. It's a place you can still visit today, just above an Arab bus station outside the Damascus Gate. It is known as Golgotha—the very site where a group of Roman soldiers erected three crosses 2,000 years ago—the very site where the New Testament states the Son of God was willingly sacrificed for the sins of the world—the very site where Abraham offered his own son as a sin offering! We're just getting started (see map on page 135).

THE UNNAMED SERVANT

In Genesis 24, Abraham commissions his eldest servant to go and gather a bride for Isaac. In the story we see that Abraham's servant is compelled to swear an oath that the bride will not be "from the daughters of the Canaanites, among whom I dwell." That is, Abraham specifically requested a *gentile bride* for his son Isaac.[172]

The servant then travels to a distant land, qualifies the candidate (Rebecca) by a well, and after she agrees to accept a bridegroom (Isaac) whom she has never met, the servant arranges for her to return with him, giving her gifts along the way.

Then we come to the climactic scene where Isaac first meets Rebecca, by the Well of Lahai Roi.

Here is another interesting biblical "type." We need to understand, however, the role of the "eldest servant." He is not a menial; he was the steward of, and stood to inherit in the absence of issue, all of Abraham's wealth. Abraham, the Father, commissioned him (the eldest servant) to gather a bride for Isaac. Abraham is again in the role of the Father, Isaac the Son.

If the bride is in the role of the Church, it would seem that this servant is in the role of the Holy Spirit. It is particularly provocative that whenever the Holy Spirit appears in a "type" He is always an unnamed servant. However, earlier in Genesis 15:2 we are told that the name of Abraham's eldest servant is Eliezer, which means "Comforter!"

In the New Testament Jesus told his disciples that he must go away, but after his departure he would send the disciples a "Comforter"—identified as the Holy Spirit! Furthermore, Jesus stated that the Comforter "would not speak of Himself," but His role would be to testify of Jesus.[173]

In the story of Eliezer and Rebecca, we see that Eliezer (the Comforter) woos Rebecca (the gentile bride) by testifying of Isaac and the great riches bestowed to him by his father.

But there's more.

THE MISSING PERSON

In Genesis 22 after the offering is completed, verse 19 lists the people that went home:

> "So Abraham returned to his young men, and they rose up and went together to Beersheba; and Abraham dwelt at Beersheba."

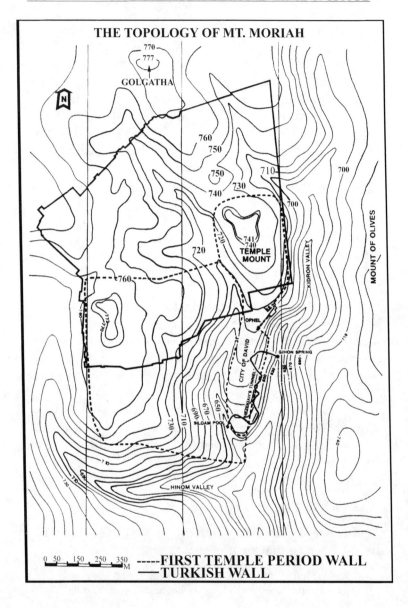

THE TOPOLOGY OF MT. MORIAH

The two young men were still waiting at the bottom of the hill with the donkey. So they all went home.

There's one small problem: *Where's Isaac?*

Obviously, we all assume that he joined them on the return trip. But notice that he is not mentioned.

In fact, Isaac is edited out of the record from the time that he is offered, *until he is united with his gentile bride* at the Well of Lahai Roi ("well of the Living One seeing me"), two chapters later.

A LOVE STORY WRITTEN IN BLOOD

The parallels found in Abraham's offering of Isaac are astonishing. Isaac, the "only son"[174] (an "error" introduced by the Holy Spirit to make the typology fit) of Abraham allows himself to be ceremonially sacrificed on the top of Mountain of Moriah (the place called Golgotha). Isaac is then edited from the text (in effect, absent from the scene) from the time of his "resurrection," until he is united with a gentile bride (Rebecca), who, having never seen Isaac, comes by faith to meet her groom at the wooing of the "Comforter," Eliezer, the eldest servant of Abraham (the Father).

Two thousand years later another Father (God) offers his only Son (Jesus) on a wooden cross to atone for the sins of the world. After his resurrection, the Son of God (Jesus) physically departs the world scene until a future time when he will be united with his gentile bride (the church).

The lengths to which the Holy Spirit has gone to make the types work out is incredible. To the casual observer the story seems like a sick joke played on Abraham. However, when the story is examined in the light of the many "types" we have seen, the story is an incredible example of a skillfully designed supernatural message system.

Isn't God awesome! Isn't it amazing how far He has gone to show His love for us? A love story written in blood, on a wooden cross, 2,000 years ago.

This was all arranged so that we might have life with

Him throughout eternity. Wow! Where's "Isaac" in your life?

THE NUMERICAL EVIDENCE FOR DESIGN

The numerical structure of the Bible has been studied closely, being the subject of numerous volumes in the past. But none are more provocative than the works of Dr. Ivan Panin.[175],[176]

Ivan Panin was born in Russia on December 12, 1855. Having participated in plots against the Czar at an early age, he was exiled and, after spending some years studying in Germany, he came to the United States and entered Harvard University. After graduation in 1882, he converted from agnosticism to Christianity.

In 1890 he discovered some of the phenomenal mathematical designs underlying both the New Testament Greek text and the Old Testament Hebrew text. He devoted over 50 years of his life, painstakingly exploring the numerical structure of the scriptures, generating over 43,000 detailed, hand-penned pages of analysis.[177]

THE HEPTADIC STRUCTURE

The recurrence of the number seven—or an exact multiple of seven—is found throughout the Bible and is widely recognized. The Sabbath on the seventh day; Egypt's seven years of plenty followed by seven years of famine; the seven priests and seven trumpets marching around Jericho; and the Sabbath Year of the land are well-known examples.

Also, Solomon's building the Temple for seven years; Naaman's washing in the river for seven times; as well as the seven churches, seven lamp stands, seven seals, seven trumpets, seven bowls, seven stars, and so on in the Book of Revelation, all show the consistent use of the number seven.

But there turns out to be much more *below the surface*. Ivan Panin noted the amazing numerical properties of the

Biblical texts—both the Greek of the New Testament and the Hebrew of the Old Testament. These are not only intriguing to discover, they also demonstrate an intricacy of design which testifies to a supernatural origin!

VOCABULARY

One of the simplest—and most provocative—aspects of the Biblical text is the vocabulary used. The number of vocabulary words in a passage is normally different from the total number of words in a passage. Some words are repeated. It is easy, for example, to use a vocabulary of 500 words to write an essay of 4,000 words.

AN EXAMPLE

The first 17 verses of the Gospel of Matthew are a logical unit, or section, which deals with a single principal subject: the genealogy of Jesus Christ. It contains 72 Greek vocabulary words in these initial 17 verses.[178] The number of words which are nouns is exactly 56, or 7 x 8. The Greek word "the" occurs most frequently in the passage: exactly 56 times, or 7 x 8. Also, the number of different forms in which the article "the" occurs is exactly 7.

There are two main sections in the passage: verse 1–11, and 12–17. In the first main section, the number of Greek vocabulary words used is 49, or 7 x 7.

Why not 48, or 50?

Of these 49 words, the number of those beginning with a vowel is 28, or 7 x 4. The number of words beginning with a consonant is 21, or 7 x 3.

The total numbers of letters in these 49 words is 266, or 7 x 38—exactly! The number of vowels among these 266 letters is 140, or 7 x 20. The number of consonants is 126, or 7 x 18—exactly.

Of the 49 words, the number of words which occur more than once is 35, or 7 x 5. The number of words occurring *only once* is 14, or 7 x 2. The number of words which occur in only one form is exactly 42, or 7 x 6. The number of words appearing in more than one form is also 7.

The number of the 49 Greek vocabulary words which are nouns is 42, or 7 x 6. The number of words which are not nouns is 7. Of the nouns, 35 are proper names, or exactly 7 x 5. These 35 names are used 63 times, or 7 x 9. The number of male names is exactly 28, or 7 x 4. These male names occur 56 times or 7 x 8. The number which are not male names is 7.

Three women are mentioned—Tamar, Rahab, and Ruth. The number of Greek letters in these three names is 14, 7 x 2.

The number of compound nouns is 7. The number of Greek letters in these 7 nouns is 49, or 7 x 7.

Evidence of Design in the Genealogy of Matthew Chapter 1

Try designing a genealogy—even from fiction—that meets the following criteria:

1) The number of *words* in it must be divisible by 7 evenly (In each of these constraints, it is assumed that the divisions are without remainders.)

2) The number of *letters* must also be divisible by 7.

3) The number of *vowels* and the number of *consonants* must also each be divisible by 7.

4) The number of words that *begin with a vowel* must be divisible by 7.

5) The number of words that *begin with a consonant* must be divisible by 7.

6) The number of words that *occur more than once* must be divisible by 7.

7) The number of words that *occur in more than one form* shall be divisible by 7.

8) The number of words that *occur in only one form* shall be divisible by 7.

9) The number of *nouns* shall be divisible by 7.

10) Only 7 words shall *NOT* be nouns.

11) The number of *names* in the genealogy shall be divisible by 7.

12) Only 7 *other kinds of nouns* are permitted.

13) The number of *male names* shall be divisible by 7.

14) The number of *generations* shall be 21, also divisible by 7.

A remarkable evidence of the numerical structure of Scripture: These are met in the first 11 verses (in Greek) found in Matthew Chapter 1. Based on the insights of Dr. Ivan Panin (1855-1942).

Only one city is named in this passage, Babylon, which in Greek contains exactly 7 letters.

And on it goes. To get an indication of just how unique these properties are, try the example in the inset.

GAMETRIA

There are even more features in the numerical structure of the words themselves. As you may know, both Hebrew and Greek use the letters of the alphabet for numerical values. Therefore, any specific word—in either Hebrew or Greek— has a numerical value of its own by adding up the values of the letters in that particular word. The study of the numerical values of words is called *gametria*.

The 72 vocabulary words add up to a gametrical value of 42,364, or 7 x 6,052. Exactly. If one Greek letter was changed, this would not happen.

The 72 words appear in 90 forms—some appear in more than one form. The numeric value of the 90 forms is 54,075, or 7 x 7,725. Exactly.

It becomes immediately obvious that hidden below the surface are aspects of design that cannot be accidental or just coincidence. Remember, the rabbis say that "coincidence" is not a kosher word!

OTHER IMPLICATIONS

There are words in the passage just described that *occur nowhere else* in the New Testament. They occur 42 times (7 x 6) and have 126 letters (7 x 18). How was this organized?

Even if Matthew contrived this characteristic into his Gospel, how could he have known that these specific words—whose sole characteristic is that they are found nowhere else in the New Testament—were *not going to be used by the other writers?* Unless we assume the absurd hypothesis that he had an agreement with them, he must have had the rest of the New Testament before him when he wrote his book. The Gospel of Matthew, then, must have been written *last*.

It so happens, however, that the Gospel of Mark

exhibits the *same* phenomenon. It can be demonstrated that it would have had to be written "last." The same phenomenon is found in Luke, John, James, Peter, Jude and Paul. Each would have had to write *after* the other in order to contrive the vocabulary frequencies! You can demonstrate that each of the New Testament books had to have been "written last."

There is no human explanation for this incredible and precise structure. It has all been supernaturally designed. We simply gasp, sit back, and behold the skillful handiwork of the God who keeps His promises.

We are indebted to the painstaking examinations and lifetime commitment of Dr. Ivan Panin for uncovering these amazing insights.

CHANCE OR DESIGN

The evidence examined in this chapter represents only a small fraction of the hundreds of hints of the supernatural engineering of the biblical text. The evidences we have examined in this chapter are either the result of random chance or intelligent contrivance.

To believe that these evidences of design arose by chance is akin to a faith in spontaneous generation. There are some that will admit that chance is insufficient to produce the design features examined herein. Thus, they conclude, they were carefully and meticulously placed there by ancient scribes. However, to believe this we must conclude that ancient rabbis conspired to place the Gospel of Jesus Christ in the genealogy of Genesis five as well as the Akedah, the offering of Isaac in Genesis chapter 22! This is obviously an appeal to absurdity.

The evidence speaks for itself. These 66 books, penned by over 40 authors, over thousands of years, are an integrated message system, supernaturally engineered, by a Being who dwells outside the space-time domain![179]

In the next chapter we examine evidence for the extradimensional nature of God.

156 E. W. Bullinger, *Numbers in Scripture*, Kregel Publications, pg.123.
157 Gerald Schroeder, *Genesis and the Big Bang*, Chapter 2.
158 Many study aids can prove rather superficial. However, a good dictionary of Hebrew roots is very beneficial.
159 Alfred Jones, *Dictionary of Old Testament Proper Names*, Kregel Publications, Grand Rapids Ml, 1990; Arthur W. Pink, *Gleanings in Genesis*, Moody Bible Institute, Chicago IL, 1922; Ray G. Stedman, *The Beginnings*, Word Books, Waco TX, 1978.
160 Genesis 4:25.
161 Genesis 4:26 is often mistranslated. Onkelos, et al, read, "Then men began to profane the name of the LORD."
162 The precise denotation is somewhat elusive; some study aids even assume that Kenan is synonymous with "Cainan."
163 Genesis 5:21, 24.
164 Genesis 5:24.
165 Genesis 4:19-25; See also, Rabbi Aryeh Kaplan, *The Living Torah*, Maznaim Publishing Corporation, Jerusalem, 1981.
166 For a detailed and fascinating look at these see *Types in the Old Testament*, by Ada Habershon, Kregel Publications.
167 Genesis 17:19.
168 Genesis 22:14.
169 Genesis 22:5.
170 Hebrews 11:17-19.
171 1 Chronicles 21:18-26.
172 Even though Abraham and the Canaanites were technically gentiles at that time, for the purpose of completing the typology, the Holy Spirit saw fit to point out that the bride of Isaac was from a land that would always be of the gentiles.
173 John 16:7-14 KJV.
174 God did not recognize Ishmael, the son of Hagar and Abraham, because he was the result of an adulterous relationship and, in effect, a son of the flesh and not God's chosen son of the Abrahamic covenant.
175 R. McCormack, *The Heptadic Structure of Scripture*, Marshall Brothers Ltd., London, 1923; E.W. Bullinger, *Numbers of the Scriptures;* F.W Grant, *The Numerical Bible* (7 vols.); Browne, Ordo Saeculoreium, et al.
176 Ivan Panin (various works), *Bible Numerics*, P.O. Box 206, Waubaushene, Ontario, LOK 2C0.
177 It is important to distinguish between the study of "Biblical Numerics" and "Numerology." The former is simply the study of the numerous numerical "structural coincidences"

in the biblical text. Numerology is a Neo-occultic practice
whereby numerical oddities are interpreted as "secret mes-
sages," prophecies or directions.

178 The verse divisions are man's allocations for convenience,
added in the thirteenth-century A.D.

179 See *Personal Update* July, 1993, March 1993, February 1993
for some additional examples of design of the biblical text.
Available at 1-800-KHOUSE 1.

CHAPTER EIGHT

BIBLE PROPHECY:
PROOF OF ITS
SUPERNATURAL ORIGIN

"'Present your case,' says the LORD. 'Bring forth your
strong reasons,' says the King of Jacob. 'Let them bring
forth and show us what will happen; let them show the
former things, what they were, that we may consider
them, and know the latter end of them; or declare to us
things to come. Show the things that are to come here-
after, that we may know that you are gods....'"

    Isaiah 41:22–23a (NKJV)

Since the dawn of time human beings have held both
apprehension and fascination with the future. As we
approach the final stage of the twentieth century, it
seems that anxiety about the future is growing. Corporate
executives, stock brokers, heads of state and millions of
Americans regularly look to their horoscopes for clues to
their future. Ann Landers reportedly gets thousands of
letters a day from people who are terrified about what
their future might bring.

    Throughout history there have always been those who
claim to know the future. Even in our time predictions
about the future are rampant. Every New Year the public
is treated to the supermarket tabloid predictions for the
coming year. To date, however, killer UFO's have not
taken over Moscow and Elvis is apparently still dead.

    The abysmal record of these contemporary prophets,
along with an increasing anti-supernatural bias among

the intellectual elite, have caused many to doubt the veracity of all forms of prophecy. As a result, the nearly universal acceptance of the supernatural origin of biblical prophecy has been replaced by widespread skepticism.

Throughout its pages the Bible dares to make the claim that its text is from a Transcendent Being who created and ordered the physical universe. However, the Bible authenticates this claim by accurately foretelling historical events which are yet future. In the eighth century B.C., God said through the prophet Isaiah:

> "Remember the former things of old, for I am God, and there is no other; I am God, and there is none like Me, declaring the end from the beginning, and from ancient times things that are not yet done, saying, 'My counsel shall stand, and I will do all My pleasure,'" Isaiah 46:9–10 (NKJV)

In this fascinating verse the God of the Bible asserts, in effect, that He is transcendent—that He exists beyond our space-time domain. To authenticate this claim He appeals to His supernatural ability to accurately foretell future events within our own time domain.

In chapter two we saw that the creation of the physical universe necessitates the work of an intelligent being with a transcendent nature. Such a being would not only have the ability to act within our space-time domain, but because He exists outside the time domain, He would also be able to "declare the end from the beginning."

A simple illustration will help to clarify the notion of God's transcendent nature. The flow of time in our universe is often represented by a parade. The beginning of the parade represents the beginning of time. Each float that passes the reviewing stand represents the passage of time in each successive generation. As finite beings, trapped within the confines of our space-time domain, we can only know of events occurring on our own "float" and those that have passed before. However, God's perspective on the parade is much different. By simultaneously existing within and without the dimensions of our space-time domain, God is able to, in effect, "see" the events on our time line just as an observer in the carriage of a blimp can *simultaneously* view the beginning and the end of the Rose Parade! Without a transcendent nature no knowledge of the future would be possible. This ability, God declares, proves He exists beyond time and space!

Because the Bible declares that God is eternal, we often think of Him as someone who simply has a lot of time on his hands. However, with the advent of modern physics we now know this to be a very naive view. One of the most startling discoveries of the twentieth century is the fact that time is itself a physical property of our universe. Consequently, as the very Creator of the physical universe, God is not someone who simply has a lot of time on His hands—He is outside of space-time altogether! Isaiah confirms this when he states:

> "For thus says the High and Lofty One *Who inhabits eternity,* whose name is Holy: 'I dwell in the high and holy place, with him who has a contrite and humble spirit, to revive the spirit of the humble, and to revive the heart of the contrite ones.'" Isaiah 57:15 (NKJV)

The transcendence of God, declared by the ancient biblical prophets and confirmed by His ability to foretell history, is the burden of proof for this chapter.

THE SKEPTIC RETURNS

When confronted with such claims, the skeptic's rebuttal is immediate and predictable. If it can be confirmed that the Bible contains a detailed knowledge of future events then the existence of an intelligent, transcendent, "Super Being" is established. Understanding this, through the centuries skeptics have simply asserted that biblical prophecies were written after the fact. That is, they assert that the biblical prophecies are in reality a record of history and not the supernatural foreknowledge they claim to be.

In the last 200 years the field of biblical "higher criti-

cism" has emerged from this foundation of skepticism in
its attempt to discredit any and all of the supernatural
claims in the Bible. However, scientific discoveries in the
last few hundred years attest to the supernatural origin of
the Bible.

Ironically, while the "higher critics" have pounded
away at the authenticity and supernatural claims of the
Bible, the field of archaeology has proven the Bible to be
an incredibly accurate and ancient historical document.
Quite unexpectedly the authenticity of Bible prophecy has
in turn been bolstered. There are numerous and very
detailed Bible prophecies which cannot be dismissed as
mere history. They were, in fact, written hundreds of years
before the events they foretold.

THE NATURE OF BIBLICAL PROPHECY

By some estimates, up to one-third of the Bible's text
is prophetic in nature. Although the Bible declares that its
prophetic utterances are from the mind of God, they were
penned by men of God between the fifteenth century B.C.
and the first century A.D.[180] Regarding the source of
Bible prophecy the Apostle Peter wrote in the first century A.D.:

> "Knowing this first, that no prophecy of Scripture is of
> any private interpretation, for prophecy never came by
> the will of man, but holy men of God spoke as they were
> moved by the Holy Spirit." II Peter 1:20-21 (NKJV)

The Apostle Paul echoed this when he wrote to his
companion Timothy:

> "All Scripture is given by inspiration of God, and is prof-
> itable for doctrine, for reproof, for correction, for instruc-
> tion in righteousness," II Timothy 3:16 (NKJV)

The purpose of Bible prophecy was to reveal God's will
in a supernatural way so that those who heard it would
honor and obey Him. In addition to predictive prophecy
(foretelling history), the prophets of God were also called

to be preachers of righteousness. They encouraged the people of God to turn from their evil deeds, obey His will and avoid disaster. As you might expect, their message was very unpopular and frequently resulted in death.

The scope of Bible prophecy is very broad. In the book of Daniel we find detailed prophecies about the rise and fall of world empires. Yet in many other places we find prophecies which foretell the future of just a single individual. Though many of the Bible's prophecies are general descriptions of events yet future, there are hundreds of Bible prophecies which are astonishingly detailed and specific. For example, there are dozens of detailed biblical prophecies that deal with the destiny of the nation of Israel. Finally, perhaps the most important theme of Bible prophecy is the foretelling of the birth, lineage, mission and destiny of Israel's Savior and Redeemer—the Messiah (the Anointed One).

The modern day prognostications of astrologers, seers and self-proclaimed prophets are for the most part taken very lightly. When ninety-five percent of the predictions made by Jean Dixon go routinely unfulfilled, no one seems to care. In stark contrast to this, the vocation of "biblical prophet" was taken very seriously. To be upheld in the eyes of Israel as a true prophet of God required an accuracy of no less than one hundred percent. If even one prophecy failed to be fulfilled the prophet's career was over. In the book of Deuteronomy, Moses sets forth the criterion for a prophet of God:

> "But the prophet who presumes to speak a word in My name, which I have not commanded him to speak, or who speaks in the name of other gods, that prophet shall die.... When a prophet speaks in the name of the LORD, if the thing does not happen or come to pass, that is the thing which the LORD has not spoken; the prophet has spoken it presumptuously; you shall not be afraid of him."[181] Deuteronomy 18:20, 22 (NKJV)

Were this standard still applied today there would certainly be very few applicants for the position of prophet. We will now turn our attention to a number of Bible prophecies which were written hundreds of years before they were fulfilled.

THE DESTRUCTION OF TYRE

In the year 606 B.C. Nebuchadnezzar, the son of the Babylonian emperor Nabopolassar, defeated Pharaoh Necho and the Egyptian army in the battle of Carchemish. Turning north, he sacked the city of Jerusalem and took thousands of Israelites captive, including the Hebrew prophet Daniel. This began the seventy-year Babylonian captivity that was predicted by the prophet Jeremiah, and others, many years earlier. Despite Jeremiah's warnings, the Jewish people, under the vassal king Jehoiakim, rebelled against the Babylonian rule and were again besieged by the armies of Babylon in 597 B.C. The Babylonians then seized Jehoiakim and brought back to Babylon thousands of the most talented artisans and craftsmen, including the young prophet Ezekiel. The final destruction of Jerusalem and Solomon's temple came in 586 B.C. with the third siege of Nebuchadnezzar.

While he was captive in Babylon, Ezekiel lived in Tel-abib, a city on the river Chebar. In the eleventh year of the captivity of Jehoiakim (586 B.C.), Ezekiel was given an astonishing prophecy regarding the ancient city of Tyre.

The city of Tyre, located in the modern day country of Lebanon, was at that time a large, thriving city and a great enemy of Israel. Regarding the future destiny of this city, God revealed to Ezekiel:

> "Thus says the Lord God: 'Behold I am against you O Tyre, and will cause many nations to come up against you, as the sea causes it's waves to come up. And *they* shall destroy the walls of Tyre and break down her towers; I will also scrape her dust from her and make her like the top of a rock. It shall be a place for the spreading of nets....

> For thus says the Lord GOD: 'Behold I will bring
> against Tyre from the north King Nebuchadnezzar,
> King of Babylon....
>
> ...he will slay your people by the sword and your strong
> pillars will fall to the ground. They will plunder your
> riches and pillage your merchandise; they will break
> down your walls and destroy your pleasant houses; they
> will lay your stones, your timbers, and your soil in the
> midst of the water.
>
> I will make you like the top of a rock; you shall be a
> place for the spreading of nets, and you shall never be
> rebuilt, for I the Lord have spoken....' For thus says the
> Lord GOD to Tyre, 'will the coastlands not shake at the
> sound of your fall.... Then all the princes of the sea will
> come down from their thrones, lay aside their robes, and
> take off their embroidered garments...and be aston-
> ished at you.'" Ezekiel 26:3–5,7,11–12,14–16 (NKJV)

The specific predictions for the city of Tyre, foretold
nearly 2600 years ago, are as follows.

1. Nebuchadnezzar will destroy the mainland city of
   Tyre.
2. More than one nation will come against Tyre.
3. Tyre will become flat like the top of a rock.
4. Fishermen will spread their nets over the site.
5. The stones and the timbers will be thrown into the
   water.
6. The city will never be rebuilt.
7. Princes of nearby coastlands will be astonished by
   Tyre's fall and give up their thrones.

THE HISTORY OF TYRE

In the year 586 B.C. Nebuchadnezzar, then king of the
Babylonian Empire, began his siege on the city of Tyre.
Although the Babylonian army was one of the greatest
fighting forces in history, it took thirteen years for them to
finally break through the walls of Tyre. When the
Babylonian army finally breached the walls of Tyre they
found that the majority of the people had moved to an

island one-half mile from the coast of the mainland city of Tyre. (Prediction number one fulfilled).

Two hundred and fifty-four years later Alexander the Great was in the midst of one of the greatest military campaigns in the history of the world. In a few short years he conquered the known world and established the renowned Greek Empire. Because of his incredible genius and military might, many of the countries he conquered submitted to him without a fight. However, in the year 332 B.C., Alexander the Great laid siege against the island city of Tyre because they would not submit to his authority. (Prediction number two fulfilled).

The island city of Tyre was a well fortified city with high walls along its entire perimeter. Look-out towers along the perimeter allowed the Tyrians to easily defend the city's high walls. Consequently, in order to overcome this island fortress, Alexander the Great devised a brilliant strategy. The Encyclopedia Britannica confirms that Alexander's army threw the debris (the stones, timbers and dirt) of the mainland city of Tyre into the ocean to make a causeway or jetty, thereby connecting the mainland to the island city of Tyre:

> "Alexander III, after defeating Darius III at the battle of Issus (333 B.C.), marched southward toward Egypt, calling upon the Phoenician cities to open their gates... the citizens of Tyre refused to do so, and Alexander laid siege to the city. Possessing no fleet, he demolished old Tyre, on the mainland, and with the debris built a mole (jetty) 200 ft. wide across the straits separating the old and new towns, erecting towers and war engines at the farther end."182

This unprecedented strategy employed by Alexander certainly contributed to his reputation as one of the greatest military strategists in history. It also fulfilled two of the predictions of Ezekiel's prophecy. (Predictions number two and five fulfilled).

Regarding Tyre's present condition historian Phillip Myers stated in his textbook of history:

> "Alexander the Great reduced Tyre to ruins in 332 B.C. Tyre recovered in a measure from this blow, but never regained the place she had previously held in the world. The larger part of the site of the once great city is now as bare as the top of a rock—a place where the fishermen that still frequent the spot spread their nets to dry."[183]

In this remarkable admission by a secular historian we see that the third and fourth predictions of Ezekiel were literally fulfilled.

Prior to its final destruction by the Moslems in A.D. 1291, the city of Tyre persisted in varying degrees of strength. Currently, according to Myers, "The causeway still remains...uniting the rock [the island] with the mainland."[184] The foundation where the ancient city of Tyre once stood is as "bare as the top of a rock—a place where the fishermen that still frequent the spot spread their nets to dry." Other than a few nearby small fishing villages, there is no evidence of the formerly great city (prediction number six fulfilled).

Historians record that when Alexander the Great defeated the city of Tyre, many of the neighboring kings submitted to his authority without a battle, thus fulfilling Ezekiel's prediction that "all the princes of the sea will come down from their thrones, lay aside their robes, and take off their embroidered garments...and be astonished at you."

How could Ezekiel have known these things would happen? A good guess? Not a chance. Ezekiel served the Creator of the universe—the God of the Bible who told Isaiah, Ezekiel and the other prophets that He would inform them of events *before they happened* so that when these events took place the people would know He was truly God.

THE SKEPTICS REPLY

The skeptic immediately responds that the book of Ezekiel must have been written after these events took place. However, archaeological finds have provided Ezekiel texts, some dating as far back as 400–600 B.C. In this century, for example, a nearly complete Ezekiel text inscribed on stone tablets has been found. Paleographic studies of the Hebrew text on these tablets indicates that they were probably chiseled around the time of Ezekiel (500-600 B.C.).[185,186] There are scholars who believe that these stone tablets may even be from the hands of Ezekiel himself!

The antiquity of the book of Ezekiel is further supported by its very early translation. According to rabbinical tradition, beginning around the year 285 B.C., seventy-two Hebrew scholars translated the Hebrew scriptures into Greek, the common language of the time. The book of Ezekiel was included in this translation called the Septuagint (meaning "Seventy"). No one knows exactly when the book of Ezekiel was accepted as part of the canon of Hebrew scripture. However, the fact that it was included together with the other books of the Bible in the Septuagint is powerful evidence that it had long been accepted as a genuine prophetic book by the Jews.

Alexander the Great didn't invade the city of Tyre until 332 B.C., long after the oldest known texts and certainly after the book was accepted as part of the Hebrew canon of scripture. The final fulfillment of the prophecy did not happen until its final destruction by the Moslems in A.D 1291—over 1700 years after it was penned by the prophet Ezekiel. The skeptic's ax is incapable, therefore, of explaining this prophecy away.

DANIEL'S PROPHECY OF THE 70 WEEKS

One of the most authenticated books of the Bible is the book of Daniel. Daniel was a Hebrew youth when he was taken captive by the Babylonian army in 606 B.C.[187] As a youth Daniel was trained for service in the palace of King Nebuchadnezzar. However, only two years after being taken captive, Daniel was made "ruler over the whole province of Babylon" after he correctly interpreted King Nebuchadnezzar's dream.[188] Many years later, near the end of the Babylonian servitude, the angel Gabriel appeared to Daniel and gave him a four verse prophecy that is unquestionably the most remarkable passage in the entire Bible (Daniel 9:24–27).[189]

Near the end of the Babylonian captivity, Daniel had apparently heard reports of the persistent desolation of Jerusalem. Daniel knew from his study of the book of Jeremiah that the captivity of Israel was almost over. Therefore, Daniel began praying for the people and nation of Israel when the angel Gabriel stated that he had come to give Daniel "skill and understanding" regarding the future of the nation.

In the book of Daniel we find the angel's statement:

"Seventy weeks are determined for your people and for your holy city, to finish the transgression, to make an end of sins, to make reconciliation for iniquity, to bring in everlasting righteousness, to seal up vision and prophecy, and to anoint the Most Holy. Know therefore and understand, that from the going forth of the command to restore and build Jerusalem until Messiah the Prince, there shall be seven weeks and sixty-two weeks; the street shall be built again, and the wall, even in troublesome times.

And after the sixty-two weeks Messiah shall be cut off, but not for Himself; and the people of the prince who is to come shall destroy the city and the sanctuary. The end of it shall be with a flood, and till the end of the war desolations are determined. Then he shall confirm a covenant with many for one week; but in the middle of the week he shall bring an end to sacrifice and offering. And on the wing of abominations shall be one who makes desolate, even until the consummation, which is determined, is poured out on the desolate." Daniel 9:24–27 (NKJV)

The scope of these four verses is very broad. It covers a time span from the fifth-century B.C. even to the present day. However, for our purposes (examining fulfilled predictive prophecy) we will focus on the portion which pinpoints the time of the coming of the "Messiah the Prince" (Meschiach Nagid in Hebrew).[190]

The angel Gabriel told Daniel that the focus of this prophecy was to be upon "thy people and upon thy holy city." That is, upon Israel and Jerusalem. However, at the time of this angelic visitation, Jerusalem was completely desolate. The majority of Israelites had been taken captive by the Babylonians and the city of Jerusalem, including Solomon's Temple, had been destroyed by the Babylonian army nearly 70 years earlier. However, at the time this prophecy was given (circa. 537 B.C.) the Jews were about to be freed by the Medo-Persian king Cyrus.

Verse 24 states that "*seventy weeks are determined for your people and for your holy city.*" In Hebrew the word translated as "weeks" is pronounced "shabua" and literally means a week of years. The word shabuim would readily be understood as seven years in this context, much like the word decade means ten years in English.

Verse 25 then declares that Daniel should "*know and understand, that from the going forth of the command to restore and rebuild Jerusalem until Messiah the Prince, there shall be seven weeks and sixty two weeks.*" This verse is a precise mathematical prediction of the time of Messiah's coming! In effect, the angel Gabriel told Daniel that after sixty-nine weeks of years the Messiah would be revealed to the nation of Israel!

If a "shabuim" is a week (seven) of years, it therefore follows that 69 sevens is 483 years (69 x 7= 483 years). Furthermore, it is well documented that the ancient Jewish and Babylonian calendars were based on a 360 day year.[191] According to some scholars, the current 365.25 day calendar year came about because of an ancient cosmic catastrophe such as a close passing of Mars or a mete-

or or comet striking the earth. Such an event, it is believed, lengthened the time the earth takes to rotate one time around the Sun to the current 365.25 days per year.[192]

For the final elucidation of this prophecy we are deeply indebted to the work of Sir Robert Anderson, former head of Scotland Yard, who made a remarkable discovery when he applied the principle of a 360-day calendar year to the 69 weeks (483 years). His famous book, *The Coming Prince*, meticulously details the fulfillment of this prophecy.[193]

After careful examination of Old Testament chronological factors, Sir Robert Anderson demonstrated that the Jews also used a 360-day calendar year for purposes of prophetic calculations. Anderson applied this fact and multiplied the 360 days per calendar year by the 483 years to get 173,880 days. Gabriel was, in effect, telling Daniel that 173,880 days after the command was given to "restore and rebuild Jerusalem" the Messiah would come. Remember, at the time this prophecy was given the city of Jerusalem was desolate.

Is there a record of a command such as this recorded anywhere in history? Yes!

In the fifth century B.C. a Hebrew named Nehemiah, then cup bearer to the Medo-Persian king Artaxerxes, wrote of the command to restore and rebuild Jerusalem:

> "And it came to pass in the month of Nisan, in the twentieth year of the reign of Artaxerxes, when wine was before him, I took wine and gave it to the king. Now I had never been sad in his presence before. Therefore, the king said to me 'why is your face sad, since you are not sick?'" Nehemiah 2:1–2 (NKJV)

Nehemiah went on to explain that he was sad because he had heard reports that the city of his people, Jerusalem, was still desolate. Nehemiah requested that he be allowed to go back to Jerusalem and rebuild the city. King Artaxerxes granted his wish on the spot and gave him official "letters" or documents for easy passage. This occurred, we are told, in the month of Nisan, in the twentieth year of Artaxerxes Longimanus' reign.

Artaxerxes Longimanus ascended to the throne of the Medo-Persian empire in July 465 B.C.[194] The twentieth year of his reign would have begun in July 446 B.C. The decree occurred approximately nine months later in the month of Nisan (March/April on our calendar). By Hebrew tradition, when the day of the month is not specifically stated (as in Artaxerxes decree), it is given to be the first day of that month. Consequently, the very day of Artaxerxes' decree was the first day of the Hebrew month Nisan in 445 B.C. The first day of Nisan in 445 B.C. corresponds to the 14th day of March. These dates were confirmed through astronomical calculations at the British Royal Observatory and reported by Sir Robert Anderson.[195]

The prophecy states that 69 weeks of years (173,880 days) after the command goes forth to restore and rebuild the city of Jerusalem the Messiah will come. If we count forward 173,880 days from March 14th, 445 B.C., we arrive at April 6th, 32 A.D.

Here are the calculations.

March 14th, 445 B.C. to March 14th, 32 A.D. is 476 years.

(1 B.C. to 1 A.D. is one year. There is no year zero)

476 years x 365 days per year = 173,740 days

Add for leap years = 116 days[196]

March 14th to April 6th = 24 days

total = 173,880 days!

What happened on April 6th, 32 A.D.? According to Anderson's calculations a humble carpenter rode into the east gate of Jerusalem on a donkey while the crowds cried "Hosanna! Hosanna! Blessed is He who comes in the name of the Lord!"[197] This man's name was Jesus of Nazareth.

This was the first day that He allowed his followers to

proclaim Him as their Messiah. He had previously told them that His day had not yet come.

It is fascinating to realize that during the ministry of Jesus Christ there were several occasions in which the people attempted to promote Him as King Messiah, but He carefully avoided it. "Mine hour is not yet come," was His response on these occasions.[198]

Then one day, He meticulously arranges it! On the day that Jesus presents himself as "King Messiah" to the nation of Israel, He arranged for a donkey to be His personal transportation. While riding into the city of Jerusalem on a donkey He specifically fulfilled the prophecy of Zechariah that the Messiah would present himself in just that way:

> "Rejoice greatly, O daughter of Zion! Shout, O daughter
> of Jerusalem! Behold, your King is coming to you; He is
> just and having salvation, lowly and riding on a donkey,
> a colt, the foal of a donkey." Zechariah 9:9 (NKJV)[199]

This is the *only* occasion that Jesus presented Himself as King. According to precise biblical and secular historical benchmarks, Robert Anderson demonstrated that this occurred on April 6th, 32 A.D.—exactly 173,880 days after the command went forth "to restore and rebuild Jerusalem!!!"

How could Daniel, writing in 537 B.C., have known this in advance? How could anyone have contrived to have this prediction documented over five centuries in advance?

Skeptical? Read on.

There is, in fact, another way to check the accuracy of this date. In the Gospel of Luke, chapter three, it states that in the 15th year of the reign of Caesar Tiberius, Jesus was baptized by John the Baptist and began His ministry. It is well established that the reign of Caesar Tiberius[200] began with his coronation on August 19th in the year A.D. 14. Most scholars believe Jesus was baptized in the fall season. It therefore follows that the ministry of Jesus started with his baptism in the Fall of A.D. 28, the 15th year of the reign of Caesar Tiberius.[201] The ministry of Jesus spanned four Passovers or about three and one half years.

The first Passover of Jesus' ministry would have been in the Spring of A.D. 29. The fourth Passover of His ministry was the day of His crucifixion and would have fallen in the year A.D. 32.[202] The Passover in that year fell on April 10th.[203] Remarkably, according to Robert Anderson and the British Royal Observatory, the Sunday before that Passover was April 6th—the very day Jesus presented Himself as King and exactly 173,880 days after the decree of Artaxerxes!!

According to the principles of biblical higher criticism, this prophecy proves that the book of Daniel was written after the Gospel of Luke! This is, of course, absurd because Daniel was translated into Greek nearly three centuries before Jesus was even born.

This prophecy is one of the most astonishing proofs that God transcends time and is able to see the end from the beginning with incredible precision!

THE ANCIENT RABBIS AND DANIEL'S 70 WEEKS

Some of you may be thinking that the application of this prophecy to the Messiah is a Christian contrivance. In fact, most modern rabbis try to deny the messianic application of this prophecy. However, it is well established that ancient Jews believed that this prophecy pinpointed the time of Messiah's coming. In fact, many in the Qumran community (the writers of the Dead Sea Scrolls) believed that they were living in the very generation to which this prophecy pointed![204,205]

In the Babylonian Talmud, compiled between A.D. 200–500, ancient rabbis commented on the time of Messiah's coming and Daniel's seventy weeks prophecy.

Regarding the times referred to in Daniel's prophecy,

Rabbi Judah, the main compiler of the Talmud, said:

> "These times were over long ago"
> Babylonian Talmud Sanhedrin 98b and 97a

In the 12th Century A.D., Rabbi Moses Ben Maimon (Maimonides), one of the most respected rabbis in history, and a man who rejected the messianic claims of Jesus of Nazareth, said regarding Daniel's seventy weeks prophecy:

> "Daniel has elucidated to us the knowledge of the end times. However, since they are secret, the wise [rabbis] have barred the calculation of the days of Messiah's coming so that the untutored populace will not be led astray *when they see that the End Times have already come but there is no sign of the Messiah*" (Emphasis added). *Igeret Teiman*, Chapter 3, p. 24.

Finally, Rabbi Moses Abraham Levi said regarding the time of Messiah's coming:

> "I have examined and searched all the Holy Scriptures and have not found the time for the coming of Messiah clearly fixed, except in the words of Gabriel to the prophet Daniel, which are written in the 9th chapter of the prophecy of Daniel." *The Messiah of the Targums, Talmuds and Rabbinical Writers,* 1971

THE INTERVAL BETWEEN THE 69TH AND 70TH WEEK

After the coming of the "Messiah the Prince," the prophecy continues that *"after the sixty-two sevens the Messiah shall be cut off, but not for himself; and the people of the prince who is to come shall destroy the city and the sanctuary* (verse 26)." The word here translated as "cut off" is the Hebrew "karath." This word literally means to be put to death (usually by being pierced) for a capital crime. Jesus was arrested, tried and convicted for blasphemy and for insurrection against the Roman Empire, both capital crimes punishable by death. Jesus was then "pierced" by crucifixion on a Roman cross.

After the Messiah is "cut off," Gabriel told Daniel that *"the people of the prince who is to come shall destroy the city and the sanctuary."* In the year A.D. 70, 38 years after Jesus was crucified, Titus Vespasian, with the fifth, tenth, twelfth, and fifteenth Roman Legions leveled the city of Jerusalem and the Second Temple, exactly as Daniel had predicted. The first-century historian Flavius Josephus graphically records that the city of Jerusalem was burned to the ground and millions of Jews were starved to death, cannibalized, or killed by the Roman Legions.[206]

The destruction of Jerusalem was also foretold by Jesus Himself. On the very day that He presented himself to the nation of Israel as "King Messiah," while descending the Mount of Olives on a donkey, Jesus stopped and wept saying:

> "...If you had known, even you, especially in this your day, the things that make for your peace! But now they are hidden from your eyes. For the days will come upon you when your enemies will build an embankment around you, surround you and close you in on every side, and level you, and your children within you, to the ground; and they will not leave in you one stone upon another, because you did not know the time of your visitation." Luke 19:42–44 (NKJV)

Days later Jesus' Messianic claim was rejected by the Jewish leadership and He was crucified as a common criminal on a Roman cross.

In this passage in Luke we can feel the passion that Jesus held for the people and nation of Israel. And yet, He held those same people accountable for not recognizing "the time of their visitation." The 173,880 days were up and Jesus held them responsible for this fact.

A final note on the first sixty-nine weeks. This entire prophecy was written by Daniel at a time when the temple in Jerusalem was desolate. Destroyed in 587 B.C., there was no indication in Daniel's day that it would be rebuilt. However, Daniel states that after the temple is rebuilt, the Messiah would come and then "the prince of the people who is to come" would then destroy it again. So the Messiah *had to come* to the Second Temple before it was destroyed!

THE SEVENTIETH WEEK OF DANIEL

There is one 'seven' or week of years remaining to be fulfilled. In a private briefing for His disciples, Jesus himself points to this final seven-year period as the key to end-time prophecy.[207] In the final verse of the seventy weeks prophecy we are told:

> "Then he shall confirm a covenant with many for one week; but in the middle of the week he shall bring an end to sacrifice and offering. And on the wing of abominations shall be one who makes desolate, even until the consummation, which is determined, is poured out on the desolate." Daniel 9:27 (NKJV)

The "he" in this verse is the "ruler that shall come" of verse 26, otherwise known as the Anti-Christ. This future world leader will make a treaty with "the many" (a Hebrew idiom for Israel), but in the middle of the seven-year period he will set up his own idol to be worshipped in the temple itself. This event, called the "abomination of desolation," triggers the final three and one-half years of earth history known as "the great tribulation."

The seventieth week of Daniel culminates with the second coming of Jesus Christ. This entire prophecy of the "Seventy Weeks" is powerful proof of the supernatural, transcendent origin of the biblical text. If the first coming of the Messiah was foretold with such impeccable accuracy, it is indeed safe to assume that the prophecy of His second coming will also occur in God's perfect timing—a time known only to Him.

UNTIL SHILOH COMES

In the 49th chapter of the book of Genesis there is another specific prophecy regarding the time of Messiah's coming. In verse one we read of the last blessing that Jacob bestowed to his sons.

> "And Jacob called his sons and said, 'Gather together, that I may tell you what shall befall you in the last days'" Genesis 49:1 (NKJV)

When he had gathered them together he began to prophesy over each of them. When he got to his son Judah, he gave a prophecy concerning the Messiah:

> "The scepter shall not depart from Judah, nor a lawgiver from between his feet, until Shiloh comes; and to him shall be the obedience of the people." Genesis 49:10

This strange prophecy has a few words that need to be defined in order to be fully understood. The word "scepter" has been understood by the Rabbis to mean the "tribal staff" or "tribal identity" of the twelve tribes of Israel. This "tribal identity" was linked, in the minds of the Jews, to their right to apply and enforce Mosaic law upon the people, including the right to adjudicate capital cases and administer capital punishment, or *jus gladii*.[208]

Secondly, it is well documented that the word "Shiloh" has been understood for millennia to be an idiom for the Messiah.[209]

Therefore, according to this prophecy, the tribal identity or scepter of the tribe of Judah would not cease until the Messiah came. Judah was not only the name of the son of Jacob, but it was also the name of the southern kingdom of the divided nation of Israel.

With these definitions in place we can restate the prophecy as follows:

"The [National identity of Judah, which includes the right to enforce Mosaic law, including the right to administer capital punishment upon the people, as called for in the Torah] shall not depart from [the southern kingdom (Judah)], nor a lawgiver from between his feet, until Shiloh [the Messiah] comes; and to him shall be the obedience of the people."

This prophecy gives specific indicators regarding the time of the coming of the Messiah! The prophecy declares that He would come before the right to impose Jewish law (which includes capital punishment) is rescinded and before the national identity of Judah was removed!

During the 70-year Babylonian captivity, from 606–537 B.C., the southern kingdom of Israel, Judah, had lost its national sovereignty, but it retained it's tribal staff or national identity.[210] It is very significant that in the book of Ezra we read that during the 70-year Babylonian captivity the Jews still retained their own lawgivers or judges.[211] The Jews maintained their identity and judicial authority over their own people even during 70 years of slavery. The scepter had not been lost during the Babylonian captivity.

During the next five centuries the Jews suffered under the yoke of the Medo-Persian, Greek and Roman Empires. Yet, Judah retained its tribal identity up until the first quarter of the first century A.D.

In the first quarter of the first century A.D. the Jews were under Roman dominion when an unprecedented event occurred. According to Josephus (Antiquities 17:13) around the year A.D. 6–7, the son and successor to King Herod, a man named Herod Archelaus was dethroned and banished to Vienna, a city of Gaul.[212] He was replaced, not by a Jewish king, but by a Roman Procurator named Caponius. The legal power of the Sanhedrin was then immediately restricted.

With the ascension of Caponius, the Sanhedrin lost their ability to adjudicate capital cases. This was the normal policy toward all the nations under the yoke of the Romans. The province of Judea had, however, been spared from this policy up to this point. However, Caesar Agustus had had enough of the Jews and finally removed the judicial authority from them at the ascension of Caponius. This transfer of power was recorded by Josephus:[213]

"And now Archelaus' part of Judea was reduced into a

province, and Caponius, one of the equestrian order of the Romans, was sent as a procurator, *having the power of life and death put into his hands by Caesar!*" (Emphasis added).

The power of the Sanhedrin to adjudicate capital cases was immediately removed. In the minds of the Jewish leadership, this event signified the removal of the scepter or national identity of the tribe of Judah!

If you think that this is a Christian contrivance, think again. Here are several ancient rabbinical references that indicate that the rabbis believed that Genesis 49:10 was referring to the Messiah.

In the Targum Onkelos it states:

"The transmission of dominion shall not cease from the house of Judah, nor the scribe from his children's children, forever, *until Messiah comes.*" [214]

In the Targum Pseudo-Jonathan it states:

"Kings and rulers shall not cease from the house of Judah...until King Messiah comes" [215]

The Targum Yerushalmi states:

"Kings shall not cease from the house of Judah...*until the time of the coming of the King Messiah*...to whom all the dominions of the earth shall become subservient." [216]

In the Babylonian Talmud, Sanhedrin 98b, Rabbi Johanan said:

"The world was created for the sake of the Messiah, what is this Messiah's name? The school of Rabbi Shila said 'his name is Shiloh, for it is written; until Shiloh come.'"

These amazing commentaries should eliminate any doubt that the Jews that lived prior to the Christian era believed that one of the names of the Messiah was Shiloh. Furthermore, these quotes should eliminate all doubt that the ancient rabbis believed that the Messiah would come before the removal of the scepter from Judah!

"WOE UNTO US, FOR MESSIAH HAS NOT APPEARED!"

So far we have established that Shiloh is an idiom for the Messiah and that the scepter (that is, the tribal identity, associated with the right to impose capital punishment) had departed from the kingdom of Judah early in the first quarter of the first century. What was the reaction of the Jews when the right to adjudicate capital cases (the *jus gladii*) was removed from Judah? Did they view the removal of their authority on capital cases as the removal of the scepter from Judah? The answer can be categorically stated as YES!

When Archelaus was banished, the power of the Sanhedrin was severely curtailed. Capital cases could no longer be tried by the Sanhedrin. Such cases were now transferred to the Roman Procurator, Caponius. This transfer of power is even mentioned in the Talmud:

> "A little more than forty years before the destruction of the Temple, the power of pronouncing capital sentences was taken away from the Jews." [217]

This certainly corresponds to the same event recorded by Josephus we saw earlier. In Antiquities 20:9 Josephus again points out that the Sanhedrin had no authority over capital cases:

> "After the death of the procurator Festus, when Albinus was about to succeed him, the high-priest Ananias considered it a favorable opportunity to assemble the Sanhedrin. He therefore caused James the brother of Jesus, who was called Christ, and several others, to appear before this hastily assembled council, and pronounced upon them the sentence of death by stoning. All the wise men and strict observers of the law who were at Jerusalem expressed their disapprobation of this act.... Some even went to Albinus himself, who had

departed to Alexandria, to bring this breach of the law
under his observation, and to inform him that Ananias
had acted illegally in assembling the Sanhedrin without
the Roman authority."

This remarkable passage not only mentions Jesus of
Nazareth and his brother James as historical figures, but
it also declares that the Sanhedrin had no authority to
pass the death sentence upon any man!

The *jus gladii,* the right to impose the death sentence,
had been removed. The remaining authority of Judah had
been taken away by the Romans in the early years of the
first century. The scepter had departed from Judah. Its
royal and legal powers were removed; but where was
Shiloh?

The reaction of the Jews to these monumental events
is recorded in the Talmud. Augustin Lemann, in his book
Jesus before the Sanhedrin, records a statement by Rabbi
Rachmon:

> "When the members of the Sanhedrin found themselves
> deprived of their right over life and death, a general con-
> sternation took possession of them: they covered their
> heads with ashes, and their bodies with sackcloth,
> exclaiming: '*Woe unto us for the scepter has departed
> from Judah and the Messiah has not come*'"[218,219,220]
> (emphasis added).

The scepter was smitten from the hands of the tribe of
Judah. The kingdom of Judea, the last remnant of the
greatness of Israel, was debased into being merely a part
of the province of Syria. While the Jews wept in the streets
of Jerusalem, there was growing up in the city of Nazareth
the young son of a Jewish carpenter, Jesus of Nazareth.
The inescapable conclusion was that Shiloh had come!
Only then was the scepter removed!

THE NATION OF ISRAEL

One of the most remarkable aspects of Bible prophecy
is its ability to foretell the history of nations and king-

doms. Throughout its text the Bible has foretold the future destiny of nearly every nation and kingdom within a thousand miles of Israel. However, the most remarkable example of such prophecies are those regarding the nation of Israel itself. Israel's history is absolutely without parallel in the history of the world and is one of the most remarkable proofs of God's existence.

BIRTH OF A NATION

The nation of Israel was born out of a promise that God gave to Abram (later called Abraham), a gentile from an idol-worshipping nation in the Middle East called the land of Ur. In this promise, given around 2000 B.C., God declared that Abraham would be the father of many nations. Among those nations would be His chosen people, the nation of Israel:

> "Now the LORD said to Abram: 'Get out of your country, from your family and from your father's house, to a land that I will show you. I will make you a great nation; I will bless you and make your name great; and you shall be a blessing.'" Genesis 12:1–2 (NKJV)[221]

This promise, penned by Moses centuries later, saw its fruition when the descendants of Abraham finally occupied the land of Israel shortly after Moses' death.

THE FIRST EXILE BABYLON

Shortly before his death, Moses recorded incredibly grim details regarding the future destiny of the nation of Israel. Under the inspiration of the Holy Spirit, Moses foreknew that after his death the people of Israel would soon rebel against their God. The tragic result would be the destruction of the nation and the captivity of its people by an invading foreign power:

> "The LORD will bring a *nation* against you from afar, from the end of the earth, as swift as the eagle flies, a nation whose language you will not understand, a nation of fierce countenance, which does not respect the

elderly nor show favor to the young." Deuteronomy 28:49–50

In the subsequent verses, Moses foretells in gruesome detail a time of famine, moral chaos, murder, cannibalism and generalized social collapse.[222]

In the eighth century B.C. the prophet Isaiah added more detail regarding Israel's impending destruction: it would be at the hands of the Babylonians, a minor power in the region during Isaiah's time.[223]

Why would God allow this to happen to His chosen people? The reason can be traced back to the Law of God given many years earlier. In the book of Leviticus, penned by Moses himself, God commanded the people to rest the land of Israel every seventh year:

> "And the LORD spoke to Moses on Mount Sinai, saying, 'Speak to the children of Israel, and say to them: When you come into the land which I give you, then the land shall keep a Sabbath to the LORD, *Six years you shall sow your field, and six years you shall prune your vineyard, and gather in its fruit; but in the seventh year there shall be a Sabbath of solemn rest for the land, a Sabbath to the LORD.* You shall neither sow your field nor prune your vineyard.'" Leviticus 25:1–4 (NKJV)

Shortly after Moses died, Joshua led the people into the promised land of Israel. However, while they were in the land, the Jews did not rest it. Centuries later the prophet Jeremiah foretold that the Jews would be removed from the land for seventy years so that the land could enjoy its Sabbath rest:

> "'Behold, I will send and take all the families of the north,' says the LORD, 'and Nebuchadnezzar the king of Babylon, My servant, and will bring them against this land, against its inhabitants, and against these nations all around, and will utterly destroy them, and make them an astonishment, a hissing, and perpetual desolations...'*And this whole land shall be a desolation and an astonishment, and these nations shall serve the king of Babylon seventy years.*" Jeremiah 25:9,11

In the summer of 606 B.C., centuries after Moses' death, Nebuchadnezzar, the eldest son of Babylonian king Nabopolassar, besieged the nation and people of Israel.[224] In his first campaign, Nebuchadnezzar seized Jehoiakim, king of Judah and appointed him as his vassal.[225] Upon hearing of his father's death, Nebuchadnezzar returned to Babylon to receive his throne. It was during this first siege that Nebuchadnezzar took captive the prophet Daniel along with "young men...gifted in all wisdom, possessing knowledge and quick to understand...."[226] This campaign initiated a seventy-year period known biblically as the "servitude of the nation," foretold by the prophet Jeremiah.[227]

Three years later Jehoiakim rebelled against the authority of Nebuchadnezzar. In 597 B.C. Nebuchadnezzar encamped against the city of Jerusalem. Ironically, by the time Nebuchadnezzar broke through the walls of Jerusalem, Jehoiakim was already dead. Nebuchadnezzar overcame the rebellion in Judah, took Jehoiachin[228] (Jehoiakim's son) captive and appointed Zedekiah as his vassal.

In the ninth year of Zedekiah, 589 B.C., the Jews again rebelled against the authority of Babylon. For the third and final time the Babylonian army attacked Judah. Nearly two years later, after unrelenting assault and severe famine, the Babylonians broke through the walls of Jerusalem and destroyed the city and the temple of God.[229] Zedekiah and his family tried to escape in the desert, but they were quickly captured. Nebuchadnezzar then killed the sons of Zedekiah and plucked out the eyes of Zedekiah.

According to 2 Chronicles 36:17 the Babylonians, whose language *the Jews did not understand*, were incredibly vicious in their attack:

> "Therefore He [GOD] brought against [the Jews] the king of the Chaldeans, who killed their young men with the sword in the house of their sanctuary, and had no

compassion on young men or virgin, on the aged or the weak; He gave them all into his hand."

This final siege, in 587 B.C., initiated a seventy-year period known biblically as the "Desolations of Jerusalem."[230,231]

This catastrophe, brought on by the corporate sin of Israel, fulfilled in detail the predictions given by Moses centuries earlier. By the will of God, "A nation of fierce countenance" (Babylon), whose language (Chaldean) the Jews did not understand, decimated the people, burned their cities and destroyed the "House of God." Those that did not die by the sword were taken captive to serve a foreign king—exactly as Moses and Jeremiah had foretold.

THE RETURN FROM CAPTIVITY

In 537 B.C, exactly seventy years after the first siege of Jerusalem, the servitude of the nation ended with the decree of Cyrus, the Medo-Persian Emperor.[232,233] In his decree Cyrus acknowledged the God of Israel and allowed the Jews the freedom to return home to rebuild the temple of God. Furthermore, Cyrus gave back the vessels that Nebuchadnezzar had plundered from Solomon's Temple and contributed financially to the construction of their second temple. About 50,000 Jews responded to this royal proclamation and returned to Jerusalem under the leadership of Zerubbabel.[234]

Seventeen years later, in 520 B.C., exactly seventy years after the third siege of Nebuchadnezzar, the "Desolations of Jerusalem" were fulfilled when the foundation of the second temple was laid by those who had returned to Jerusalem.[235] Thus, the "Servitude of the Nation" and the "Desolations of Jerusalem" were both accomplished in exactly seventy years!

EXILED AGAIN

From 537 B.C. until 70 A.D. the Jews remained in the land of Israel. After their return from Babylon, the nation of Israel survived under the authority of the Medo-Persian, The Grecian and finally the Roman empires. However, in A.D. 70, Titus Vespasian, with the fifth, tenth, twelfth, and fifteenth Roman Legions leveled the city of Jerusalem.[236] According to Josephus, over a million Jews were killed by starvation, crucifixion, cannibalism and the Roman sword. Those who escaped death were taken captive by Rome and dispersed "among the nations."[237]

For the second time in its history, the House of God and the city of Jerusalem were destroyed. Remarkably, this second destruction was also foretold by the prophet Daniel at least six centuries before it transpired!

As we saw earlier in Daniel chapter 9, the angel Gabriel told Daniel that after the coming of the Messiah the Prince, "...the people of the prince who is to come *shall destroy the city and the sanctuary....*"[238] When Daniel penned this prophecy (circa. 538 B.C.) the first temple had long since been destroyed. From this historical context we know that the term "the city and the sanctuary" must therefore refer to the city of Jerusalem and the *second* temple which was rebuilt shortly after Daniel penned this prophecy.[239]

For the skeptic who might argue that this prophecy in the book of Daniel was written after the destruction of Jerusalem in A.D. 70 we have bad news. The book of Daniel, long accepted as part of the Hebrew Bible, was translated into Greek as a part of the "Septuagint" in 285 B.C.[240]

Finally, as we saw earlier, Jesus of Nazareth also foretold the destruction of the second temple and the city of Jerusalem in Luke chapter 19.

Because of these facts, the skeptic has not a leg to stand on when he argues that the second destruction of Jerusalem is only a record of history and not the fulfillment of divinely given prophecy.

"FROM THE FOUR CORNERS OF THE EARTH"

From the year A.D. 70 until May 14, 1948 the Jewish people lived dispersed and geographically isolated among the nations of the world. Despite this fact, they retained their cultural and religious identity for nearly two thousand years. This fact is unprecedented in history. In virtually every other case, when a people or nation is reduced to a small remnant and dispersed around the world, they lose their cultural identity within just a few generations as they are "absorbed" into the local population.

Remarkably, the fact that the Jewish people would be re-gathered to the land of Israel from the four corners of the earth was also foretold by a number of prophets thousands of years earlier.

When David Ben Gurion announced the rebirth of the nation of Israel on May 14, 1948, he used as his authority the ancient prophecies of the book of Ezekiel!

In the book of Ezekiel, written over 2500 years ago, the prophet predicts a time when the Jewish people would be regathered to the land of Israel a second and final time. However, quite unlike the prophecies of the Babylonian exile and the first restoration, those referring to the second restoration speak of the people being regathered from among the *nations* (plural) of the earth.

> "'Then say to them, 'Thus says the Lord GOD: 'Surely I will take the children of Israel *from among the nations, wherever they have gone,* and will gather them from every side and bring them into their own land; and I will make them one nation in the land, on the mountains of Israel; and one king shall be king over them all; they shall no longer be two nations, nor shall they ever be divided into two kingdoms again.'"[241] Ezekiel 37:21–22 (NKJV)

In the verses that follow God declares that once His people are regathered into the land He will pour out His Spirit on them and they will remain in the land "forever."[242] Therefore, we know that Ezekiel cannot be speaking of the return from Babylon because they were removed again in 70 A.D.!

Lest the skeptic think we are "reading into the text" the concept of two exiles and two restorations, the prophet Isaiah comes to the rescue. In the eighth century B.C., nearly 2700 years before the second restoration of the nation of Israel, the prophet Isaiah wrote:

> "It shall come to pass in that day that the LORD shall set His hand again the *second time* to recover the remnant of His people who are left, from Assyria and Egypt, from Pathros and Cush, from Elam and Shinar, from Hamath and the islands of the sea. He will set up a banner for the nations, and will assemble the outcasts of Israel, and gather together the dispersed of Judah from the *four corners of the earth*." Isaiah 11:11–12 (NKJV)

In this prophecy, written long before the *first restoration* in 537 B.C., the prophet Isaiah speaks of a time when God will re-gather the "remnant of His people" a *second time*.[243] Why not "the third time" or "the fourth." How did Isaiah know that there would be a second restoration? Could it be that Isaiah possessed "inside information" from a being outside time and space? As we see time and again the biblical prophecies fulfilled in minute detail, even the most devout skeptic must be pricked with a measure of awe and wonder.

Of necessity our overview of Bible prophecy is by no means comprehensive. However, we have attempted to review a small number of prophecies *in detail* to give the believer and skeptic alike an appreciation for the incredible accuracy and detail of prophetic fulfillment. There are, of course, hundreds of additional Bible prophecies that have been fulfilled in minute detail. But given even the small number that we have reviewed, the reader can see that there is ample evidence to believe in the divine inspiration of Scripture.

CHANCE OR DESIGN? THE SKEPTICS DILEMMA

Throughout this book we have attempted to anticipate the skeptic's reply to the evidence presented. In the case of the origin of the universe and life on earth, as we have seen, there are only two possible explanations—chance or design. In each case a balanced examination of twentieth-century scientific evidence has led a number of world authorities to conclude that appealing to chance is akin to faith in supernatural miracles! In effect, to believe that the universe "just happened," the skeptic must place as much faith in the arbitrary and purposeless laws of physics and chance chemistry as the Christian does in the God of the Bible.

In this section we have examined wide ranging evidences for the supernatural, extra dimensional origin of the biblical text. For many, such evidence is overwhelming proof of God's existence and His authorship of the Bible. On the other hand, there will be those who remain unconvinced. But what options remain? If there is not an extra-dimensional, supernatural Agency who authored the biblical text, how then are we to interpret the evidences of its supernatural origin? Luck? Collusion? Chance?

When all the arguments are broken down, we find that each of the evidences for the supernatural origin of the Bible are either the result of design or the result of an abundance of fortuitous slips of the pen by prophets and scribes alike.

To argue that the evidences for biblical inspiration are the result of a myriad of lucky guesses requires an enormous measure of faith. Such an assertion requires us to believe that ancient fishermen, tent makers, shepherds, kings and paupers, who were separated by 1,500 years on three different continents, could consistently, and without error, describe the nature of the universe, planet earth and it's life forms, in a way that is fully consistent with twentieth-century science. It requires us to believe that those same men wrote history in advance—all of this *without* the guidance of One with supernatural "inside information." It requires us to believe that ancient scribes colluded with their contemporary rabbis to place the gospel of Jesus Christ—a man whom they would ultimately reject as Messiah—in the genealogy of Genesis chapter five!

Ironically, to hold the view that the evidences for biblical inspiration are the result of chance is akin to believing that the universe and its life forms arose without intelligent guidance. This unfailing appeal to "chance" is required if the skeptic is to maintain a world view void of any supernatural influences.

In the twentieth century we often smile when we think of the ancients who worshipped idols of wood and stone. Certainly we are too sophisticated to participate in such pagan idolatry. However, in the twentieth century, our public educational systems, the media and the major think-tanks are governed by individuals who pay homage to, bow down to and worship at the throne of the god called "Chance." How much more must the Creator be offended by the worship of "nothingness and purposelessness."

---

180 Many scholars believe that the book of Job was written as early as 2,000-2,500 B.C.

181 See also Deuteronomy 13:5, Jeremiah 14:14-15, Zechariah 13:3.

182 Encyclopedia Britannica. vol. 15/xiii. pg. 452 (1970).

183 Phillip Myers, *General History for Colleges and High Schools*. pg. 55 Boston, Ginn & Co.

184 Myers, *op. cit.*, pg. 153.

185 Paleography is the study of ancient writing. A document can often be reliably dated based on the style and structure of its letters. When compared with other documents of known age,

a date or era is assigned to the document.

186 See David Allen Lewis, *Prophecy 2000*.

187 There are some scholars that place this event at 605 B.C. The difference is due to a technicality regarding the way one dates the ascension of Babylonian Kings and whether Daniel used this method.

188 Daniel Chapter 2:48.

189 Portions of this chapter were adapted from "The Babylon Report" by Hal Lindsey and Chuck Missler.

190 For a detailed look at Daniel's 70 Weeks prophecy see *The Seventy Weeks of Daniel* Chuck Missler, Koinonia House, PO box D, CDA, Idaho, 83816-0317. 1-800-KHOUSE1.

191 See *Footprints of the Messiah*, Chuck Missler, Koinonia House, PO box D, CDA, Idaho, 83816-0317.

192 See *Signs in the Heavens*, Chuck Missler, Koinonia House, PO box D, CDA, Idaho, 83816-0317.

193 See *The Coming Prince*, Sir Robert Anderson.

194 Encyclopedia Britannica, 1990 ed.

195 Robert Anderson, *The Coming Prince*, Kregel. Reprinted in 1984.

196 Leap years do not occur in century years unless divisible by 400 (therefore, we must add three less leap years in four centuries).

197 See The New Testament, Luke Chapter 19.

198 John 7:6, 8, 30.

199 In the Babylonian Talmud, written by ancient rabbis, we find that Zechariah 9:9 was believed to be a Messianic prophecy. See *The Search for Messiah*, Mark Eastman, Chuck Smith, The Word for Today, 1993.

200 The Encyclopedia Britannica, 1990. Micropedia.

201 The day that a Roman ruler ascends to the throne begins his first year.

202 There are some scholars that place the crucifixion at A.D. 33. The disagreement is due to the method one uses in calculating the ascension of Caesar Tiberius. Some believe that his first year began the day he took office. In this case the fifteenth year begins in A.D. 28 and the crucifixion would be in A.D. 32. If one begins counting the first year of Tiberius' reign on his 1st anniversary, then A.D. 29 is the year Jesus was baptized and His crucifixion would be in A.D. 33.

203 The Passover holiday always occurs on the 14th day of Nisan in the Hebrew calendar. This corresponds to the first full moon after the Spring equinox.

204 *Biblical Archaeology Review*, Nov/Dec 1992, pg. 58.

205 For a detailed analysis of the ancient Jewish beliefs regarding this prophecy see The Search for Messiah, Mark Eastman, M.D., Chuck Smith, The Word for Today, 1993, chapter 6.

206 See *The Writings of Josephus: Wars of the Jews.*

207 Matthew 24-25.

208 The *jus gladii* is a legal term which refers to the legal authority to adjudicate capital cases and impose capital punishment.

209 For a detailed discussion see *The Search for Messiah*, Mark Eastman, Chuck Smith, Pg 74. The Word for Today. (800) 272-WORD.

210 Paraphrased from *Evidence That Demands a Verdict*, Josh McDowell, Here's Life Publishers, pg. 168

211 See Ezra 1:5, 8 where we read of the priests and prince of Judah, still in existence after 70 years away from Israel.

212 Archelaus was the second son of Herod the Great. Herod's oldest son, Herod Antipater, was murdered by Herod the Great, along with a number of other family members. Archelaus' mother was a Samaritan, giving him only one quarter or less, Jewish blood. At the death of Herod the Great in 4 B.C. Archelaus was placed over Judea as "Entharch" by Caesar Augustus. However, he was never accepted by the Jews and was removed from office in 6 or 7 A.D.

213 *Wars of the Jews*, Book 2, chapter 8.

214 *The Messiah: An Aramaic Interpretation; The Messianic Exegesis of the Targum*, Samson H. Levy (Cincinnati: Hebrew Union College Jewish Institute of Religion, 1974), pg. 2.

215 *ibid.*, pg. 7.

216 *ibid.*, pg. 8.

217 Jerusalem Talmud, Sanhedrin, folio 24.

218 Babylonian Talmud, Chapter 4, folio 37.

219 *Jesus Before the Sanhedrin*, by Augustin Lemann, 1886, Translated by Julius Magath, NL# 0239683, Library of Congress# 15-24973.

220 See also the monumental work Pugio Fidei, Martini, Raymundus, published by De Vosin in 1651. For a detailed discussion of this reference see The Fifty Third Chapter of Isaiah According to Jewish Interpreters, preface pg.iv S.R. Driver, A.D. Neubauer, KTAV Publishing House, Inc. New York 1969.

221 See also Genesis 17:4-5.

222 See also Deuteronomy 28:41.

223 See also Isaiah 39:6.

224 This happened in the third year of Jehoiakim.

225 A vassal king is one who held land from a feudal lord and received protection in return for homage and allegiance.

226 Excerpted from Daniel 1:4.

227 Jeremiah 25:9, 11.

228 Also known as Jeconiah.

229 2 Chronicles 36:19, Jeremiah 39:2.

230 2 Chronicles 36:13-21.

231 The "Servitude of the Nation" and the "Desolations of Jerusalem" are often confused by Bible commentators as synonyms. They are, in fact, two independent periods, largely overlapping, but both lasting seventy years. The "desolations of Jerusalem" began with the annihilation of the city of Jerusalem and Solomon's Temple in 587 B.C. According to Jeremiah it was punishment for not yielding to the "Servitude of the Nation." which began in 606 B.C., with the first siege of Nebuchadnezzar. See Jeremiah 27:6,8,11; 38:17-21. Cf. Jeremiah 29:10, Daniel 9:2.

232 As discussed earlier, for the purposes of prophetic calculations the Jews employ a 360-day calendar year. The period from the summer of 606 B.C., (the first siege) to the summer of 537 B.C. (the decree of Cyrus) is exactly 25,200 days. This corresponds to 70 years of 360 days duration!

233 See Ezra chapter 1, Jeremiah 29:10.

234 Ezra 2:64-65.

235 Ezra 6:15.

236 Remarkably, this destruction also took place on the very day, the 9th of Av, as the destruction of the first temple.

237 *The Complete Works of Josephus, Wars of the Jews*, Book 4.

238 Daniel 9:26.

239 At the beginning of the 9th chapter of Daniel we are told that Daniel is seeking God regarding the city of Jerusalem (verse 12, 16, 25) and God's sanctuary (Daniel 9:17).

240 Tradition holds that seventy-two Hebrew scholars translated the Hebrew text of the Bible into Greek in Alexandria Egypt beginning in 285 B.C. This translation is called the "Septuagint," meaning "seventy."

241 See also Ezekiel 39:26-29.

242 Ezekiel 37:23-28.

243 See also Isaiah 43:5-6 and Jeremiah 23:8.

CHAPTER NINE

THE CREATOR BEYOND
TIME AND SPACE

"For thus saith the high and lofty One that inhabiteth eternity, whose name is Holy; 'I dwell in the high and holy place, with him also that is of a contrite and humble spirit, to revive the spirit of the humble, and to revive the heart of the contrite ones.'"

Isaiah 57:15 (KJV)

In the fifteenth century Nicolas Copernicus (1473–1543) began a revolution when he showed the earth was not the center of our solar system. His findings were strongly opposed by the church "establishment" because they contradicted the dogma of an earth-centered universe. Ironically, at the end of the twentieth century the stage has been set for a similar paradigm shift. This time the scientific establishment's dogma of an eternal universe, free of any extra-dimensional (i.e. supernatural) influence, is imploding.

Three centuries ago a small but vocal group of intelligentsia in Europe asserted that the Copernican revolution was the beginning of an "Age of Enlightenment"—an age where the notion of a Transcendent Creator, a finite universe and a supernaturally-inspired Bible was an aging, irrational paradigm. In the last three centuries the "high priests" of this new paradigm have been incredibly successful in their evangelistic efforts to replace the God of the Bible with the god called "Chance" within the world's educational institutions and "Think Tanks." Ironically, scientific discoveries in this century have, in one fell swoop, destroyed the notion of an eternal universe and bolstered the biblical world view of a finite universe, and a personal, Transcendent Creator.

Today many physicists and astronomers speak openly about the existence of a *Transcendent Creator*. While it is true that belief in God is a matter of faith, the fact that scientists recognize the necessity of a *Transcendent Creator*, purely on scientific grounds, is indeed remarkable.

While the notion of a fully Transcendent Creator is a logical construct to explain a finite universe, it is quite unique among religious writings. The Bible is the only "holy book" on planet earth that speaks of a finite universe and a transcendent, eternally existent Creator who is capable of simultaneously acting, unencumbered, within and without the dimensions of our space-time domain. All other religious writings teach either an eternal universe, a world view where God is confined to the dimensions of the universe, or they place limitations on the Creator's transcendence.[244]

As we approach the new millennium, the overwhelming evidence of twentieth-century scientific inquiry now calls for another "Age of Enlightenment"—an age where the biblical world view of a finite universe and a Transcendent Creator now seems to be the only rational alternative!

THE ONE THAT INHABITS ETERNITY

Throughout the Bible we find a progressive revelation of a transcendent, eternal God. In the Old Testament God is presented as the Transcendent Creator of the universe—the One who gave breath to mankind—the One who sustains us, provides for us, and ultimately, the Holy and Righteous One who redeems us through the ultimate act of love—sending His only begotten Son, the Messiah, to die for the sins of mankind![245] Although God "inhabits eternity,"[246] because of His transcendent nature, He manifests Himself within the dimensions of time and space in a number ways in both New and Old Testaments.

In the New Testament, written between A.D. 50–100, Jesus of Nazareth is presented as the supernatural Son of God who was born of the virgin Mary, as a descendant of King David and the very fulfillment of over three hundred Old Testament messianic prophecies. According to the New Testament, Jesus healed the blind, the lame, the deaf, cured leprosy, walked on water, stilled a raging storm and even raised the dead! Though His ministry spanned only three and one-half years, He drew multitudes to Himself and His message of salvation through faith in *Him* alone. Finally, Jesus of Nazareth is presented as a Transcendent Being, the Creator of our universe, who existed *before* time began—something foretold in the Old Testament hundreds of years before His birth.

The Bible clearly teaches that there is only one God. This is a dominant theme throughout its text. And yet, within its pages we find that the God of the Bible is presented as a Being who manifests Himself as three separate persons; God the Father, God the Son (Jesus of Nazareth) and God the Holy Spirit. This fact has led to the biblical doctrine of the tri-unity of God.

Among those groups that hold the Bible sacred there is no controversy that God the Father is, in fact, God. However, there are many groups which deny the deity of Jesus Christ. For this reason, as we examine the claims of Jesus we will show that all the attributes and works of God are applied specifically to Jesus. In fact, a careful examination of both testaments reveals that all the attributes and works of God are applied to *all three persons* of the Trinity.

GOD MANIFEST IN THE FLESH!

There is no doubt about it—Jesus of Nazareth is the most radical, the most controversial, the most despised, the most loved and the most influential individual that has ever lived. On the one hand, He has been worshipped by billions as the Son of God, the Messiah (Anointed One) of Israel and the very Creator of the physical universe. On the other hand, He has been despised, rejected and branded as a liar, a lunatic or a legend by untold millions, including the Jewish leadership of His day. Even to this day His life and claims create more division than any man in world history.

In the first century A.D., the mood of Israel was ripe for a national redeemer. For over seven centuries the Jews had suffered mightily under the yoke of the Assyrian, Babylonian, Medo-Persian, Grecian and Roman empires. During that same time the Hebrew prophets had foretold the coming of a future prophet and redeemer, the Messiah, who would restore the nation of Israel to its former greatness and rule and reign forever on the throne of David. Thus, when Jesus came preaching that the "kingdom of God is at hand," His message was greeted with great enthusiasm by those that followed His ministry.[247]

A STONE OF STUMBLING

The life, message and ministry of Jesus of Nazareth was unlike any rabbi or prophet that had preceded Him. Born in the city of Bethlehem, He spent His first night in a feeding trough![248] Such an entry into time and space can hardly be considered fit for a king, not to mention the Creator of the universe. And yet, His entry was a fitting foreshadowing of the simplicity, humility and paradoxical themes that would distinguish His future ministry.

At the age of thirty, Jesus began His ministry with His Baptism at the hands of John the Baptist.[249] From the very beginning of His ministry His claims and His actions created division among the people and ire among the Jewish leadership. Throughout the New Testament records we find that Jesus was frequently at odds with the leaders of Israel.

The ministry of Jesus was a ministry of service. He was concerned about people, about their pain, their physical suffering and about their spiritual separation from God. Consequently, He healed on the Sabbath day, pointed out religious hypocrisy, and ate with sinners, tax collectors and prostitutes. As He put the needs of men before the traditions of the Jewish leadership, He revealed His disregard for their authority and offended the leadership. So, as the Gospel of John points out, "For this reason the Jews persecuted Jesus, and sought to kill Him, because He had done these things on the Sabbath."[250]

Ultimately, the division between Jesus and the Jewish leadership led to His rejection, His cruel death on the cross and the fulfillment of His ultimate purpose on earth—to atone for the sins of mankind through His own substitutionary, sacrificial death!

---

244 See Walter Martin, *The Kingdom of the Cults*, Bethany House Publishers, 1985 ed.
245 See Isaiah 52-53.
246 Isaiah 57:15.
247 Mark 1:5.
248 Luke 2:7.
249 See Luke chapter 3.
250 John 5:16.

CHAPTER TEN

WHO DO YOU SAY THAT I AM?

"When Jesus came into the region of Caesarea Philippi, He asked His disciples, saying, 'Who do men say that I, the Son of Man, am?' So they said, 'Some say John the Baptist, some Elijah, and others Jeremiah or one of the prophets. He said to them, 'But who do you say that I am?' And Simon Peter answered and said, 'You are the Christ, the Son of the living God.'"

Matthew 16:13–16 (NKJV)

Throughout the New Testament we see that Jesus had a peculiar habit of forcing people to decide the question of His identity. In first century A.D. nearly everyone in Israel had an opinion about this carpenter from Nazareth. To the Pharisees He was a devil who did His miracles by the powers of Satan. To some He was John the Baptist risen from the dead; to others, Elijah or one of the prophets. To His disciples He was the Son of God and the very Creator of the universe.

Today in America most people have an opinion about Jesus. To some He is a legend—a non-historical figure. To others a lunatic or a deceiver. Some, including many Jewish people, believe that Jesus was just a good rabbi who was "messianized" by His disciples. According to this theory, the disciples of Jesus erroneously applied a number of Old Testament Scriptures to the life and ministry of Jesus.

In December, 1994, *Life* magazine did a cover story on Jesus called "Who Was He?"[251] In this article a number of theologians, atheists and philosophers were asked their opinion about the carpenter from Nazareth.

John Murray, president of the American Atheists Society said regarding Jesus:

> "There was no such person in the history of the world as Jesus Christ. There was no historical, living, breathing sentient human being by that name. Ever. The Bible is a fictional, non-historical narrative. The myth is good for business."

Barbara Thiering, author of a book on the Dead Sea Scrolls, stated:

> "It is in the scrolls if you really study the codes. It was not a resurrection. He was put on the cross. Those with his own party, trying to help him to commit suicide, gave him poison (The sponge dipped in vinegar). He was unconscious but not dead. His side was pierced, blood came out. A dead body does not bleed. So his followers knew that he was not dead. They put him in the cave. He lived until his seventies, and it was he, Jesus, acting behind Paul, who led their party out of Judaism and to Rome. He married Mary Magdalene and had four children."

Predictably, *Life* magazine never bothered to examine the claims of Jesus or His disciples. In this chapter we will do just that.

JESUS THE LEGEND?

For centuries there have been those who have attempted to deny the historicity of Jesus of Nazareth. The proponents of this theory will argue that the only ancient historical references to Jesus are in the New Testament manuscripts and the writings of the early church fathers. However, even a cursory review of ancient rabbinical and Roman historical documents destroys this claim.[252]

JOSEPHUS

In the first century A.D. a Jewish priest by the name of Joseph ben Matthias (later given the Roman name Flavius Josephus) was commissioned by the Roman government to write a history of events in Judea. In his book, *Antiquities of the Jews,* Josephus makes one of three references to Jesus and His disciples:

> "Now there was about this time Jesus, a wise man. If it be lawful to call Him a man, for He was a doer of wonderful works. He was the Christ.[253] And the tribe of Christians so named from Him. are not extinct to this day."[254]

This is an important historical reference to Jesus of Nazareth because it's from a source that can hardly be considered as biased.

ANCIENT JEWISH SOURCES

From A.D. 200 to 500 ancient rabbis compiled their commentaries on the Bible, Jewish social customs and historical events in the Talmud.[255] Because it was compiled by rabbis who were the leaders in rabbinical academies, the Talmud is considered to be very authoritative by Jews, even to this day.

In the Babylonian Talmud there are numerous references to the historical existence of Jesus. In the tractate Sanhedrin, 43A, there is a fascinating historical reference to Jesus:

> "It has been taught on the eve of the Passover they hanged Yeshua. And an announcer went out in front of him for forty days saying, 'He is going to be stoned because He practiced sorcery and enticed and led Israel astray. Anyone who knows anything in His favor, let him come and plead in His behalf.' But, not having found anything in His favor, they hanged him on the eve of the Passover."

In this remarkable reference to Jesus (Yeshua in

Hebrew) a number of aspects of Jesus' ministry are confirmed. First, the fact that He performed supernatural feats, which they attribute to sorcery, is confirmed as a cause for His rejection. Secondly, the fact that He was crucified (hanged is an idiom for crucifixion) on the eve of the Passover is a remarkable confirmation of the historical events recorded in the New Testament Gospels.

Again, the value of this reference stems from its unbiased source. Certainly no one would argue that ancient rabbis, who despised Christians, would bolster the claims of the church by making such a reference to a man who *never existed*.

Among the writings of the ancient Romans and Jews there are dozens of additional historical references to Jesus of Nazareth.

THE DISCIPLES' CLAIMS

The impact Jesus had on the lives of His disciples is one of the most powerful evidences for His messiahship and deity. The crew that Jesus chose to turn the world "right-side up" was comprised of fishermen, tax collectors, tent makers and the like. With the exception of Paul the Apostle, a well educated rabbi, it is unlikely that they would have been voted "most likely to succeed" by their classmates. And yet, they changed the known world with unparalleled devotion and sacrifice to their "Lord and Savior," Jesus Christ. However, it didn't begin that way.

The disciples were ordinary men with the same desires, fears and weaknesses as any one of us. They *were not* "supermen." Although they were "eye witnesses"[256] to Jesus' majesty and His command over the forces of nature, when He was arrested on the night before His crucifixion, the disciples scattered like sheep, fearing for their own lives. Peter, the one who stated Jesus was "the Christ, the Son of the Living God," denied even knowing Jesus after His arrest. At the moment of truth, at the foot of the cross, as Jesus hung dying, only a small contingent of women and the Apostle John were there at His side.

However, the cowardice of the disciples was short lived. After the bodily resurrection and ascension of Jesus Christ the disciples boldly proclaimed Jesus as Messiah and Savior in the most dangerous place on earth—the Temple in Jerusalem.[257]

A PRINCE AND SAVIOR

Throughout the New Testament the disciples claim that Jesus is the Savior of the world and the only way to salvation. After the resurrection and ascension of Jesus, we read in the book of the Acts of the Apostles this very claim by the Apostle Peter:

> "The God of our fathers raised up Jesus, whom ye slew and hanged on a tree. Him hath God exalted with his right hand to be a Prince and a Saviour, for to give repentance to Israel, and forgiveness of sins." Acts 5:30–31 (KJV)

This same claim was made by angels at the birth of Jesus:

> "And there were in the same country shepherds abiding in the field, keeping watch over their flock by night. And, lo, the angel of the Lord came upon them, and the glory of the Lord shone round about them: and they were sore afraid. And the angel said unto them, Fear not: for, behold, I bring you good tidings of great joy, which shall be to all people. For unto you is born this day in the city of David a Savior, which is Christ the Lord." Luke 2:8–11 (KJV)

The remarkable thing about the title of Savior is its application in the Old Testament. In the book of Isaiah this very title is applied *exclusively* and *only* to God! In Isaiah 43, God, speaking through Isaiah states of Himself, "I, even I am the LORD and beside me there is no Saviour."[258,259]

In this verse the word LORD (all capitals) is the English translation for the holiest name of God, Jehovah or Yahweh, otherwise known as the "tetragrammaton." This name is so holy that the Jews will not even pronounce it.

Throughout the Old Testament we find the name Yahweh coupled to the title Savior as an indication of God's covenant relationship to Israel. The exclusivity of Yahweh's role as Savior is amplified in Isaiah, chapter 45 where God states:

> "Tell ye, and bring them near; yea, let them take counsel together: who hath declared this from ancient time? Who hath told it from that time? Have not I the LORD? And *there is no God else beside me*; a just *God and a Saviour; there is none beside me*." Isaiah 45:21 (KJV)

In this verse Yahweh, the Creator of the universe, the God of the Bible, wants us to know that He alone is God and He alone is Savior. According to these two Old Testament verses there cannot be two saviors! Consequently, either Jesus and Yahweh are One and the same or there is a major contradiction in the Bible.

In the New Testament this paradox is anticipated in Paul's letter to Titus:

> "Paul, a servant of God, and an Apostle of Jesus Christ, according to the faith of God's elect, and the acknowledging of the truth which is after godliness; In hope of eternal life, which God, that cannot lie, promised before the world began; but hath in due times manifested his word through preaching, which is committed unto me according to the commandment of *God our Saviour*; To Titus, mine own son after the common faith: grace, mercy, and peace, from God the Father and the *Lord Jesus Christ our Saviour*." Titus 1:1–4 (KJV)

Paul the Apostle was a rabbi and a Pharisee who was rigorously trained in the Old Testament Scriptures all of his life. Paul knew the book of Isaiah and he knew that God (Yahweh) alone is the Savior of the world. Consequently, for Paul to apply the title of Savior to Jesus Christ and God in the same sentence is a powerful indication that Paul believed that Jesus was indeed God!

GOD MANIFEST IN THE FLESH!

Throughout the New Testament we find the remarkable claim by the disciples that Jesus of Nazareth is God in the flesh.

Before the ministry of Jesus even commenced there were those that recognized the deity of Jesus.

When Mary, the mother of Jesus, was told by an angel that she would conceive the Messiah in her womb, she was also told that Elisabeth, her relative, was with child. Mary arose immediately and went to visit Elisabeth to share the wonderful news. In Luke, chapter one, we read the remarkable declaration of Elisabeth regarding the child in Mary's womb:

> "And it came to pass, that, when Elisabeth heard the salutation of Mary, the babe leaped in her womb; and Elisabeth was filled with the Holy Ghost. And she spake out with a loud voice, and said, 'Blessed art thou among women, and blessed is the fruit of thy womb. And whence is this to me, that the mother of my Lord should come to me?'" Luke 1:41–43 (KJV)

"The mother of my Lord!" Elisabeth recognized the greatness of the child in Mary's womb and the fact that this child is the very Lord of the universe!

Apparently, Elisabeth taught her son well. Thirty years later John the Baptist, Elisabeth's son, was drawing great multitudes to his message of repentance and forgiveness of sins. News of his ministry reached the Pharisees, and so a delegation was sent to John to ask him who he was. The response of John is recorded in all four Gospels.

In the Gospel of John we read the details of this inquiry:

> "Now this is the testimony of John, when the Jews sent priests and Levites from Jerusalem to ask him, 'Who are you?' He confessed, and did not deny, but confessed, 'I

am not the Christ. And they asked him, 'What then? Are
you Elijah?' He said, 'I am not.' 'Are you the Prophet?'
And he answered, 'No.' Then they said to him, 'Who are
you, that we may give an answer to those who sent us?
What do you say about yourself? He said: 'I am 'The
voice of one crying in the wilderness: Make straight the
way of the LORD,' as the prophet Isaiah said.'" John
1:19–23 (NKJV)

In his statement John tells us plainly that he is quoting the prophet Isaiah and that his ministry was to go
before the LORD, to make *His way* straight. The casual
reader might continue on and miss an incredible insight
placed in the book of Isaiah by the Holy Spirit.

In John 1:19–23 John the Baptist claimed that he was
'The voice of one crying in the wilderness: Make straight
the way of the LORD,' as the prophet Isaiah said.'" It turns
out that John is quoting Isaiah 40:3. In this verse the
prophet Isaiah speaks of a time when another prophet, yet
future, would be:

> "The voice of one crying in the wilderness: 'Prepare the
> way of the LORD; make straight in the desert a high-
> way for our God.'" (NKJV)

In the text of Isaiah 40:3 the word LORD is again the
English translation for the Hebrew word Yahweh.

John the Baptist was claiming that he was going
before and making straight the path for Yahweh, the very
Creator of the universe! However, in the next few verses
we see unequivocally that John was speaking of Jesus of
Nazareth, the one whose path he was making straight;

> "And they which were sent were of the Pharisees. And
> they asked him, and said unto him, 'Why baptizest thou
> then, if thou be not that Christ, nor Elias, neither that
> prophet?' John answered them, saying, 'I baptize with
> water: but there standeth one among you, whom ye
> know not; He it is, who coming after me is preferred
> before me, whose shoe's latchet I am not worthy to
> unloose.' These things were done in Bethabara beyond
> Jordan, where John was baptizing. The next day John

seeth Jesus coming unto him, and saith, 'Behold the
Lamb of God, which taketh away the sin of the world.
This is he of whom I said, After me cometh a man which
is preferred before me: for he was before me.'" John
1:24–30 (KJV)

In these verses John identifies Jesus as the One whom
he preceded, the One "whose shoe's latchet [he is] not worthy to unloose," the One who Isaiah said was Yahweh!

The disciple's belief that Jesus was indeed God, "manifest in the flesh," is unequivocally proclaimed by the
Apostle Paul in I Timothy 3:16:

"And without controversy great is the mystery of
Godliness. God was manifested in the flesh, justified in
the Spirit, seen by angels, preached among the gentiles,
believed on in the world, and received up in glory." I
Timothy 3:16 (KJV)

When was God "received up in glory?" In the book of
the Acts of the Apostles, chapter one, Jesus of Nazareth
ascended into heaven from the mount of Olives forty days
after his resurrection. Skeptical? Read on.

THE FEET OF GOD!

In the book of the prophet Zechariah, written at least
four hundred years before the birth of Jesus, we are given
a glimpse of the last days:

"Then shall the LORD go forth, and fight against those
nations, as when he fought in the day of battle. And His
feet shall stand in that day upon the mount of Olives,
which is before Jerusalem on the east, and the mount of
Olives shall cleave in the midst thereof toward the east
and toward the west, and there shall be a very great valley; and half of the mountain shall remove toward the
north, and half of it toward the south." Zechariah 14:3–4
(KJV)

In this portion of Scripture we are told that Yahweh
("LORD") will manifest himself in time and space in a
body *with feet* and stand on the mount of Olives.

In the book of the Acts of the Apostles, the identity of
this person is further clarified in chapter one. The scene
depicted is forty days after the resurrection of Jesus. He
has just told His disciples that He is going to send the
Holy Spirit. In the very next verse we read:

> "And when he had spoken these things, while they
> beheld, he was taken up; and a cloud received him out
> of their sight. And while they looked steadfastly toward
> heaven as he went up, behold, two men stood by them in
> white apparel; Which also said, 'Ye men of Galilee, why
> stand ye gazing up into heaven? this same Jesus, which
> is taken up from you into heaven, shall so come in like
> manner as ye have seen him go into heaven.' Then
> returned they unto Jerusalem from the *mount called
> Olivet*, which is from Jerusalem a Sabbath day's jour-
> ney." Acts 1:9–11 (KJV)

This is another one of those places where a casual
reading of the text fails to uncover an astonishing nugget
which reveals the supernatural engineering of the biblical
text.

In Acts, chapter one, the scene is the ascension of
Jesus Christ into heaven. Can you imagine the look on the
disciples faces as they watched this event. As they are
staring in awe, two angels (men in white apparel) tell the
disciples that Jesus' return will be, in effect, a re-run of
His ascension into heaven. Then the Holy Spirit inspired
Luke, the author of Acts, to insert a seemingly insignificant commentary that they returned "unto Jerusalem
from *the mount called Olivet*."

In other words, when Jesus comes a second time, He
will descend from heaven and set His feet on the place
from which He ascended—the mount of Olives!

The Book of Zechariah states that this event will be
accomplished through a physical manifestation of
Yahweh. The New Testament says it's Jesus. Either we
have an irreconcilable contradiction, or Jesus and Yahweh
must be One and the same!

"THOU SHALT WORSHIP NO OTHER GOD"

The claims of Jesus' disciples leave little doubt that they believed He was indeed, "God manifested in the flesh." This shared belief is further supported by the fact that they willingly worshipped Him as God.

In Matthew's Gospel we read the story of the Magi—the wise men—who came to honor the baby Jesus whom they believed was the "King of the Jews."

> "And after Jesus was born in Bethlehem of Judea in the days of Herod the king, behold, wise men from the east came to Jerusalem saying, 'Where is He who has been King of the Jews, for we have seen His star in the east and have come to worship Him.'" Matthew 2:1–2 (NKJV)

The Greek word for worship is "proskuneo," The literal meaning of this word is to fall on your face, prostrate on the ground, and to kiss at the feet of an individual. These magi wanted to worship the Messiah.

Later in the Gospel of Matthew, we read the story about the day that Jesus walked on water. Jesus instructed His disciples to go ahead of Him and cross over the sea in a boat. Late that evening a storm arose and Jesus decided to take a short-cut. So, He simply walked on the sea to meet the His disciples at the boat in the midst of the sea! The disciples, believing they had seen a spirit, "were troubled," to say the least.

Once Jesus identified Himself, Peter decided to try his hand at walking on water. However, when he took his eyes off Jesus, Peter began to sink. Then Matthew's Gospel states, "then those who were in the boat came and *worshipped* Jesus, saying, 'Truly you are the Son of God.'"

In the Book of Job we are given a little nugget that helps clarify the identity of Jesus and why the disciples worshipped Him. Speaking of God, Job states, "He alone, spreads out the Heavens and treads on the waves of the sea."[260] The word "treads" literally means to walk upon.

No wonder they worshipped Jesus! They must have thought to themselves, "Only God can walk on water."

The worship of Jesus was not a trivial matter. In fact, the Pharisees rebuked Him for receiving such worship. The reason is found in the book of Deuteronomy;

> "And it shall be, if thou do at all forget the LORD thy God, and walk after other gods, and serve them, and worship them, I testify against you this day that ye shall surely perish." Deuteronomy 8:19 (KJV)

To worship anything (literally to prostrate one's self) other than Yahweh was a sin punishable by death. Consequently, if Jesus was not God then these men were guilty of blasphemy.

THE CLAIM'S OF CHRIST

Without a doubt, the claims of Jesus are the most radical, the most exclusive, the most offensive, and the most divisive claims ever made by any man. Through the ages there have been many religious leaders that have made remarkable claims about their teachings, their identity or their relationship to God. Many have claimed to be a *way* to God. Some have claimed that their words contained eternal truths which, if applied to one's life, could bring happiness or great fulfillment. Some have claimed to be the Messiah and some have even dared to claim that they were gods. The claims of Jesus are even more radical.

During his ministry, in clear and certain terms, Jesus claimed to be the Son of God, the Messiah of Israel, and on numerous occasions He even declared equality with God. He declared that He speaks the very words of God and He claimed to be the *only way* to eternal life. Such claims were not only too much for the scribes and Pharisees to handle, they were the major reason that they wanted Jesus dead.

"DO YOU BELIEVE IN THE SON OF GOD?"

There are those who say that Jesus of Nazareth never claimed to be the Son of God. On the other hand, one of the reasons that modern rabbis reject the messianic claim of Jesus is because *He did* claim this title. Their contention is that the Messiah is just a man, and not the Son of God. Therefore, Jesus could not be the Messiah. However, when the beliefs of the *ancient* Jewish rabbis are examined in detail, we find that they did, indeed, believe that the Messiah is the Son of God.[261]

Jesus' claim to be the Son of God is found throughout the four Gospel accounts, but none more clearly than in the Gospel of John. In chapter nine we read the story of a man, blind since birth, who was healed by Jesus at the Temple of God. After the Pharisees accused him of faking the recovery of his sight, he was thrown out of the Temple and was found again by Jesus:

> "Jesus heard that they had cast him out; and when He had found him, He said to him, 'Do you believe in the Son of God?' He answered and said, 'Who is He, Lord, that I may believe in Him?' And Jesus said to him, 'You have both seen Him and it is He who is talking with you.'" John 9:35–37 (NKJV)

"MESSIAH WHO IS CALLED CHRIST"

The Messiah (Anointed One), the coming redeemer of Israel, has been the hope of every Jew for thousands of years. Arguably, the dominant theme of the Tanakh (Old Testament) was to foretell the birth, lineage, mission and destiny of this Redeemer, the "King Messiah." In fact, the Babylonian Talmud states:

> "All the prophets prophesied only of the days of Messiah." Babylonian Talmud, Sanhedrin 99a

In the Old Testament, there are literally hundreds of messianic prophecies which foretell nearly every aspect of the Messiah's life, mission and destiny. During His life,

Jesus of Nazareth fulfilled over three-hundred prophecies that were definitely recognized by ancient Jews as messianic. From His humble birth in the city of Bethlehem[262] to His suffering and cruel death,[263], from His rejection by Israel[264] to His acceptance by the gentile world,[265] it was all foretold hundreds of years before His birth.[266]

Despite impeccable "credentials," the messianic claim of Jesus was ultimately rejected by the leadership in Israel. To many, the rejection of Jesus by the leadership of Israel is evidence enough that He *was not* the Messiah. "After all," the skeptic argues, "shouldn't the learned men of Israel, the scribes and the Pharisees, recognize the Messiah when He comes?" To the biblically naïve this argument seems reasonable. However, when the Messiah's mission is examined in the light of the Old Testament prophecies, we discover that His suffering, rejection and death are, in fact, the fulfillment of a supernatural plan devised before the creation of our space-time domain!

There is no doubt that Jesus took upon Himself the title of Messiah in numerous places in the four Gospel narratives. However, His messianic claim was usually affirmed in response to an inquiry about His personal identity or a discussion about the Messiah in the third person.

For example, in John, chapter four, we read the story of a Samaritan woman that Jesus met at Jacob's well. This meeting was remarkable because, as the woman noted, "Jews have no dealings with Samaritans." Centuries of animosity between the Samaritans and the Jews resulted in a tradition where the Jews would literally go around Samaria rather than risk contact with a Samaritan. After inquiring why Jesus would even talk to her, the woman said to Him, "I know that Messiah is coming who is called Christ.... When He comes, He will tell us all things.' And Jesus said to her, "I Who speak to you am He."[267]

"I AND MY FATHER ARE ONE"

Throughout the four Gospels Jesus made many astonishing claims about Himself and His relationship to God His Father. However, none of them offended the Pharisees more than His claims of deity. In the Gospel of John, chapter 10, we find a dramatic encounter and the most incredible claim ever made by Jesus:

> "Now it was the Feast of Dedication in Jerusalem, and it was winter. And Jesus walked in the temple, in Solomon's porch. Then the Jews surrounded Him and said to Him, 'How long do You keep us in doubt? If You are the Christ, tell us plainly.'
>
> Jesus answered them, 'I told you, and you do not believe. The works that I do in My Father's name, they bear witness of Me. But you do not believe, because you are not of My sheep, as I said to you. My sheep hear My voice, and I know them, and they follow Me. And I give them eternal life, and they shall never perish; neither shall anyone snatch them out of My hand. My Father, who has given them to Me, is greater than all; and no one is able to snatch them out of My Father's hand. *I and My Father are one.*'
>
> Then the Jews took up stones again to stone Him.
>
> Jesus answered them, 'Many good works I have shown you from My Father. For which of those works do you stone Me?'
>
> The Jews answered Him, saying, 'For a good work we do not stone You, but for blasphemy, and because You, being a Man, make Yourself God.'" John 10:22–33 (NKJV)

Among the Sanhedrin, the ruling body in Israel, there were those who wanted to believe that Jesus was the Messiah. Eventually, some of them did. However, when Jesus declared that He and His Father were One, they couldn't handle it. There was no doubt in their minds what Jesus had just declared. He was applying to Himself the

very nature and essence of God the Father, the Creator of
the universe, the God of Abraham, Isaac and Jacob!

Those that heard this incredible claim had a choice.
They had seen many miraculously healed; they had heard
His unparalleled words. Either this man was the Messiah
of Israel and God in the flesh, or a deceiver and a blas-
phemer. They chose the latter. Why? Because He, "being a
Man, makes himself God."

Throughout the Gospel of John, Jesus made dozens of
similar declarations regarding His equality with God. In
John chapter 14, we find an incredible discourse between
Jesus and His disciples. Speaking of His Father, Jesus
said:

> "'If you had known Me, you would have known My
> Father also; and from now on you know Him and have
> seen Him.' Philip said to Him, 'Lord, show us the Father,
> and it is sufficient for us.' Jesus said to him, 'Have I
> been with you so long, and yet you have not known Me,
> Philip? He who has seen Me has seen the Father; so how
> can you say, 'Show us the Father'?" John 14:7–9 (NKJV)

In John, chapter 12, speaking of the Father, Jesus
made a similar declaration when He stated, "...he who
sees Me sees Him who sent Me."[268]

Jesus' claim that He is the very image of God is echoed
in a number of places in the New Testament.

Speaking of His majesty, Paul the Apostle declared
that Jesus is:

> "...*the image of the invisible God*, the firstborn of all cre-
> ation. For by Him all things were created that are in
> heaven and that are on earth, visible and invisible,
> whether thrones or dominions or principalities or pow-
> ers. All things were created through Him and for Him."
> Colossians 1:15-16 (NKJV)

In Hebrews 1:3 the author, speaking of Jesus, states:

> "who *being the effulgence of His [God's] glory, and the
> very image of His substance,* and upholding all things by

the word of His power, when He had made purification of sins, sat down on the right hand of the Majesty on high."

In I John 5:20, the Apostle John makes an incredible statement regarding the identity of Jesus:

"And we know that the Son of God is come, and hath given us an understanding, that we know him that is true, and we are in him that is true, even in his Son Jesus Christ. *This is the true God, and eternal life.*"

Such radical claims about Him and by Him are unparalleled in human history. No wonder the Temple officers who were charged with capturing Jesus said "...No man ever spoke like this Man!"[269]

THE TITLES OF GOD

Within the Old Testament there are a number of majestic titles that are exclusively applied to God. In many cases we find that God jealously guards these titles, declaring that they apply to Him "alone." It is fascinating to discover that many of those titles exclusively applied to God in the Old Testament are applied to Jesus of Nazareth in the New Testament as well. In fact, a careful examination of both testaments reveals that most of the names of God are applied to all three persons of the Trinity (Table 1).

In the book of Revelation, the Apostle John was caught up in the spirit and given a panoramic vision of earthly and heavenly events at the end of the age. During his vision, John was given a preview of the throne of God where he saw Jesus Christ as "a Lamb as it had been slain." John was also given a preview of the cataclysmic events on planet earth that will take place during the last 3 1/2 years of earth history known as the "Great Tribulation."

In Revelation, chapter 19, John is given a vision of an event called the "marriage supper of the Lamb," where the saints (the church) are treated to a meal by the Lord Jesus himself. Then the Apostle John states he saw "heaven open" and a man riding on a white horse, whose robe was dipped in blood. This rider, called the "Word of God," is unequivocally identified by scholars as Jesus Christ. What is remarkable about this rider is that verse 16 states "...He has on His robe and on His thigh a name written 'King of Kings, and Lord of Lords.'"[270]

This presents a small problem because this very same title is exclusively applied to Yahweh in the Old Testament.[271]

> "For the LORD, [Yahweh] your God, is the God of Gods and the Lord of Lords. The great God, mighty and awesome, who shows no partiality nor takes a bribe." Deuteronomy 10:17

The title "LORD of lords," by its very nature, can only apply to one individual. There cannot be two "LORD of lords." So, either Jesus of Nazareth and Yahweh are One and the same, or there is another major contradiction in the Bible. But wait, there's more.

In the book of Revelation, chapter one, there is a similar paradox. The Apostle John was exiled to the island of Patmos when he heard behind him a "great voice" who identified himself as the "Alpha and Omega, the First and the Last."[272] Stunned by this encounter, John "fell at his feet as dead." Then the One who spoke to John laid His right hand on him and said:

> "...Do not be afraid; I am the First and the Last. I am He who lives, and was dead, and behold, I am alive forevermore. Amen. And I have the keys of Hades and of Death." Revelation 1:17b–18

The identity of this individual is, of course, Jesus Christ. Only Jesus could make the claim, "I am He who lives, and was dead, and behold, I am alive forevermore." The problem is that the title "First and the Last," here applied to Jesus, is also applied exclusively to Yahweh in the Old Testament.

In the book of Isaiah we read:

> "Thus says the LORD, the King of Israel, and his Redeemer, the LORD of hosts: 'I am the First and I am the Last; besides Me there is no God.'" Isaiah 44:6 (NKJV)

In this verse we see another hint of the supernatural engineering of the Biblical text. Notice first that there are two distinct personages spoken of here; Yahweh, King of Israel and Yahweh of Hosts. These *two* individuals refer to themselves as "I." Notice, they do not state, "We are the First and the Last." Here we see a hint of at least two personages making up the God of the Bible.

Secondly, notice that Yahweh states, "besides Me there is no God." There are not two Yahwehs. Consequently, since the title, "the First and the Last," is applied to Jesus Christ, then He must be a physical manifestation of Yahweh, the Transcendent Creator of the universe.

THE GREAT 'I AM'

In the book of Exodus, Moses took his flock to the back of mount Horeb, the "mountain of God," and had an encounter with a burning bush that was not consumed. Frightened, Moses turned away and the voice of God spoke to Moses out of the burning bush. God told Moses that he has seen the affliction of his people in Egypt and that he was about to deliver them from their servitude.

Although Moses was quite impressed with his encounter, he wasn't convinced that he was the man that God was looking for. After some reassurance from God, Moses asked:

> "...when I come unto the children of Israel, and shall say unto them, The God of your fathers hath sent me unto you; and they shall say to me, What is His name? what shall I say unto them?" Exodus 3:13 (KJV)

The Names of God

God's Name	The Father	The Son	Holy Spirit
Yahweh	Throughout	Isaiah 6:1-3; Isaiah 45:21; Jer 23:5-6; John 1:23	Isaiah 11:2
El	Throughout	Isaiah 9:6	Exodus 31:3
Almighty	Genesis 17:1	Rev 1:8	Job 33:4
True God	Jer 10:10	1 John 5:20	
Blessed God	Throughout	Romans 9:5	
Great God	Deut 10:17	Titus 2:13; Rev 19:17	
God	Throughout	Isaiah 7:14; 1 Tim 3:16	Acts 5:3-9
"I Am"	Exodus 3	John 8	
First and Last	Isaiah 41:4; 44:6; 48:12	Rev 1:17-18	
LORD of lords	Deut 10:17; Psalm 136:1-3	1 Tim 6:15; Rev 19:16; Rev 17:14	

Table 1

Imagine Moses' predicament. He was about to go to three million Jewish exiles and tell them that a burning bush had just spoken to him and told him that he was their deliverer. Moses was hoping to bring some impressive evidence that would convince the people his story was true. What was God's response?

> "And God said unto Moses, 'I AM THAT I AM:' and he said, 'Thus shalt thou say unto the children of Israel, I AM hath sent me unto you.'"[273]

The name of the God of Abraham, Isaac and Jacob is "I AM."

The literal meaning of this Hebrew word, *haw-yaw* (I AM), is the existent One, the becoming One, the One who is. The term "I AM" eventually became so sacred that it was considered blasphemous to apply it to one's self. Despite this tradition, on numerous occasions Jesus of Nazareth applied that very title to Himself.

In John, chapter eight, we find Jesus teaching in the treasury of the temple with the scribes and Pharisees listening in. After declaring that He was "the light of the world," the scribes and Pharisees were indignant because Jesus was testifying of Himself. A few moments later Jesus accused them of being from "beneath" and He made a staggering declaration about Himself:

> "I said therefore unto you, that ye shall die in your sins: for if ye believe not that *I Am*, ye shall die in your sins." John 8:24 (KJV)

All they could say in response is, "Who are you?" A few verses later Jesus replied,

> "...When ye have lifted up the Son of man, then shall ye know that *I Am*, and that I do nothing of myself; but as my Father hath taught me, I speak these things." John 8:28 (KJV)[274]

Not only did Jesus claim that he was the "I Am," the voice of the burning bush, He also declared to the scribes and Pharisees that when they kill Him ("lift up the Son of man"), He will prove it to them, presumably by resurrecting Himself from the dead!

In John 8:58 Jesus said again to the scribes and Pharisees, "Verily, verily, I say unto you, Before Abraham was, *I Am*." There are some groups that claim that Jesus wasn't really declaring His deity in this verse. However, the response of the scribes and Pharisees indicates that they believed He was. In the very next verse it says, "Then they took up stones to cast at Him: but Jesus hid Himself, and went out of the temple, going through the midst of them, and so passed by."[275]

Clearly, the leadership of Israel believed that Jesus did, on many occasions, declare His equality with God.

THE WORKS AND ATTRIBUTES OF GOD

One of the most fascinating discoveries the diligent Bible student can make is to find the major works and attributes of God applied to all three persons of the Trinity. From the creation of the universe to the resurrection of Jesus from the dead, from the Omnipresence of God to His eternal existence, they are all applied to God the Father, the Messiah and the Holy Spirit.

In the New Testament we find many of the works of God applied to Jesus by His disciples (See Table 2). Others, He claimed of Himself. For example, in John 2:19 and John 10:17 Jesus declared that He has the power to resurrect His own body. In John 5:21 Jesus declared that He has the power to resurrect anyone.

Regarding the attributes of God, in the Gospel of John chapter 17 verse 5, while praying before His crucifixion Jesus claimed He shared the glory of God:

> "And now, O Father, glorify Me together with Yourself, with the glory which I had with you before the world was."

THE WORKS OF GOD

Work of God	The Father	The Son	Holy Spirit
Creation of Universe	Psa 102:25-26	Col 1:16; John 1:1-3	Gen 1:2; Job 26:13
Creation of Man	Gen 2:7; Gen 1:26; Eccl 12:1; Isaiah 54:5	Col 1:16	Job 33:4
Incarnation of Messiah	Hebrews 10:5; John 3:16	Phil 2:7	Luke 1:35
The Death of Christ	Psalm 22:15; Romans 8:32; John 3:16	John 10:18; Gal 2:20	Hebrews 9:14
The Atonement	Isaiah 53:6,10	Eph 5:2	Hebrews 9:14
The Resurrection of Jesus	Acts 2:24; Romans 6:4	John 10:17,18; John 2:19	1 Pet 3:18; Romans 8:11
The Resurrection of Mankind	John 5:21	John 5:21, John 6:40,54	Romans 8:11
Scriptures Inspired by	2 Tim 3:16	1 Pet 1:10,11	2 Pet 1:21
Minister's Authority	2 Cor 3:5-6	1 Tim 1:12	Acts 20:28
Indwelling Presence	Eph 4:6	Col 1:27	1 Cor 6:19
The Work of Sanctification	Jude 1:1	Hebrews 2:11	1 Cor 6:11

Table 2

Jesus' claim that He shared the very glory of God the Father presents another difficulty. In Isaiah 42:8 Yahweh declared that He will not share His glory with anyone:

> "I am the LORD [Yahweh]: that is my name: and *my glory will I not give to another*, neither my praise to graven images."

Either Jesus of Nazareth and Yahweh are One, or Jesus was committing blasphemy. God will not share His glory with anyone.

Additional attributes applied to Jesus are omnipotence, omnipresence, omniscience, eternal existence and the holiness of God (See Table 3).

ATTRIBUTES OF GOD

Attribute	The Father	The Son	Holy Spirit
Eternal Existence	Psalm 90:2; Isaiah 57:15	Isaiah 9:6; Micah 5:2; Rev 1:8, 17; John 1:2	Hebrews 9: 14
Infinite Power	1 Peter 1:5	2 Cor 12:9	Romans 15:19
Omniscience	Jer 17:10	Rev 2:23	1 Cor 2:11
Omnipresence	Jer 23:24	Matt 18:20	Psalm 139:7
Glory of God	throughout	John 17:5	
Holiness	Rev 15:4	Acts 3:14	everywhere
Truth	John 7:28	Rev 3:7; John 14:6	1 John 5:6
Benevolence	Romans 2:4	Eph 5:25	Neh 9:20
Our Fellowship With:	1 John 1:3	1 John 1:3	2 Cor 13:14

Table 3

THE SKEPTIC RETURNS

Some will argue that the New Testament's claims of the divine nature of Jesus are a cleverly engineered fabrication. They assert, "over-zealous disciples of Jesus erroneously applied dozens of Old Testament Scriptures to the life and ministry of this simple carpenter from Nazareth."

However, even without the claims of Jesus and His disciples, the Old Testament presents the Messiah as an eternally existent, extra-dimensional, divine Being—One who stepped out of eternity into time in the form of a man—One who is called God and worshipped as God in many places. Finally, in the Bible there is an abundance of evidence that the God of the Bible is a plural Being—One God who manifests Himself in more than one personage.

"IN BEGINNING ELOHIM"

Within the pages of Scripture we find it clearly stated that there is indeed, only *one* God.[276] This is a fundamental belief of Judaism and Christianity. However, there are indications in the very first verse of Genesis that God is a plural Being.

> "In the beginning God created the heavens and the earth"

The word used for God in Genesis 1:1 is "Elohim," which is a form of the word "Eloa." In the context of Genesis 1:1, there can certainly be no doubt as to who is doing the creating. In the Hebrew language the "im" ending imputes plurality. Therefore, "Elohim" is the plural form of the word "Eloa," one of the names of God.

It is interesting to note that each usage of this word throughout the Bible is grammatically incorrect. It is a plural noun used with singular verbs. According to Genesis 1:1, the Creator of the Universe, Elohim, exists as a plural being.

If this were not so then the word "Eloa" or perhaps Yahweh would have been used. However, the Holy Spirit chose to use the word "Elohim," the plural form of the name of God in the very first place where the name of God is proclaimed.

"LET US MAKE MAN IN OUR IMAGE"

> "And God said, 'Let Us make man in Our image, after Our likeness; and let them have dominion over the fish of the sea, over the fowl of the air, and over the cattle, over all the earth and over every creeping thing that

creeps on the earth.'" Genesis 1:26, (Jewish Publication Society version, 1917)

The plurality of God is also discovered in the creation of man. According to this fascinating verse, man was created by God in His own image. However, there is something provocative and unexpected in this verse. Prior to the creation of man we find a conversation between God (Elohim) and an unidentified being ("*let Us make* man in Our image"). Who is this person with whom God is speaking?

This person, or intelligent being, has some attributes that we can glean from the text. First, the personage is able to speak with God "on His turf", that is, in the realm of timeless eternity.

Secondly, this being apparently has the same kind of creative ability as God ("Let US make"). This describes a cooperative effort between Elohim and the person with whom He is speaking.

Finally, the likeness or image of this being is comparable to God's ("In Our image, after Our likeness").

When confronted with this passage, modern rabbis often claim that God is speaking to the angels. However, this explanation fails to recognize a number of problems.

First, there is no indication in the Bible that angels can create life. Secondly, nowhere is it indicated that angels are made in the image of God. Finally, there is no indication that mankind was made in the image of angels either!

We may conclude that the person with whom Elohim is conversing lives in the eternal realm, has His creative power and exists in the image or likeness of God. No angel, no man, no created being in heaven or on earth could possibly fit these criteria.

The plurality of God is also seen in Genesis 3:22. After Adam and Eve sinned in the garden of Eden we find a fascinating conversation:

"Then the LORD God said, 'Behold, the man has become

like one of Us, to know good and evil. And now, lest he put out his hand and take also of the tree of life, and eat, and live forever.'" Genesis 3:22 (NKJV)

"Man has become like one of Us." To whom is the LORD talking?

Again in Genesis 11:7, God is discussing His solution to the whole earth having one language at the time of the Tower of Babel:

"Come, let Us go down and there confuse their language, that they may not understand one another's speech." Genesis 11:7 (NKJV)

The fact that the LORD (Yahweh) refers to Himself in these passages as "Us," is indeed a fascinating hint of the plurality of God.[277]

THE "CREATORS" OF THE UNIVERSE?

The plurality of the Creator seen in Genesis 1:1 has been dismissed by some as simply a description of God's plural majesty. However, the plurality of the Creator is also seen in a number of very provocative verses.

In Ecclesiastes 12:1 we read:

"Remember also thy *Creators* in the days of thy youth, While that the evil days come not, Nor the years have arrived, that thou sayest, 'I have no pleasure in *them*.'" (Young's Literal Translation, 1898)

The word Creators is a plural form of the word "bara," which means to create out of nothing.[278],[279]

The notion of plural Creator is also seen in Isaiah 54:5, where the prophet states:

"For thy Maker is thy husband, Jehovah of Hosts is His name, And thy Redeemer is the Holy One of Israel, 'God of all the earth,' He is called.'" (Young's Literal Translation, 1898)

In this verse the word "Maker" is the plural form of the word "asa," which means to form or make.

In the last section we saw that the creation was attributed to God the Father, the Messiah and the Holy Spirit (Table 2). So it should come as no surprise that we find verses which speak of a plural Being, "Elohim," and the concept of "Creators" or "Makers" for the universe.

These verses present a remarkable paradox. The Bible clearly teaches that there is but one God and one Creator. Yet this one God is a plurality of more than one personage, each of which has the attributes of God and performs the works of God.

Surprisingly, the solution to this paradox may be found in one of the strongest monotheistic passages in the entire Bible, Deuteronomy 6:4:

"Hear, O Israel: The LORD our God, the LORD is one LORD!" Deuteronomy 6:4 (KJV)

In this verse we are told that God is One. However, when we examine the word "echad," translated "one," we discover an interesting meaning. This word, "echad," comes from a Hebrew root which means "to unify" or "to collect together," a "united one."

We can get a better feel for it's usage by examining a couple of additional verses. After the creation of man we find the establishment of the marriage relationship:

"Therefore shall a man leave his father and his mother, and shall cleave unto his wife, and they shall be one (echad) flesh" Genesis 2:24 (Jewish Publication Society version, 1917)

Regarding the people of the earth after the flood we read:

"And the LORD said: They are one (echad) people, and they have all one language." Genesis 11:6 (Jewish Publication Society version, 1917)

In each of these verses we see the idea of separate persons viewed as a unified "one." The man and woman become "one flesh." The people of the earth become unified

together as "one people." This unification in these verses
obviously does not mean that they physically unite into a
single being. The individuals still retain their personal
identity and distinct personage. The word "one" here
implies a "compound unity."

It is in this sense that we can understand the "One
God" in Deuteronomy 6:4—He is clearly One God, yet He
manifests Himself in more than one distinct personage—
something totally compatible with the Christian concept
of the Trinity.

The word "yachiyd" (pronounced "yaw-kheed") is used
to indicate "one and only one." This word is frequently
translated into the English word "only." However, it literally means "only one" or "solitary one." It is a word which
suggests an indivisible one as opposed to the compound
unity implied by the word "echad."

If God was an indivisible unity, as opposed to the com-
pound unity implied by "echad," then surely the Holy
Spirit would have inspired Moses to use the word
"Yachiyd."

This problem was recognized by the great
Maimonides, a twelfth-century Hebrew Sage.
Maimonides, a Jewish rabbi who denies the messiahship
and deity of Jesus, recognized that the word "echad" in
Deuteronomy 6:4 implies a compound unity—a plurality
of personages in Yahweh. Consequently, Maimonides stated that Moses used the wrong word when he wrote the
book of Deuteronomy![280]

Finally, we see a hint of the Trinity, the three in One,
in a number of provocative verses which declare the holiness of God. In Isaiah 6:1–3 we read:

> "In the year that King Uzziah died, I saw the Lord sit-
> ting on a throne, high and lifted up, and the train of His
> robe filled the temple. Above it stood seraphim; each one
> had six wings: with two he covered his face, with two he
> covered his feet, and with two he flew. And one cried to
> another and said: 'Holy, holy, holy is the LORD of hosts;

the whole earth is full of His glory!" Isaiah 6:1–3
(NKJV)

In Revelation, chapter four, John is given a view of the
four living creatures around the throne of God:

"And the four living creatures, each having six wings,
were full of eyes around and within. And they do not
rest day or night, saying: 'Holy, holy, holy, Lord God
Almighty, Who was and is and is to come!'" Revelation
4:8 (NKJV)

Why "Holy, holy, holy?" This is just another hint of the
plurality of God and the three in one seen throughout the
Scripture.[281,282]

DEITY OF MESSIAH IN THE OLD TESTAMENT

In the Old Testament there are a number of additional proofs of the deity of the Messiah. We have already seen
a number of the titles of God applied to Jesus Christ in the
New Testament. However, there are those that will dis-
miss such titles as mere plagiarism. The New Testament
authors, they claim, simply applied Old Testament titles
to Jesus, thus making Him something He was not.
However, in the Old Testament, the Messiah is called God
no less than three times and He is worshipped as God at
least twice.

"MIGHTY GOD"

"For unto us a child is born, unto us a Son is given; And
the government will be upon his shoulder; And his name
will be called Wonderful, Counselor, Mighty God,
Everlasting Father, Prince of Peace" Isaiah 9:6 (NKJV)

Isaiah the prophet lived during a time of great despair
for the nation of Israel. Yet, in his prophecies there are
rays of hope for the future inhabitants of Israel. In this
fascinating verse we see the incredible messianic hope

declared. Deliverance would come through a "son" who is born physically into the world, a redeemer who would be called "Mighty God." The words "Mighty God" come from the Hebrew "El Gibbor," literally, "God the Mighty." This very word is used a number of times as a definite reference to Jehovah God.[283]

Among ancient rabbis the identity of this person was almost universally believed to be the Messiah. Presently, however, most rabbis deny the messianic application of this verse with its obvious Christian connotation. If this is not the Messiah, then who else? Surely no prophet or priest is worthy of the title, "The Mighty God, The Everlasting Father and the Prince of Peace."

"GOD WITH US"

> "Therefore the Lord himself will give you a sign: behold, a virgin shall conceive, and bear a son, and shall call his name Immanuel." Isaiah 7:14 (KJV)

The book of Isaiah is considered by many Jewish scholars to be the greatest book of messianic prophecy in the entire Bible. In Isaiah we are told more about the origin, nature, ministry and destiny of the Messiah, than in any other prophetic book.

In Isaiah 7:14 we are told that a child was born into the world as a sign to mankind. The name of the child was to be called Immanuel. This word, Immanuel, means "with us is God." It is derived from the root words "El" which means God, and the word "Im," which is translated "with."

Today the identity of the child "Immanuel" is a point of great contention. However, ancient rabbinical sources clearly believed it was a reference to the Messiah.[284] In fact, ancient rabbis believed that the child Immanuel is the same person identified as "the Root of Jesse's stock", in Isaiah 11:1 and the "Mighty God, Everlasting Father, Prince of Peace," in Isaiah 9:6, verses which were clearly believed to be messianic.[285]

"THE LORD OUR RIGHTEOUSNESS"

> "Behold the days are coming, saith the LORD, that I
> will raise unto David a righteous shoot, and he shall
> reign as king and prosper, and shall execute justice and
> righteousness in the land. In His days Judah shall be
> saved, and Israel shall dwell safely; and this is the name
> whereby he shall be called, The LORD Our
> Righteousness." Jeremiah 23:5-6 (Jewish Publication
> Society Version 1917)

Jeremiah the prophet was a witness to the destruction
of Jerusalem and the abduction of the people of Israel by
the Babylonians. In the midst of his prophetic book, after
many chapters of doom and gloom, Jeremiah includes this
beautiful prophecy regarding the future redeemer of Israel
and the security of the nation under His reign.

This remarkable verse declares that a future King of
Israel, from the line of David (the "righteous shoot", some-
times translated the "Branch") will bring justice, righteousness and salvation to Israel, and will be called The
LORD (Yahweh) Our Righteousness! The word LORD is
again the "tetragrammaton," the name Yahweh, the holiest name of God.

Who is this person, this "righteous shoot," the one who
will be called "Yahweh our righteousness?" If He is the
God of Abraham, Isaac and Jacob, then how could He also
be a descendant of David? Why is this person described as
a *physical being*, born of the line of David, one who will
reign as king, the one who, "in His days," will save Judah.

Some might argue that this is simply a prophetic declaration that God will rule over the people of Israel at
some point in the future. However, an omnipresent Being
cannot fit the bill here. Such a Being isn't born into time
and space with a beginning or end of days. Furthermore,
God, in His spiritual, omnipresent state, cannot be a
descendant of David. What kind of a being could possibly
fulfill such criteria?

The solution is simple, yet profound. To fulfill these

requirements God would need to enter our space-time domain by manifesting Himself in a physical body, be born supernaturally as a descendant of David, then "reign as king and prosper, and...execute justice and righteousness in the land!"

All these criteria could be solved by God in just such a way. He could be a descendant of David, yet still be the God of Abraham, Isaac and Jacob. Furthermore, by entering our space-time continuum at a finite point, He would technically have a beginning to His physical earthly days.

An examination of ancient rabbinical writings reveals that they clearly believed that this verse was a reference to the Messiah. In an ancient Aramaic paraphrase (written by rabbis) of the Hebrew Scriptures, called the Targumim, Jeremiah 23:5–6 is applied to the Messiah:

"And I will raise up for David the Messiah the Just."[286]

Rabbi Kimchi (1160–1235 A.D.), a highly respected Rabbi in his time, wrote of this prophecy:

"By the righteous branch is meant Messiah"[287]

If the ancient rabbis are correct, then the obvious and startling conclusion is that the Messiah (the righteous shoot) will be born into the world as a literal and physical manifestation of Yahweh, the Creator of the universe, the great I Am, the LORD of Lords, the One who was dead and now lives!

For those who might argue that this is not the Messiah, then the obvious question is again, "to whom else could it refer?" What other man could deserve the title "The LORD Our Righteousness?"

PLACES WHERE MESSIAH IS WORSHIPPED

"ONE LIKE UNTO A SON OF MAN"

"And I saw in the night visions, and behold, there came

with the clouds of heaven one like unto a son of man,
and he came even to the ancient of days, and he was
brought near before him. And there was given him
dominion, and glory, and a kingdom, that all the peoples, nations, and languages should serve him; his
dominion is an everlasting dominion, which shall not
pass away, and his kingdom that which shall not be
destroyed" Daniel 7:13–14 (Jewish Publication Society
version, 1917)

Throughout the Bible the people of God are admon-
ished to serve and worship the God of Israel only, and not
to serve and worship other gods. This is absolutely foundational to the beliefs of the observant Jews and
Christians.

However, in the above passages, Daniel 7:13–14 we
read of an individual to whom "all the peoples, nations,
and languages" will serve. Who is this individual? In the
Babylonian Talmud this person is identified as the
Messiah:

> "If Israel behaved worthily, the Messiah would come in
> the clouds of heaven, if otherwise, humble riding on a
> donkey." (Babylonian Talmud, Sanhedrin 98a)

According to the ancient rabbis who compiled the
Talmud, the person coming in the clouds—a reference to
Daniel 7:13–14—is the same individual (the Messiah) who
rides into Jerusalem on a donkey.

A curious aspect to this prophecy, however, is that we
are told that "all the peoples, nations, and languages
should serve him." The word, *pelach*, translated serve, literally means to serve or to worship, especially in the sense
of offering service or worship to God.[288] The very same
word is used eight additional times in the book of Daniel
and each time with the idea of serving or worshipping
God.[289]

In the seventh chapter of Daniel we are given a
description of a dream and vision that Daniel had in the
first year of the reign of Belshazzar. Daniel is shown a suc-

cession of four beasts which represent the four gentile kingdoms of the earth. These were to be the kingdoms that would arise prior to the coming kingdom of the Most High God, a kingdom that will be everlasting. After a description of the four kingdoms we are told:

> "Then the kingdom and dominion, and the greatness of the kingdoms under the whole heaven, shall be given to the people, the saints of the Most High. His kingdom is an everlasting kingdom, and all dominions shall serve (pelach) and obey him." Daniel 7:27 (Jewish Publication Society version, 1917)

Here we find the very same Hebrew word, *pelach*, used in reference to "all dominions" (that is all peoples) serving the Most High God. This is the very same word and the very same activity that Daniel said, in chapter seven, verse 14, would be reserved for the Messiah.

However, God absolutely forbids that we serve or worship anything other than himself, the true and living God of Israel.

Deuteronomy 8:19 tells us what will happen if we worship other gods: "you shall surely perish."

According to Daniel 7:14, the group that will serve the Messiah is composed of "all the peoples, nations, and languages." That is, every person on earth will serve him. However, Daniel 7:27 states that the same all inclusive group will be serving "the Most High" God.

If everyone on earth is serving the Messiah, who is left to serve the "Most High" God? Has Daniel contradicted himself? How do we reconcile this dilemma? The obvious solution is that the Messiah must be a physical manifestation of the eternal God!

In serving the Messiah, all humanity will truly be serving the LORD, the God of Israel!

"LET ALL THE ANGELS OF GOD WORSHIP HIM"

In the New Testament we find a fascinating verse in

the book of Hebrews which also speaks of the worship of
Messiah:

> "God, who at various times and in different ways spoke
> in time past to the fathers by the prophets has in these
> last days spoken to us by His Son, whom He has
> appointed heir of all things, through whom also He
> made the worlds; who being the brightness of His glory
> and the express image of His person, and upholding all
> things by the word of His power, when He had by
> Himself purged our sins, sat down at the right hand of
> the Majesty on high, having become so much better
> than the angels, as He has by inheritance obtained a
> more excellent name than they. For to which of the
> angels did He ever say: 'You are My Son, today I have
> begotten You'?[290] And again: 'I will be to Him a Father,
> and He shall be to Me a Son'?[291] But when He again
> brings the firstborn into the world, He says: 'Let all the
> angels of God worship Him.'" Hebrews 1:1–6

In this portion of the book of Hebrews the writer
(widely held to be Paul the Apostle) quotes a number of
Old Testament passages and then attributes them to
Jesus Christ. After describing Jesus as God's Son and "the
brightness of His (God's) glory and the express image of
His person," the writer then goes on to state, "...when He
again brings the firstborn into the world, He says: 'Let all
the angels of God worship Him.'" In this verse the writer
is quoting from the Septuagint version of Deuteronomy
32:41–43.

The Septuagint is a Greek translation of the Hebrew
Scriptures that was commenced in 285 B.C. During the
period from the first century B.C. to the second century
A.D. it was the most commonly used translation by the
synagogues. In fact, many of the New Testament references to the Old Testament are from the Septuagint version.

In the book of Deuteronomy we find the following rendering:

> "For I will sharpen my sword like lightning, and my

hand shall take hold of judgment; I will render judgment to my enemies, and will recompense them that
hate me. I will make my weapons drunk with blood, and
my sword shall devour flesh, it shall glut itself with the
blood of wounded, and from the captivity of the heads of
their enemies that rule over them. Rejoice, ye heavens,
with him, and *let the angels of God worship him;* rejoice
ye Gentiles, with his people, and let all the sons of God
strengthen themselves in him; for he will avenge the
blood of his sons, and he will render vengeance, and recompense justice to his enemies, and will reward them
that hate him; and the LORD shall purge the land of his
people." Deuteronomy 32:41–43 (Septuagint Version)

In this portion of Scripture, Deuteronomy 32:41–42,
God tells the children of Israel of His power, His glory and
how He will render judgment upon His enemies.

In the very next verse we read of someone who will,
"avenge the blood of his sons, and he will render
vengeance, and recompense justice to his enemies."

What is astonishing about this individual is that God
states that His [God's] angels will worship Him! "Rejoice,
ye heavens, with him, and let the angels of God worship
him." This phrase is also found in the Dead Sea Scroll
fragment of Deuteronomy 32.

Who is this individual? Why would God have His
angels worship him?

It is obvious that this person could not be a mere mortal. No king, priest or prophet could qualify for worship.
Not even an angel may receive worship. The Bible tells us:

"...for you shall worship no other god, for the LORD,
whose name is Jealous, is a jealous God...." Exodus
34:14

And as we saw earlier:

"Then it shall be, if you by any means forget the LORD
your God, and follow other gods, and serve them and
worship them, I testify against you this day that you
shall surely perish." Deuteronomy 8:19 (NKJV)

We can see by these verses that God takes worship seriously. The penalty for worshipping anything other than Him is death! Consequently, the person sanctioned for worship by God must be a physical manifestation of God Himself. The solution to this puzzle is found in the writings of Paul in the New Testament.

"EVERY KNEE SHALL BOW "

One of the most productive and fascinating studies the student of Scripture can do is to examine the hundreds of Old Testament Scriptures that are applied to Jesus in the New Testament. Many prove the messiahship of Jesus and many prove His deity. In Paul's letter to the Philippians there is a subtle example of the latter.

In chapter two Paul makes sweeping statements about the nature and majesty of Jesus Christ:

> "Let this mind be in you which was also in Christ Jesus, who, being in the form of God, did not consider it robbery to be equal with God, but made Himself of no reputation, taking the form of a servant, and coming in the likeness of men. And being found in appearance as a man, He humbled Himself and became obedient to the point of death, even the death of the cross. Therefore God also has highly exalted Him and given Him the name which is above every name, that *at the name of Jesus every knee should bow*, of those in heaven, and of those on earth, and of those under the earth, and that *every tongue should confess that Jesus Christ is Lord*, to the glory of God the Father." Philippians 2:5–10 (NKJV)

A casual reading of this text might easily miss a fascinating proof for the deity of Jesus. Paul states that, "at the name of Jesus every knee should bow...and every tongue should confess that Jesus Christ is Lord...." Such a statement by Paul is not surprising since he clearly believed that Jesus was God. However, what is not widely known is that Paul was quoting a verse that was actually another reference to Yahweh.

In the book of Isaiah, chapter 45, we read of the

majesty and glory of Yahweh, the Creator, Redeemer and Savior of Israel. After enumerating a number of the LORD's works and attributes, we find these words of the LORD, spoken through the prophet Isaiah:

> "I have sworn by Myself; the word has gone out of My mouth in righteousness, and shall not return, that to Me every knee shall bow, every tongue shall take an oath." Isaiah 45:23 (NKJV)

According to Yahweh, "every knee shall bow, every tongue shall take an oath," to Him, the Creator and Savior of the universe. According to Paul the Apostle, every knee would bow to Jesus! This is just another proof that every verse, every place name, and every letter of God's word is there by design.

MESSIAH—GOD THE SON!

Shortly after the ministry of Jesus began, it was determined by the Sanhedrin that He must die.[292] Though His disregard for their authority and their traditions were enough for them to want Him dead, the claims He made about Himself were the final straw. Jesus even asked them why they wanted to stone Him to death. "Because you, being a man, *make yourself God*," was their response.

While most first century Jews believed that the Messiah was the Son of God, the notion of Him being God in the flesh was apparently foreign. However, according to Alfred Edersheim, a nineteenth-century Jewish believer in Jesus, the line between the nature of the Messiah and the nature of God was very fine;

> "The Messiah expected was far above the conditions of the most exalted of God's servants, even his angels; in short, so closely bordering on the Divine, that it was almost impossible to distinguish him therefrom."[293]

Shortly after Jesus raised Lazarus from the dead, the Sanhedrin met to discuss the fate of Jesus. Some believed in Him, but most wanted Him dead. Though He did many

wonders and spoke like no man, His claims were too radical and His image too meek. The crowds that gathered
everywhere He went were a threat to the tenuous but
peaceful status quo maintained by the Roman Empire.

So, as the Gospel of John says:

> "Then the chief priests and the Pharisees gathered a
> council and said, 'What shall we do? For this Man works
> many signs. If we let Him alone like this, everyone will
> believe in Him, and the Romans will come and take
> away both our place and nation.' And one of them,
> Caiaphas, being high priest that year, said to them, 'You
> know nothing at all, nor do you consider that it is expe-
> dient for us that one man should die for the people, and
> not that the whole nation should perish.'" John 11:47–50
> (NKJV)

"It is expedient for us that one man should die for the
people." These are the words of the high priest, Caiaphas.
Though he didn't know it, Caiaphas had summarized the
very reason that the Creator of the universe came in the
person of Jesus of Nazareth, the Redeemer and Savior of
all mankind.

Jesus said it Himself, "It is for this purpose that I have
come."[294]

Despite His impeccable credentials as Messiah and
God in the flesh, "...He was wounded for our transgressions, He was bruised for our iniquities; the chastisement
for our peace was upon Him, and by His stripes we are
healed...the LORD has laid on Him the iniquity of us all...
He was led as a lamb to the slaughter.... He was cut off
from the land of the living; for the transgressions of My
people He was stricken.... Yet it pleased the LORD to
bruise Him...by His knowledge My righteous Servant
shall justify many, for He shall bear their iniquities....
Therefore I will divide Him a portion with the great...
because He poured out His soul unto death, and He was
numbered with the transgressors, and He bore the sin of
many, and made intercession for the transgressors."[295]

251 *Life* magazine, December, 1994, pgs. 67-82.
252 For a detailed examination of ancient historical references to Jesus see Josh Mc Dowell, *He Walked Among Us*, Here's Life Publishers, 1988.
253 For a more detailed examination of this historical reference see *The Search for Messiah*, Mark Eastman, Chuck Smith. The Word for Today, 1993 ed.
254 *The Antiquities of the Jews*, book 18, chapter 3.
255 There are actually two Talmuds. The Babylonian Talmud, complied by Jews in Babylonia, and the Jerusalem Talmud compiled by Jews in Israel.
256 2 Peter 1:16.
257 Acts 5.
258 Isaiah 43:11.
259 See also Isaiah 43:3; 45:15; 45:21; 49:26; 60:16; Luke 1:47.
260 Job 9:8 (NKJV).
261 This has been thoroughly documented in *The Search for Messiah*; Mark Eastman, Chuck Smith; The Word for Today, Coats Mesa , CA. (800) 272-WORD.
262 Micah 5:2.
263 Isaiah 53, Psalm 22, Zechariah 12:10.
264 Isaiah 8:14.
265 Isaiah 11:10.
266 See *The Search for Messiah*; Mark Eastman, Chuck Smith; The Word for Today, P.O. Box 8000, Costa Mesa, Ca 92628.(800) 272-WORD.
267 John 4:1-25.
268 John 12:45b (NKJV).
269 John 7:46 (NKJV).
270 See also Rev 17:14.
271 See also Psalm 136:1-3.
272 Revelation 1:11.
273 Exodus 3:14.
274 In many English translations the translators inserted the word "He" in italics after the words "I Am." However, this word is not in the original Greek texts nor does the context require it. Jesus said that He would prove that He was God (the I Am) after they killed Him. Clearly Jesus used the term as declaration of His deity.
275 John 8:59.
276 Deuteronomy 6:4, Isaiah 45:5-6.
277 See also Isaiah 6:8.
278 The is the same word used in Genesis 1:1 "Elohim created (bara)."

279 In most English translations this plurality is not carried through. However, it is there in the original Hebrew text.

280 In Moses Maimonides' work *Articles of Faith* (12th century A.D.) he wrote that Moses should have written, "Hear, O Israel: the LORD our God, the LORD is one (<u>Yachid</u>)."

281 See also Matthew 28:19; 2 Corinthians 13:14; John 15:26.

282 For a detailed discussion of the Trinity see the two tape briefing package, *The Trinity*, by Chuck Missler, available at 1-800-KHOUSE1.

283 See Jeremiah 32:18;Isaiah 10:21; Nehemiah 9:32; Deuteronomy 10:17.

284 See the chapter, "Messiah God the Son?" in *The Search for Messiah*, Eastman, Smith.

285 ibid. chapter 9.

286 See Babylonian Talmud Babha Bathra 75b, Midrash on Psalm 21.

287 Baron, David, *Rays of Messianic Glory: Christ in the Old Testament*, Grand Rapids, Michigan, Zondervan, 1886.

288 See *Wilson's Old Testament Word Studies*, pg. 382, Kregel Publications, 1987.

289 Daniel 3:12,14,17,18,28. Daniel 6:16,20. Daniel 7:14,27.

290 A reference to Psalm 2.

291 A reference to 2 Samuel 7:14.

292 John 5.

293 Edersheim, Alfred, *The Life and Times of Jesus the Messiah*, pg. 179.

294 John 12:27.

295 Excerpts from Isaiah 53:5-12 (NKJV).

CHAPTER ELEVEN

THE TRANSCENDENT ONE

"But you, Bethlehem Ephrathah, though you are little among the thousands of Judah, yet out of you shall come forth to Me the One to be ruler in Israel, Whose goings forth have been from of old, from everlasting."

Micah 5:2

O ver and over Jesus made the incredible claim that He was not of this world. To the Pharisees Jesus stated, "You are from beneath; I am from above. You are of this world; I am not of this world."[296] On the night before He was crucified, He said to His disciples, "I came forth from the Father, and am come into the world: again, I leave the world, and go to the Father."[297] And as He prayed for Himself, He said to His Father, "And now, O Father, glorify Me together with Yourself, with the glory which I had with You before the world was."[298] Within these few verses is the unparalleled claim by Jesus that He is a Transcendent Being from beyond time and space.

Jesus' claim that He "is not of this world" is provocative indeed. The Greek word translated to the English "world," is the word *kosmos*. While this word has a number of meanings, it is most often translated as "world," or "universe" in more contemporary literature. In the New Testament it is also frequently used to mean the "world system."

When Jesus said to the Pharisees, "You are from beneath; I am from above. You are of this world; I am not of this world," He clearly implied that He was not of this "universe." By itself, this is an astonishing declaration. However, when He prayed to the Father, "...glorify Me together with Yourself, with the glory which I had with You before the world (*kosmos*) was," He not only claimed that He shared the glory of God, He claimed that He existed before time began!

FROM EVERLASTING

In the twentieth century, Einstein's Theory of Relativity has confirmed that time itself is a physical property of the universe, and not just a construct of the human mind. As evidence is the fact that time can be compressed or stretched when influenced by extreme velocity, acceleration or gravity. Because of this, anyone that claims to be the Creator of this universe must be able to demonstrate an existence which is independent of the time domain. Throughout the Bible, in both testaments, this claim is made of the Messiah, Jesus Christ.

Within the Old Testament there are a number of clear references to the eternal existence of the Messiah. The book of Isaiah is widely held to be the greatest book of messianic prophecy in the entire Bible. Within its pages we find virtually every aspect of the Messiah's life and ministry foretold. In the ninth chapter of Isaiah we find two verses which speak of the Messiah's eternal existence:

> "For unto us a Child is born, Unto us a Son is given; And the government will be upon His shoulder. And His name will be called Wonderful, Counselor, Mighty God, Everlasting Father, Prince of Peace. Of the increase of His government and peace, there will be no end. Upon the throne of David and over His kingdom, to order it and establish it with judgment and justice from that time forward, even forever. The zeal of the LORD of hosts will perform this." Isaiah 9:6–7 (NKJV)

Within this scripture we find a description of a Being whose existence is indeed independent of the time domain.

According to this verse, this person is the "Everlasting Father." Some translations call Him the "Father of Eternity." By default, such a Being must have existed before the creation of the time domain. With the arrival of our time domain, this "Son" manifested Himself in time and space through His birth as a child on planet earth.

Ultimately, this Being regains His eternal, time-independent nature, to rule on the throne of David "from that time forward, even forever." With rare exception, the ancient Rabbis believed that this person is the Messiah of Israel, the "Son" of God, the One who "will be called Wonderful, Counselor, Mighty God, Everlasting Father and the Prince of Peace."

The remarkable thing about this verse is that it describes a Being who lives in eternity, enters time and space, then re-enters an eternal realm again. This phenomenal ability to enter and exit the time domain could only be accomplished by a transcendent, extra-dimensional Being.

There is one last point that needs to be made about this scripture. When this "Prince of Peace" came into time and space, He took on the form of a man. However, within this text is a hint that this "Wonderful Counselor" remains in the form of a man forever! This is supported by New Testament scriptures as well.

The eternal existence and transcendent nature of the Messiah is further confirmed in the book of the prophet Micah. In this undeniable messianic verse, the prophet foretells the place where the eternal One is born into space-time:

> "But you, Bethlehem Ephrathah, though you are little among the thousands of Judah, yet out of you shall come forth to Me the One to be ruler in Israel, Whose goings forth have been from of old, from everlasting." Micah 5:2 (NKJV)

Here again we see the likes of a Transcendent Being. Though He inhabits eternity, He took upon Himself the limitations of a human body, born in the city of Bethlehem, to be ruler in Israel.

In an ancient rabbinical commentary, called the Targum of Jonathan, we find the unequivocal application of this prophecy to the Messiah:

> "And you, O Bethlehem Ephrathah, you who were too small to be numbered among the thousands of the house of Judah, *from you shall come forth before Me the Messiah*, to exercise dominion over Israel, he whose name was mentioned before, from the days of creation."[299] (emphasis added).

In his book, *The Life and Times of Jesus the Messiah*, Alfred Edersheim, a Jewish believer in Jesus, points out that at one time, the belief in the eternal existence of the Messiah was firmly rooted in the writings of the ancient rabbis:

> "Even in strictly Rabbinic documents, the premundane if not the *eternal existence* of the Messiah, appears as a matter of common belief. Such is the view expressed in the Targum on Isaiah 9:6 and on Micah 5:2"[300] (emphasis added).

The composite picture of the Messiah presented in these few verses is quite remarkable. An eternally existent Being enters time and space as a child. This child, now confined by the dimensions and laws of the physical universe, experiences birth, growth, hunger, thirst, pain, the aging process and death. He regains His transcendent nature in an eternal, glorified body, only to rule on the throne of David forever.

The nature of this "Everlasting Father"—clearly the Messiah—fulfills the requisite credentials of a transcendent, time-independent, Creator for this universe.

THE KING ETERNAL

The eternal existence and transcendent nature of Jesus Christ is also confirmed throughout the New

Testament. In some verses His preincarnate and post-res-
urrection eternal existence are emphasized. In others, it is
His ability to transcend the time domain which confirms
His deity and transcendent nature.

In John 1:1 we find what some have called the oldest
genealogy in the Bible:

> "In the beginning was the Word, and the Word was with
> God, and the Word was God. The same was in the begin-
> ning with God. All things were made by him; and with-
> out him was not any thing made that was made.... And
> the Word was made flesh, and dwelt among us, (and we
> beheld his glory, the glory as of the only begotten of the
> Father) full of grace and truth." John 1:3, 14 (KJV)

In this verse we are told that at the beginning of time
the Word (*logos*) was already in existence. This "Logos"
was with God and He was God. All things (time, space,
matter) were made by Him. Finally, this Word became
flesh and dwelt among us. This person is of course, Jesus
Christ. These verses have some striking parallels to
Isaiah 9:6–7.

Described in these verses is a Being whose existence is
again, independent of the time domain. He existed in
timelessness before "the beginning" of the time domain
which He created. He entered space-time, "taking the
form of a servant, and coming in the likeness of men."[301]
Ultimately, because "the world knew Him not," He was
killed, only to regain His transcendent nature after His
bodily resurrection.

In I Timothy 1:17 Jesus is called the "King Eternal."
In the book of Revelation, Jesus calls Himself the "Alpha
and Omega, the Beginning and the Ending...the First and
the Last."[302] To the first-century Greek mind, such titles
would readily be understood to mean existing from eternity past to eternity future.

Finally, throughout the New Testament Jesus tells His
disciples that He has the power to give them eternal
life.[303] While this ability certainly impressed His disci-

ples, it also revealed something about His nature. For
Jesus could not bestow eternal life unless it was something that He possessed Himself. If He himself didn't possess it, He couldn't give it away.

"I CAME FORTH FROM THE FATHER"

The eternal existence of Jesus is not something that
He merely possessed after His resurrection, it is one of the
attributes He possessed *before* His bodily incarnation in
the womb of the virgin. This fact is seen in a number of
statements He made during His ministry.

On the night before His crucifixion Jesus spent a time
of deep sharing and reflection with His disciples. On that
short evening together, He revealed to them some of the
greatest insights about His nature, ministry and destiny.
In John 16, Jesus warned His disciples that after He was
gone they would be despised, persecuted and killed, in the
name of God, by those that ruled in Israel:

> "They will put you out of the synagogues; yes, the time
> is coming that whoever kills you will think that he offers
> God service. And these things they will do to you
> because they have not known the Father nor Me." John
> 16:2–3 (NKJV)

Then He shared with His disciples that He was
returning to the place from where He had come, the eternal dwelling place of His Father:

> "A little while, and you will not see Me; and again a lit-
> tle while, and you will see Me, because I go to the
> Father.... I came forth from the Father and have come
> into the world. Again, I leave the world and go to the
> Father." John 16:16, 28 (NKJV)

In these few verses Jesus confirms that His eternal
dwelling place was with the Father before His incarnation.

NOW YOU SEE HIM, NOW YOU DON'T

In the 1930's British physicist Sir James Jeans admitted that the Creator of our universe must be a Transcendent Being who works "...outside time and space, which are part of his creation, just as the artist is outside his canvas."[304] Having a transcendent nature also means the Creator would be able to enter His "canvas" to order and establish the materials therein.

One of the fascinating outcomes of Einstein's relativity theories is the discovery that space and time are intimately and inseparably linked. This fact has led to the term "space-time" as a way of demonstrating this linkage. This linkage provides another fascinating way in which God might demonstrate His existence.

It's interesting that the Bible spends very little time arguing for God's existence. It simply takes His existence for granted. Nevertheless, in the book of Isaiah, God said that one of the proofs of His existence is that He is able to foretell history in advance.[305] In fact, the Bible demonstrates that its origin is from outside the time domain through predictive prophecy.

The question is, how could God demonstrate that His existence is not only independent of time, but beyond the three spatial dimensions of our universe as well? The answer is simple: He could do this by materializing out of nowhere, *ex nihilo*, and by disappearing without a trace, anywhere within the three dimensions of our universe. This ability demonstrates a nature which supersedes and is beyond the mere dimensions of our universe. Furthermore, if God could do this *anytime* He wished, it would prove that His existence is independent of both time and space.

It's interesting to discover that Jesus demonstrated this very ability before His incarnation and after His bodily resurrection from the dead.

THE CAPTAIN OF THE LORD'S HOST

In the Old Testament there are a number of pre-incarnate appearances, called "Christophanies," of Jesus Christ. After the death of Moses, Joshua was appointed to lead the children of God into the promised land of Israel. Shortly after they crossed over the Jordan river, we read:

> "And it came to pass, when Joshua was by Jericho, that he lifted up his eyes and looked, and, behold, there stood a man over against him with his sword drawn in his hand: and Joshua went unto him, and said unto him, 'Art thou for us, or for our adversaries?' And he said, 'Nay; but as captain of the host of the LORD am I now come.' And Joshua fell on his face to the earth, and did worship, and said unto him, 'What saith my lord unto his servant?' And the captain of the LORD'S host said unto Joshua, 'Loose thy shoe from off thy foot; for the place whereon thou standest is holy.' And Joshua did so." Joshua 5:13–15 (KJV)

There are differing opinions regarding the identity of this person identified as the "captain of the host of the LORD." Some claim he is an archangel. However, this interpretation is hampered by the fact that he receives worship from Joshua and tells him that the ground upon which Joshua stands is holy (This is exactly what God said to Moses when He revealed His glory at the burning bush on Mt. Horeb).[306] God forbids the worship of anything but Himself, including angels.[307]

In support of this principle is an event in the book of Revelation where the Apostle John is overcome with awe at the appearance of an angel. In Revelation 19:10, John records:

> "And I fell at his feet to worship him. But he said to me, 'See that you do not do that! I am your fellow servant, and of your brethren who have the testimony of Jesus. Worship God! For the testimony of Jesus is the spirit of prophecy.'" Revelation 19:10 (NKJV)

Because the Being who appeared to Joshua received

worship, most scholars believe that this person was none
other than Jesus Christ. In fact, some would argue that
every time that God has materialized in the form of a man,
it is in the person of Jesus Christ—the GOD-MAN.[308]

THE ROAD TO EMMAUS

In the New Testament, in all four Gospel accounts,
Jesus of Nazareth reveals His extra-dimensional nature
by materializing out of nowhere. One of the most fascinating post-resurrection appearances was when He appeared
to the two disciples on the road to Emmaus. Three days
earlier Jesus had been crucified and it was now the day of
His resurrection. In Luke 24 we read:

> "And they talked together of all these things which had
> happened. So it was, while they conversed and rea-
> soned, that Jesus Himself drew near and went with
> them. But their eyes were restrained, so that they did
> not know Him.
>
> And He said to them, 'What kind of conversation is this
> that you have with one another as you walk and are
> sad?' Then the one whose name was Cleopas answered
> and said to Him, 'Are You the only stranger in
> Jerusalem, and have You not known the things which
> happened there in these days?'
>
> And He said to them, 'What things?'
>
> So they said to Him, 'The things concerning Jesus of
> Nazareth, who was a Prophet mighty in deed and word
> before God and all the people, and how the chief priests
> and our rulers delivered Him to be condemned to death,
> and crucified Him. But we were hoping that it was He
> who was going to redeem Israel.
>
> Indeed, besides all this, today is the third day since
> these things happened. Yes, and certain women of our
> company, who arrived at the tomb early, astonished us.
> When they did not find His body, they came saying that
> they had also seen a vision of angels who said He was
> alive. And certain of those who were with us went to the
> tomb and found it just as the women had said; but Him
> they did not see.'

Then He said to them, 'O foolish ones, and slow of heart
to believe in all that the prophets have spoken! Ought
not the Christ to have suffered these things and to enter
into His glory?'

And beginning at Moses and all the Prophets, He
expounded to them in all the Scriptures the things concerning Himself.

Then they drew near to the village where they were
going, and He indicated that He would have gone far-
ther. But they constrained Him, saying, 'Abide with us,
for it is toward evening, and the day is far spent.' And
He went in to stay with them. Now it came to pass, as
He sat at the table with them, that He took bread,
blessed and broke it, and gave it to them. Then their
eyes were opened and they knew Him; and He vanished
from their sight.

And they said to one another, 'Did not our heart burn
within us while He talked with us on the road, and
while He opened the Scriptures to us?'" Luke 24:14–32
(NKJV)

What a blessed case of heartburn! There are many
provocative aspects to this portion of Scripture.

First, while the disciples of Jesus traveled on the road
to Emmaus they did not recognize Him. It's interesting to
note that on numerous occasions His disciples did not recognize Him after His resurrection.[309] Whether it was due
to the physical abuse and disfigurement He suffered, or a
supernatural change in His glorified body, we do not
know.[310] It wasn't until He broke bread with them that
they recognized that it was Jesus. Could it be that when
He broke the bread that they saw the prints of the nails,
or was it a supernatural unveiling of their eyes?

Secondly, Jesus stated, in effect, that through the
entire Old Testament, from the first five books of Moses to
the last prophet Malachi, the rejection, suffering and
death of Messiah was foretold.

Finally, after they recognized Him, He simply vanished out of their sight.

Immediately after this encounter these two disciples traveled back to Jerusalem to tell the others. When they arrived, they told the other disciples that Jesus had risen indeed. Luke records what happened next:

> "Now as they said these things, Jesus Himself stood in the midst of them, and said to them, 'Peace to you.' But they were terrified and frightened, and supposed they had seen a spirit. And He said to them, 'Why are you troubled? And why do doubts arise in your hearts? Behold My hands and My feet, that it is I Myself. Handle Me and see, for a spirit does not have flesh and bones as you see I have." Luke 24:36–39 (NKJV)

There are those who claim that Jesus did not resurrect bodily, but spiritually. However, this error is anticipated by these very verses. The disciples were afraid because, when Jesus appeared, they thought they were seeing a spirit. However, Jesus corrected them by pointing out that, "a spirit does not have flesh and bones as you see I have."

The point is that within these few verses we see the appearance, *ex nihilo*, and disappearance of the Messiah of Israel, in His glorified body, thus revealing His transcendent nature.[311]

EXTRA DIMENSIONS?

While we can only speculate as to the method Jesus used to accomplish these post-resurrection appearances, the field of dimension theory may provide at least a conceptual basis for such appearances.

We currently enjoy a universe which consists of three dimensions of space and one dimension of time. In reality, we humans only experience half of the time dimension because we can only move foreword along its course. In this century theoretical physicists believe they have discovered a basis for many more dimensions within our universe.

While the speculation in this area is plentiful indeed,

some physicists believe that at the moment of creation, the universe consisted of ten dimensions (nine spatial and one time dimension).[312] Then at 10^{43} seconds, six of them collapsed sub-microscopically, never to be seen again. Others believe that there may be an infinite number of dimensions. Whatever the case may be, the implications of dimension theory are fascinating.

According to the principles of dimension theory, if Jesus, in His pre-incarnate and post-resurrection state, possessed at least nine spatial dimensions and one additional dimension of time, He could "pop in and out" of our universe, unencumbered, anytime or anywhere He wished. Even though dimension theory may have nothing to do with how God manifests Himself in time and space, it's fascinating to discover that twentieth-century theoretical physics may provide, at the very least, a conceptual basis for what has been considered to be an unexplainable supernatural phenomenon.

THE GREAT MYSTERY

For thousands of years the Bible has taught that God is an omnipresent, omnipotent, omniscient, eternally existent and Transcendent Being. In fact, as we have seen, the Bible applies all of these attributes to all three persons of the Trinity. The difficulty for us as finite beings is to understand how an infinite God could be one and three at the same time. Secondly, How can God be everywhere at once and yet be confined to a body in the person of Jesus Christ? Furthermore, why did He even bother to walk among us?

Regarding the mystery of the triune God, Paul the Apostle said in I Corinthians 13:12, "For now we see through a glass, darkly; but then face to face: now I know in part; but then shall I know even as also I am known."[313] The word translated "darkly," is the Greek word "ainigma," which means an obscure thing, or a riddle. The blessed hope, expressed by Paul, is that one day this enigma will be cleared up. Then, as the Apostle John said, "we know that when He is revealed [made manifest], we shall be like Him, for we shall see Him as He is."314

While the enigma of a triune God cannot be solved by finite beings trapped within the dimensions of space and time, with the twentieth-century discovery that the universe is finite, our view of God's nature has been made a little clearer.

Prior to this century there were a number of biblical difficulties that could not be solved because those attempting to solve them did so from the bias that the universe was infinite. However, when viewed from the foundation of a finite universe, many of these seemingly irreconcilable paradoxes are within our grasp.

With a finite universe God could exist before its creation, He could exist outside space and time ("inhabit eternity," as Isaiah said), and He could design the universe and its life forms, outside of time. Then with the arrival of the universe, He could "fax" those concepts or "blueprints" into time and space. Furthermore, because He exists outside of time, He knows history in advance. And from our perspective, He is all-knowing (omniscient). Because He exists outside of space, He can instantaneously manifest (i.e. materialize) Himself anywhere He wishes within the dimensions of space, and therefore, He is to us, omnipresent. Finally, since all causes must be greater than their effects, God, who is greater than the sum of all the mass and energy in the universe, becomes to us, the Omnipotent One.

There are many religions that proclaim the notion of an infinite universe. The problem with such a notion is that it puts some interesting, but logical constraints on their notion of God.

By definition, if the universe is infinite, then there can be nothing else. Consequently, with such a view of the universe, God becomes an occupant of the universe rather than a Being who transcends it. Therefore, God could not dwell in eternity. He could not exist before time and space began. And because God is confined to the universe, He is subject to its laws. Therefore, God becomes either a product of the universe or the universe itself.

It's interesting that most Eastern religions and New Age philosophies believe in an infinite universe and a god who is its occupant.

However, in one fell swoop, twentieth-century discoveries have provided evidence which destroys the notion of an infinite universe, while the biblical view of a Transcendent Creator and a finite creation is now more logical than anytime in history.

"THAT WE MAY KNOW HIM"

According to Scripture, one of the purposes of Jesus coming to earth was to represent to us, in a tangible and comprehensible way, the very nature and essence of God. Indeed, according to the writer of Hebrews, Jesus is "the radiance of His [God's] glory and *the exact representation of His nature.*"[315] However, according to God, man cannot look upon Him "as He is," without dying.[316] Therefore, God needed to adapt His nature and take on a form that we could relate to with our five senses and yet survive. This process—becoming a man—was therefore not only the most rational way to accomplish this goal, but it was, to say the least, an enormous step of humility.

Paul the apostle wrote that Jesus Christ "emptied Himself, taking on the form of a bondservant."[317] In the Greek the word translated "emptied," means to make void, to render vain or to make of no reputation. However it is rendered, it implies an incredible descent to a lower, humbler state of existence. Perhaps this is why Jesus could state that His Father was greater than He.[318] And yet, He was still God! He was not a representation of God. He was not simply an extension or an appendage of God. He was not an ideal. He was and is God! But as a man, He set aside His transcendent nature to give a tangible glimpse of the true and living God.

But there is another, even greater reason why He came.

THE DEATH OF GOD!

In the 1960's philosophers confidently declared that "God is dead." While the report of God's death was greatly exaggerated, they were partly correct. Nearly two thousand years earlier, the Creator of the universe, the "Mighty God," "Immanuel," died on a Roman cross to pay the price for the sins of all mankind.

The death of Jesus Christ was not an unfortunate occurrence in a failed ministry. Nor was it an afterthought of God. "Oops," is not in God's vocabulary. Rather, the sacrificial death of "God in the flesh," was part of a plan devised "from the foundation of the world."[319]

The Bible teaches that all men "have sinned, and come short of the glory of God."[320] The word sin means "to miss the mark." God's mark or requirement is nothing less than perfection. The prophet Micah summed up God's requirement:

> "He has shown you, O man, what is good; And what does the LORD require of you, but to do justly, to love mercy, and to walk humbly with your God?" Micah 6:8 (NKJV)

The problem is that none of us have done these things all our lives. There are times when we are not just nor merciful nor humble. We may strive for this, but we all miss the mark.

In the Old Testament God set forth His laws to His people in the Ten Commandments.[321] Thou shalt not kill, lie, steal, covet, commit adultery, nor worship other gods, etc.... Obviously none of us have kept these "marks," or standards, all our lives. If you think you have, according to the Apostle John:

> "If we say that we have no sin, we deceive ourselves, and

the truth is not in us.... If we say that we have not
sinned, we make him a liar, and his word is not in us." I
John 1:8, 10 (KJV)

The problem with sin is that it separates us from God.
As the prophet Isaiah stated:

"But your iniquities have separated you from your God;
and your sins have hidden His face from you, so that He
will not hear." Isaiah 59:2 (NKJV)

So what is the remedy for our sin? In the Old
Testament, God established a system of animal sacrifice
for the atonement of sins. This principle is presented in
the book of Leviticus:

"'For the life of the flesh is in the blood, and I have given
it to you upon the altar to make atonement for your
souls; for it is the blood that makes atonement for the
soul.'" Leviticus 17:11 (NKJV)

In order to cover or atone for one's sins or transgressions, individuals were required to go to the Temple and
offer an unspotted, unblemished animal on a regular
basis. The blood of the animal was sprinkled on the mercy
seat of the Ark of the Covenant and provided a covering for
a person's sins. This sacrificial system, however, offered
only a temporary atonement, or covering for sins.
Consequently, each time a person sinned, it was necessary
to atone or cover the sin with such a sacrifice.

The writer of the book of Hebrews points out that the
sacrificial system, though effective for a time, provided
only a temporary covering for sins:

"For the law, having a shadow of the good things to
come, and not the very image of the things, can never
with these same sacrifices, which they offer continually
year by year, make those who approach perfect. For
then would they not have ceased to be offered? For the
worshipers, once purged, would have had no more con-
sciousness of sins. But in those sacrifices there is a
reminder of sins every year. For it is not possible that

the blood of bulls and goats could take away sins."
Hebrews 10:1–4 (NKJV)

The Levitical sacrificial system only covered over a person's sins. The writer of the book of Hebrews points out that such sacrifices did not take away a man's sins, but were in fact a continual reminder of one's sinfulness. If such sacrifices could permanently justify a man in the sight of God then those sacrifices would have to be done but once.

Because of the temporary nature of the sacrificial system, there needed to be something more permanent and effective that could take away a man's sins, something that the writer of Hebrews says cannot be accomplished by the blood of bulls and goats.

According to the Bible, we can pay the price for our own sins. However, the price is very high indeed. The Apostle Paul said in the book of Romans:

"For the wages of sin is death, but the gift of God is eternal life in Christ Jesus our Lord." Romans 6:23 (KJV)

However, there is another way. By placing our faith in the perfect sacrifice—the Lamb of God—the Bible states we can have a complete remission of our sins and not just a covering.

The prophet Isaiah, speaking of the sacrificial, atoning death of the Messiah, proclaimed:

"But He was wounded for our transgressions, He was bruised for our iniquities; the chastisement for our peace was upon Him, and by His stripes we are healed.

He was taken from prison and from judgment, and who will declare His generation? For He was cut off from the land of the living; for the transgressions of My people He was stricken. And they made His grave with the wicked—but with the rich at His death, because He had done no violence, nor was any deceit in His mouth.

Yet it pleased the LORD to bruise Him; He has put Him
to grief. When You make His soul an offering for sin, He
shall see His seed, He shall prolong His days, and the
pleasure of the LORD shall prosper in His hand. He
shall see the labor of His soul, and be satisfied. By His
knowledge My righteous Servant shall justify many, for
He shall bear their iniquities. Therefore I will divide
Him a portion with the great, and He shall divide the
spoil with the strong, because He poured out His soul
unto death, and He was numbered with the transgressors, and He bore the sin of many, and made intercession for the transgressors." Isaiah 53:5,8–12(NKJV)

In the New Testament we are told by Jesus Himself:

"For God so loved the world, that he gave his only begotten Son, that whosoever believeth in him should not
perish, but have everlasting life." John 3:16 (KJV)

Paul the apostle, in the book of Romans, his definitive
statement of Christian doctrine, said:

"For whosoever shall call upon the name of the Lord
shall be saved." Romans 10:13 (KJV)

"That if thou shalt confess with thy mouth the Lord
Jesus, and shalt believe in thine heart that God hath
raised him from the dead, thou shalt be saved." Romans
10:9 (KJV)

The Apostle John, known as the apostle of love, put it
this way:

"Herein is love, not that we loved God, but that He loved
us, and sent His Son to be the propitiation for our sins."
I John 4:10

Nothing less than the sacrificial death of the Creator
of the universe will do. Angels cannot save us from our
sins because they have the potential to sin.[322] Neither can
our family members and friends because their predicament is no better than ours.
    Only an unspotted, unblemished sacrifice is capable of
atoning for the sins of mankind. So the Creator of the uni-

verse became flesh and dwelt among us.[323] And as John the Baptist said when he saw Jesus at His baptism, "Behold, the Lamb of God, which taketh away the sins of the world."[324]

The love of God for us, expressed in the sacrificial death of His Son, Jesus Christ, is quite simply unfathomable.

HOW TO "WORK" YOUR WAY TO HEAVEN!

There are many among us who cannot accept that our personal salvation is a gift of God. We have a tendency to think that our salvation is something we need to earn through "good works." In fact, most non-Christian religious systems and cults involve themselves in such practices. "If you hand out enough magazines, sell enough trinkets and do enough righteous works, you can obtain a right standing with God," they assert.

According to Jesus Christ Himself, there is only one work we can do to obtain a right standing with God:

> "Jesus answered and said to them, 'This is the work of God, that you believe in Him whom He sent.'" John 6:29 (NKJV)

Believe in Him—Jesus Christ—the One whom God has sent.

Good motives cannot save you. Good works cannot save you. In fact, 700 years before Jesus was born the prophet Isaiah said of our good works:

> "But we are all as an unclean thing, and all our righteousnesses are as filthy rags; and we all do fade as a leaf; and our iniquities, like the wind, have taken us away." Isaiah 64:6 (KJV)

The Hebrew word translated as "filthy rags," means literally "used menstrual cloths." Apparently the translators felt that the public couldn't handle such a comparison. God, however, wanted us to have a vivid picture of how He views our self-attained righteousness. Surely, such a righteousness cannot justify us in the sight of God.

If our righteousnesses (good works) look like "used menstrual cloths," imagine what our sins look like to a Holy and Righteous God!

The only way to obtain a righteous standing before God is through His Son, Jesus Christ:

> "Jesus saith unto him, I am the way, the truth, and the life: no man cometh unto the Father, but by me." John 14:6 (KJV)

CHOOSE YOU THIS DAY WHOM YOU WILL SERVE

> In this twentieth-century age of skepticism it is indeed ironic to discover that more evidence has accumulated for the existence of a Transcendent Creator in this century than any time in the last 1900 years. And yet, the evidence examined points to just such a Being. One who exists outside time and has spoken history in advance. One who exists outside space and has manifested Himself within our spatial dimensions. And The One who came to die for our sins as the ultimate expression of love in the history of the universe.

> God has prepared a destiny for you so marvelous no words can describe it. It's available for the asking. However, you must choose whom you will serve: the god called chance, or The Creator Beyond Time and Space.

* * *

"And if it seems evil to you to serve the LORD, choose for yourselves this day whom you will serve, whether the gods which your fathers served that were on the other side of the River, or the gods of the Amorites, in whose land you dwell. But as for me and my house, we will serve the LORD." Joshua 24:15

MY KING DO YOU KNOW HIM?

From Pastor Lockridge

The Bible says my King is a seven-way King. He's the King of the Jews, that's a racial King. He's a King of Israel, that's a national King. He's a King of righteousness. He's the King of the Ages. He's the King of Heaven. He's the King of Glory. He's the King of Kings and He's the Lord of Lord's. That's my King.

Well, I wonder do you know Him? No means of measure can define His limitless love. No far-seeing telescope can bring into visibility the coastline of His shoreless supply. No valley can hinder Him from pouring out His blessing. He's enduringly strong. He's entirely sincere. He's eternally steadfast. He's immortally graceful. He's imperially powerful. He's impartially merciful.

Do you know Him? He's the greatest phenomenon that has ever crossed the horizon of this world. He's God's Son. He's the sinner's Saviour. He's the centerpiece of civilization. He stands in the solitude of Himself. He's august and He's unique. He's unparalleled. He's unprecedented. He's the loftiest ideal in literature. He's the highest personality in philosophy. He is the supreme problem in higher criticism. He's the fundamental doctrine of true theology. He is the total necessity for spiritual religion. He's the miracle of the ages. He's, yes He is, He is the superlative of everything good that you choose to call Him. He's the only One qualified to be an all-sufficient Saviour.

I wonder if you know Him today? He supplies strength for the weak. He's available for the tempted and the tried. He sympathizes and He saves. He strengthens and sustains. He exhorts and He guides. He healed the sick. He cleansed the lepers. He forgives sinners. He discharges debtors. He delivers the captives. He defends the feeble. He blesses the young. He serves the unfortunate. He regards the aged. He rewards the diligent and He beautifies the meek. I wonder if you know Him.

Well, this is my King. He's the King of knowledge. He's

the well-spring of wisdom. He's the doorway of deliverance. He's the pathway of peace. He's the roadway of righteousness. He's the highway of holiness. He's the gateway of glory. Do you know Him?

Well, His office is manifold. His promise is sure. His light is matchless. His goodness is limitless. His mercy is everlasting. His love never changes. His Word is enough. His grace is sufficient. His reign is righteous and His yoke is easy and His burden is light. I wish I could describe Him to you. Yes, He's indescribable. He's incomprehensible. He's invincible. He's irresistible.

Well, you can't get Him out of your mind. You can't get Him off of your hand. You can't outlive Him and you can't live without Him.

Well, the Pharisees couldn't stand Him, but they found out they couldn't stop Him. Pilate couldn't find any fault in Him. The witnesses couldn't get their testimonies to agree. Herod couldn't kill Him. Death couldn't handle Him, and the grave couldn't hold Him. Yes, that's my King. And Thine is the kingdom and the power and the glory forever and ever and ever and ever and ever. How long is that? And ever and ever and when you get through with all of the forevers, then amen. Good God Almighty. Amen. Amen. Amen.

I wonder, do you know Him?

296 John 8:23.
297 John 16:28.
298 John 17:5.
299 *The Messiah: An Aramaic Interpretation; The Messianic Exegesis of the Targum*, Samson H. Levy (Cincinnati: Hebrew Union College Jewish Institute of Religion, 1974), pg. 92.
300 Alfred Edersheim, *The Life and Times of Jesus the Messiah*,

Book II, page 175.

301 See Philippians 2:7.

302 Revelation 1:8, 11, 17-18.

303 John 5:21, 6:40, 54.

304 Jeans, *The Mysterious Universe*, (Macmillan Co. 1930) pgs. 138-39, 146, 154.

305 Isaiah 41:21-23, 46:9-10, 57:15.

306 Exodus 2:5.

307 Deuteronomy 8:19.

308 There are a number of additional Christophanies in the Old Testament. These include the One like "a Son of God," in the fiery furnace of Daniel 3:25; the One who appeared to Abraham in the terebinths of Mamre in Genesis 18; the One who wrestled with Jacob.

309 John 20:4, 15, 21:12.

310 See Isaiah 50:6, 52:14.

311 See also John 20, Mark 16:14.

312 For a more detailed discussion of dimension theory and related topics, see the two tape briefing packages, *Beyond Perception, Beyond Time and Space and Genesis and the Big Bang* by Chuck Missler, Koinonia House. 1-800-KHOUSE1.

313 See also 2 Corinthians 3:18.

314 1 John 3:2.

315 Hebrews 1:3 (NASB).

316 Exodus 33:20.

317 Philippians 2:7-8 (NASB).

318 John 14:28.

319 Revelation 13:8; Colossians 1:26.

320 Romans 3:23.

321 Exodus 20:17

322 One-third of the angels fell into sin with Satan, an angel himself.

323 John 1:14.

324 John 1:29 (KJV).